A Wonderful Boss

Forthcoming titles in the series

- A Wonderful Wife
- A Wonderful Husband
- A Wonderful Colleague

A Wonderful Boss

Great People to Work With

Virender Kapoor

B L O O M S B U R Y

LONDON • NEW DELHI • NEW YORK • SYDNEY

Bloomsbury Publishing India Pvt Ltd
Vishrut Building, DDA Complex
Building No. 3, Pocket C-6 & 7, Vasant Kunj
New Delhi 110 070

ISBN: 978-93-82951-58-2
10 9 8 7 6 5 4 3 2 1

Typeset by Eleven Arts
Printed and bound by Replika Press Pvt Ltd

The content of this book is the sole expression and opinion of its author,
and not of the publisher. The publisher in no manner is liable for any
opinion or views expressed by the author. While best efforts have been
made in preparing this book, the publisher makes no representations or
warranties of any kind and assumes no liabilities of any kind with respect
to the accuracy or completeness of the content and specifically disclaims
any implied warranties of merchantability or fitness of use for a
particular purpose.

The publisher believes that the content of this book does not violate
any existing copyright/intellectual property of others in any manner
whatsoever. However, in case any source has not been duly attributed, the
publisher may be notified in writing for necessary action.

CONTENTS

PREFACE

There are hundreds if not thousands of books on leaders and leadership, but there are very few on bosses or about being a boss. In fact, we as individuals need to deal more with bosses than leaders every day. And this is what inspired me to write a book on this often-used and discussed subject in our daily lives.

A leader will always be wearing two hats at a time, one of a leader and the other of a boss as the two roles are quite different. Yet these two roles may have some common traits that could functionally overlap. Very often people attach a negative connotation to the word 'boss'. In fact, the Oxford dictionary defines it as 'to tell someone what to do in an arrogant or annoying way.'

Though the definition itself is somewhat derogatory, I would like to dispel this notion through this book. As a believer in the law of averages and quoting from my own experience of around forty years, I would say there would be more good guys in organisational corridors of power than bad ones. Yet there is big room for improvement for the good guys too. A leader has a much larger role to play which affects the performance and progress of the entire organisation. At the core of leadership lies vision, mission, direction, wisdom, sacrifice, and also a moralistic stance. In contrast, the role of a boss is more hands-on and largely revolves around and is focused towards people management and interpersonal relations with the employees of the organisation. The boss-subordinate relationship becomes very personal and that is why one would say 'He is my boss', and you will seldom get to hear, 'he is my leader'. It is the softer part of leadership which is the hardest to manage. Putting it another way, a boss is in your immediate vicinity and with whom you deal on a daily basis, whereas a leader may be visible only from a distance. During the Gilded age, in the late 19th century, in the United States, bossism was a system of political control centreing around a single powerful figure—the boss. The central figure had tremendous clout and influence in terms of political control. In that context also, boss was to do more with control and perhaps nothing to do with leadership. In the modern environment, bossism is about atmospherics, which has a direct impact on a subordinate's performance as well his personal life and happiness. Therefore, in my opinion, bossism is skewd more towards emotional intelligence rather than the IQ of a boss.

It is often said that people don't quit jobs, they quit bosses. The Naukri.com advertisement of 'Hari Sadu', a boss who is hated by his subordinates', who then constantly look out for job opportunities elsewhere, is a good illustration of a bad boss and its ramifications. Most of us have crossed paths with bosses of all flavours—the good, the bad and some ugly. We had to live with some, tolerate others and also loved many. Many of us were lucky to get some great people to work with. Wherever we work, we will have a boss. It is a mandatory requirement for any organisation or a department to have a person in charge and, therefore, bosses are here to stay.

A team member or an employee is not so much bothered about the capability of his boss in terms of leadership like vision or wisdom. But he is highly affected—directly—by how he behaves with him or with his team members.

Boss, that one man or woman, therefore becomes the most important person in your life and is directly responsible for your happiness and hence, your well-being and productivity as well. Therefore, I believe that a good boss not only becomes a hygiene factor for the health of the organisation, but also acts like an anti-attrition glue, which helps in keeping the team together. It is not surprising then to witness a mass exodus of employees when a good boss decides to quit. If given a chance, the entire team goes and docks with him in his new assignment.

The flipside is that a nasty person in charge can generate so much of bad blood that he can break the entire team, with many of the team members looking for avenues elsewhere.

Bossism, therefore, boils down to behavioural aspects of a leader which impacts the ecosystem in his immediate vicinity, either positively or negatively.

It would not be wrong to say that leadership is about collective success or failure of a team or an organisation, whereas bossism is more about success and failure of each individual within that organisation. While wearing a leader's hat you could screw the organisation from the top, but as a boss you would start ruining people from all over your department—one on one. Therefore, bossism is a very important aspect of leadership because if every individual flourishes, the entire team will do well. In that sense, bossism is an integral part of leadership but needs to be examined separately.

I must mention an incident which triggered the idea of writing this book. One day I was out shopping in a mall with my son when he bumped into one of his former colleagues. This girl, who had been working in a team headed by my son, introduced us to her husband. She said, 'He is Samir who was my boss at Talisma and my first boss, but I must say he was the best boss I ever had, truly a wonderful boss.' The author in me immediately latched on and responded, 'This is a brilliant title to write on.' Now such bosses are in my view wonderful, otherwise how else do we justify such loyalty bordering on devotion.

The definition of a good or a great person is highly subjective and hence prone to error, a human error. Therefore, while defining such a character, we must take into account the fact that human perception would play an important role.

Another important factor about people is that while they constantly find faults with their bosses, when they become a boss they behave exactly in the same manner, and sometimes even worse, with their subordinates. Do we fail to learn or is it a human tendency to put history in the dustbin? Or many don't know how to handle authority that flows out of power—the power to harm others?

If boss or leaders are two hats for the same head, as mentioned earlier, and can bring in some nice factors into their behaviour and make people comfortable, build trust and connect with their hearts, organisations could greatly benefit.

One could also mesh into this the more tangible professional competence of a boss and his/her capacity to advise his subordinates. There could be some other qualities of an individual which can earn respect and love from the team. There is a big difference between respect and love. When people respect a boss they obey him, but when they love their boss they follow him.

If you look at it from the perspective of a boss, this book addresses the basic question, 'Can I improve and become a better boss by changing my behaviour?' The answer is a big yes. Alternatively, 'If I give this book to any boss as a gift, will he become a better boss?' The answer is again yes. Let me tell you that there are only three reasons as to why a person as a boss does not change his behaviour. The first one is that no one has ever told him that his behaviour is atrocious and he is viewed as an undesirable person by his team. For such people ignorance is bliss. The second reason, which is more serious, is that he knows that he is a difficult person for everyone, but he neither understands how damaging his behaviour is for himself as well as for the organisation and worse, when he decides to make amends he does not know how to go about it. In short, he needs help.

The third category of bosses are the ones who know that they are a pain for others but who just don't want to change. These are hard-core, hard nuts which you can never crack. They are the die-hard kinds. They learn—may be if they are lucky—when they get a big personal jolt in life. Then they find ways and means to make a change and could be repentant, and are then prepared to kneel down in front of the confession box.

This book is for all the three types of people. But bosses must understand that the buck stops with you, even when it comes to changing your behaviour. In fact, no one can motivate you to make amends. It has to come from within. This book will motivate you to make amends and will show you how.

If you look at it from the perspective of your boss, then you would realize that there is a lot you can do to have a wonderful relationship with your boss. You can look at it as a glass half empty or glass half full. But there is a third way of looking at it. The glass is half full and the rest of it is full of air! This book will also show you how to look at the glass half empty in a different perspective so that you can perform better and give your best under the existing circumstances. You need not jump for changing a job only because of one person, you have a lot at stake.

In my forty years of work experience, I have bumped into more than twenty people whom I could call as my boss because I fell into their radius of direct influence. I was fortunate that during my career I met more good guys than bad. In fact, in my case the good far outnumbered the bad. But when I sat down to write the list of my bosses it was easy to recall all names. It was still easier to tick the bad ones. It took me less than sixty seconds to mark those black sheep out of twenty names! This proves another point that you may forget the good ones but would never be able to forget the bad guys—though you may forgive them. A substantial part of my working life was spent in the armed forces. Therefore, I did not have the privilege of quitting an organisation if I was posted under a bad boss. I had to lump it. In fact, it taught me how to manage my affairs in such a hostile environment. I never quit, because I could not quit. So there is a great lesson that if you desire you can sail through a bad patch, lie low for a while till you get a chance to move out—in our case, it came every three years.

I had been planning to write a book to address this leadership gap for a couple of years but was unable to decide on the format. As I spent more time pondering over the format, I realized that such a complex subject needs a fresh treatment and a different approach.

I am fortunate to know many stalwarts in industry who have had illustrious careers and each one of them is an island of excellence in his or her own right. I wanted to learn from them and draw upon their experience. I wanted each one of them to tell me their story—the journey up the ladder. More specifically, their experiential learning from their bosses. Each one of them has also played the role of a boss several times over and could therefore reflect upon both sides of the coin.

I had a big list to choose from and considering myself privileged, I picked up people from almost every industry vertical. I was able to get CEOs and Managing Directors of large corporations to share their experiences and their 'close encounters' with their mentors and bosses. Very senior human resource professionals also came forward willingly. Journalists-turned-editors, industrialists, chief executives-turned-consultants, educationists and seasoned bureaucrats have narrated their stories.

Fortunately, by design and not accident, the representation is from almost every domain. I thought it would be important to take views from every segment of the industry and I was able to muster inputs from manufacturing, IT, banking, consulting, ITES, quality management, media, education and even pharma.

The list being exhaustive, I am not surprised by the quality, sheer expanse and the diversity of inputs. I am convinced that every aspect of boss-subordinate relationship, even however insignificant, has been touched upon. It takes into account views of almost three generations, as the stories have been told by people who are in the age group of 35 years to 75 years.

The biggest challenge for these people was to find time for penning their experiences and thoughts in writing as most of them have very tight working schedules and often travel to meet professional obligations. I had to discuss with each one of them personally about my vision and mission, and explain to them how important their inputs were for me. I wanted diversity and hence, wanted people from different verticals as well as backgrounds. To cater to gender diversity, I wanted some women to contribute as well.

As you read this book, you will find a number of suggestions jumping at you which are ideas and concepts to deal with people, your people. You will be surprised that there are more than a hundred ideas which if implemented on a day to day basis can make you a wonderful boss. A wonderful boss who is respected, who is loved by his subordinates and is also very effective while running the show.

This book is full of real stories and experiences which go a long way in shaping the reader into a good boss. It has that crunch advise for the bosses of today and tomorrow.

It contains more than four hundred years of corporate experience. It will be a guide for anyone who works for a living. None of us works in isolation, we all work in teams and teams have bosses.

A manager or an executive with even three years of work experience would have a few reportees—people for whom he or she is the boss. This book is as essential for young managers as it is for Vice Presidents, Presidents and CEOs. In fact, young managers must learn the ropes at an early stage of their career so that they can develop their own effective style of dealing with their teammates. Young minds are open to fresh ideas and ready to learn. It is better to learn from other's mistakes in the formative years rather than make costly mistakes later and regret.

It is equally useful and applicable to the top brass who are now holding fort as bosses directly controlling lives of dozens or may be hundreds of people. You could be in any profession—corporate, politics, public sector, bureaucracy, diplomacy, media, or even an entrepreneur—this book is for you and your boss.

Virender Kapoor

GOOD BOSS BAD BOSS
Where the buck *doesn't* stop

Virender Kapoor

Bosses need to be creative minded ... so that they conceive,
nurture and deliver regardless of their role.

A Myth Called a Perfect Boss

As far as human behaviour is concerned, there are no perfect people in this world. Similarly, there can be no perfect relationships as they are created, nurtured, maintained or broken between two people who themselves are never perfect. Bosses have a direct relationship with each of their team members and with efforts these relations can become cordial if not perfect. Therefore, can there be a perfect boss? If one has to stretch one's imagination a little and look at it practically, one would conclude that this is far from being true. The opinion pendulum would swing between a good and a bad boss, and in between the arch formed by these two points; there is no room for a perfect point.

Human personality being so complex, one should never expect any person to be perfect. A person may display many qualities that are considered good but would also have several negative qualities which cannot be ignored. For a boss it therefore becomes a balancing act between how good or how bad he can be.

One thing is very certain, a boss cannot be expected to be God, after all he is a human being. He is an individual and is bound to have some limitations. Let us not forget that a boss is a person-in-charge who has to deliver and is accountable to someone above him. He has to make sure that his team works, achieves targets and get things done. Therefore, however good he might be, there would be enough opportunities to label him as a bad one.

So what are we talking about? We are looking at this balancing act where a person, who is positioned as a boss, tries to cultivate more good habits and shed as many bad ones to eventually earn respect from his team members who look up to him as a good boss.

Up to What Extent Does a Boss Affect the Well-being and Progress of His Team Mates?

If a leader has a radius of influence, a boss has a radius of heat. If it becomes too hot and sticky, it becomes difficult to tolerate. In case it becomes too cold and damp it incapacitates you. At the end of the day, it is all about atmospherics and that has a direct impact on the happiness and productivity of a team.

A study conducted a decade ago concluded that employees rate having a good boss higher than perks and remuneration. It is also a fact that more than 70 percent people dread dealing with their bosses. Many of them find this to be the most stressful part of the job. Bad bosses not only give you a severe headache but could also make your stress levels reach such heights that it could trigger a heart attack. Studies point out that a terrible boss can affect your family life, health and even increase your risk for heart disease. In fact, a specific Swedish study found a correlation between 'incompetent' bosses and worker's risk for heart attack, angina and death due to other heart-related complications. Incompetent bosses cause frustration which causes tension and if it persists for a long time, results in serious health issues.

Jack Zenger and Joseph Folkman who conducted a detailed survey with organisations employing 225,000 and also 250 people conclude that your happiness, commitment, and health depends on your immediate superior or your boss.

It is important to note that work culture is a part of the organisational culture and is usually set and regulated by the top management. In a great culture too, a bad boss can make things go wrong. Your Chairman and Board of Directors may be good and may have set up a great company. But if your immediate boss or supervisor is bad and nasty to you, then for you that company is bad. In fact, bad bosses negate other organisational investments. For instance, a great career path, good salary, health cover and other perks make no difference to people who have to work with a bad boss.

Organisations Must Focus on Grooming Good Bosses

While there are many thousands of books on leadership and many workshops and intervention tools available to groom and cultivate leaders within organisations, there is little effort put; may be none at all to groom good bosses.

If I were to pick up a few simple definitions of leadership they would be:

- The capacity to establish direction, align people towards a common goal, committing them to action and making them responsible for their performance.

- Leadership is the ability to evaluate and forecast a long term plan and influence the followers towards the achievement of this plan.

- Leadership is the capacity to translate vision into reality.

- To influence the behaviour of the group and persuade them to follow a particular course of action.

Or

- Leadership is all about transforming organisations according to the changing business environment.

If you examine these definitions carefully, they mostly focus on getting things done, achieving set targets, vision, forecast, or even influencing people to move on. There is little emphasis on how you deal with people in these statements—which is the basic difference between a leader and a boss.

I feel a company will benefit if they have bosses who know how to achieve organisational goals through positive, cordial and effective relation with people within the organisation. In today's competitive world, one cannot afford to lose good people to one's competition. While a good boss acts like an anti-attrition glue, a nasty boss can act like a catalyst for a mass exodus. It would be nothing short of an organisational sin ending up in *harakiri* if you cannot tame the bosses within.

If an organisation can focus towards grooming good bosses, they would end up creating a conducive environment for its employees. As we have transited from the industrial economy to service-based economy and are now firmly entrenched in the knowledge economy, retaining good people is a big challenge. Large corporations are spending millions on hiring fresh talent but unfortunately doing little in terms of retaining them. As a retention policy, many companies have come up with Employee Stock Ownership Plans, additional perks, regular pay hikes, etc., but have not invested in grooming bosses who are custodians of their environment!

Companies now, therefore, must focus on making good bosses or supervisors. While grooming leadership is essential and efforts must continue, one must focus on cultivating good bosses as a parallel effort.

This is one organisational blind spot which has to be tackled effectively. Short interventions at the organisational level can deliver spectacular results.

There are many other aspects which are important and fall in the blind spot category which have been ignored by organisations. These are also related to bossism. For instance, in the Armed Forces, the Annual Confidential Reports (ACRs) are the basis of promotions. A boss writes the ACRs for his subordinates based on their year-long performance. Based on these reports, one is either promoted to the next rank or left out of the race. I would like to emphasise here that writing ACR is the function of bossism and not leadership. It is more about control than anything else. In fact, the Armed Forces run on the basis of ACRs and these reports are the biggest instrument of control. Having said that, it is a surprise that there is no effort to teach officers how to write ACRs. It is left to an individual to decide what and how to write. This many a times can have a devastating effect on the rank and file.

ACRs have defined parameters where the person writing a report has to give points in terms of figures. To some extent it could negate the subjectivity but a pen picture is something that describes a person being reported on and is much descriptive.

A boss who does not know how to write a suitable pen picture might end up writing a lukewarm report instead of an outstanding report which he actually wanted to write. Similarly, citations are also important, based on which people get recognised for valour in war. Unless a citation is strong, compelling and well-articulated, it may not result in an award being approved. Writing a citation is an art and forms part of bossism. Unfortunately, no organised efforts are made to teach people how to write an appropriate citation.

It is therefore essential that every organisation should make serious efforts to train people incharge of other people in handling people. In-fact, it should be a part of the top management agenda to groom bosses as this affects the productivity of the organisation and greatly impacts attrition.

I have witnessed the change in organisational dynamics when one boss replaces the other. When there is a change of guard and a good boss is replaced by a nasty one, it can have a devastating effect on the entire organisation down the line.

Can a Book Change the Behaviour of a Boss?

Do self-help books help? I have been asked this question often. Of course these books help, has been my answer, always and every time.

Books play an important role in our lives. They are great influencers and many times great levellers as well.

This book which is specially meant to change the behaviour of bosses has to have similar deliverables. I am sure that a book can influence the thought process, attitude and behaviour of a boss. Bosses are people in positions of power and influence. A common thread among all bosses is that they have some years of experience and level of maturity. While maturity helps in grasping concepts, it impedes acceptability. Maturity on many occasions gets you into a set mind mode where your ideas are set according to your belief, and you are not prepared to make amends easily. According to me and in its crudest form, too much experience results in rigor mortis of the mind which many bosses suffer from.

In such circumstances, to get optimal results, one should first unlearn and then try to learn things. If one starts with this premise, a book can change the behaviour of a boss substantially.

Another frequently asked question is, can a book transform individuals? Books can greatly influence, but rarely transform. Well written books, presenting fresh ideas in palatable formats can certainly act as triggers to a much larger change process. This change process at some point of time may itself become a transformer.

If I have to be optimistic, I would take the maturity of an individual as a positive for him to affect change that he seeks in himself. As regards this book, a reader with even a little experience will be able to absorb many fresh ideas. This book is full of rich experiences of industry captains which they have shared for the benefit of the readers.

Mature readers will be able to map these experiences with their own journey and validate their own beliefs. Therefore, for the experienced reader, such a book becomes an effective sounding board.

Bossism, like leadership, is not a science but is an art. I am sure no boss on earth would be either totally on the right track, or off track. Yet, in every case there is room for improvement.

If a reader picks up a few good ideas from this book and implements these in his/her style of functioning, the results can be nothing short of spectacular.

What Do Employees Expect from a Boss?

One of the main objectives of this book is to answer this question. Therefore, it may not be appropriate to attempt addressing all the aspects regarding employee expectations right here. I would only highlight those aspects which are quintessential for building a harmonious and fruitful relation between a boss and his team. At the end of it, this entire book will drive home more than hundred major lessons for bosses to become wonderful bosses and great people of substance.

Majority of employees have realistic expectations from their bosses. In most cases they want to work with just a decent guy. Therefore, to be an OK boss and sail through your time, you do not require God-like skills. But to be a great boss, you need a lot more under your belt.

Let us look at the armed forces, where a person gets transferred every two to three years. In such circumstances, a good boss is one of the most important factors which determine your happiness quotient over and above the location, which could be hazardous. I have seen people turning a hell like location in the middle of a desert into a heaven just by their good behaviour. On the other hand, a bossy person can make everybody's life miserable, even in beautiful places like Shimla or Ooty.

First and foremost, a teammate would look for decency and good conduct. If a boss is gentlemanly, polite, courteous and humane, half the requirement is met. If he or she is considerate, not vindictive and doesn't humiliate you emotionally and publicly, then he or she is a perfect person to work for. Being good hearted therefore, is a must-have trait. Who would like to work with a brilliant engineer or a financial wizard who is a horrible person?

The professional chunk comes later, always and every time. In the professional competence arena, people first expect basic morals to be in place. Integrity, honesty, fair play, no favourites, no politics, impeccable character and being upright are those sterling qualities which are highly respected by subordinates.

Next in the professional cluster come certain management skills which subordinates look for in their bosses. Who wants an impractical boss? Every subordinate wants his boss to be realistic. They also want a boss who can withstand external pressures and can give out quick decisions and hold their hands during a crisis or if they make a mistake.

If you distil what I have mentioned above, it boils down to just three things in the following order. First, being humane; second, having a strong moral fibre; and third, a sound professional knowledge and disposition.

What Does a Good Boss Expect from his Team?

Looking at the lowest common denominator, any person-in-charge, a manager or a boss who is responsible to get certain tasks done from his team, would expect his subordinates to have some basic character related qualities and some sound professional traits.

Responsiveness, punctuality, being respectful, maturity, responsibility, integrity, being flexible and professional seriousness would be on top of a boss's mind. As an employee if you expect your boss to be humane, polite, understanding and a gentlemanly, you should expect your boss to expect the same from you. Obviously, your boss would expect you to be a well behaved person who respects him or her and the team.

Since you have been hired for professional competence, will it be too much for him or her to ask for basic job skills from you? Of course, these become a hygiene factor as far as a boss is concerned.

The preceding paragraphs raised and answered a few very pertinent questions. It is now time to delve deeper into those areas which takes a boss from being good to being great.

Good Bosses Focus on Creating a Great Culture

The most important task for a boss is to ensure he extracts the best out of his team. A team can deliver optimally if the work environment is good. I, therefore, feel that to create  a good, vibrant and a healthy culture should be the prime task of the person incharge. In fact, this is on top of the agenda for every company worth its salt. But the irony is that leaders visualise the culture, but bosses mess it up. In most cases, the same person does both the things simultaneously wearing two different hats!

Now here is a nice little story about organisations.

There was a person working for a company which was a big international name in the Fast Moving Consumer Goods (FMCG) sector and had a worldwide presence. He had in his office a parrot named Chipper. One day a friend visited him and was delighted to see Chipper in a cage on his friend's table. I will show you what my Chipper can do, his friend exclaimed while opening the cage and letting the bird fly out, and everybody watched in excitement. Chipper was flying high chirping but was flying with only one wing! Seeing this unique ability of the parrot, he expressed his desire to buy the parrot from his friend and somehow convinced him to sell it for five thousand rupees.

As a proud new owner of a super smart bird he took Chipper to his office to impress his colleagues. "Hi guys, this is Chipper and I will show you how he flies only with one wing," letting him out of the cage. Chipper moved out, looked around and rose up to fly high. He was flying alright, but with both his wings! His new owner was let down as Chipper flew with both his wings every time he was let out of the cage.

To settle the score with the guy from whom he had bought Chipper, he marched into his friend's office the next day and yelled, "You have cheated me, your parrot cannot fly with one wing!"

His friend refuted the charge and promised to demonstrate Chipper's prowess once again. As the cage was opened, Chipper came out, looked around and flew with one wing only. "But in my office this bird flies with both the wings. I tried so many times."

His friend smiled and said, "It flies with one wing only in our office, because here everybody works with one hand, using the other to cover their backs."

In simple words, this is trust deficit that reduces the efficiency of an organisation to 50 percent.

 Basis of a good culture is trust and this is built top down. People on top, managers and bosses, are directly responsible to build an environment where everyone trusts everybody. Whereas, a paranoid culture breeds suspicion.

My experience tells me that in actuality to build trust is not difficult. In fact, it is one of the easiest things to do. A few things could be handy. Declare the first day there will be no politics in your department and then ensure you yourself don't do politics. Don't listen to back biters, tell people to be honest and face each other if they have complaints. Be transparent and open with everyone. Communicate individually and collectively, and communicate often with your team. I have seen good people leaving their well paying jobs with great brands only because of office politics. To stop or start this is entirely in the hands of a boss.

Let there be emotional harmony among team members. It is not that only a boss should be caring, he should ensure that each member of the team cares for the rest and vice-versa. Involving people in decision-making, taking everybody's suggestions and building a consensus is an important task of a Boss. People should feel that their opinion matters.

Another healthy practice is to provide a level playing field to everyone in your team. Give opportunities to each team member. Allow room for mistakes, and don't create that zero error syndrome. Allow people to learn from mistakes wherever possible. You cannot allow blunders to take place but, simultaneously, you should not put everyone on a tight leash. Provide limited and calculated freedom for risk-taking. In every case treat people equally and follow the rules—what applies to one also applies to the others.

Hiring the right person with a right cultural fit is also important. But it may not always be possible as people transit between organisations with different, sometimes diametrically opposite cultures.  In such cases, give a person time to absorb and settle down.

Pride is one thing that cannot be compromised. Everybody who works for a company works for a cause. People should not only be happy doing their jobs, they must be proud of it too. Ensure that you don't build a rigid, coercive organisation which is highly red taped or much process oriented. To an extent systems are very important, but they should never supersede people.

As the head of a team, imagine yourself sitting at the head of the table where everybody is watching you. You need to build respect for yourself and that can come if you build a conducive environment and demonstrate to your team that you will not compromise on what you have defined as culture.

If you are incharge of one of the units or departments in a large organisation, don't be under the impression that you cannot do your bit. In such an environment, there may be an existing culture. But within your radius of influence, within your department, you can make things better. If a bad boss in a good company can mess up things for people in his department, then by the same logic, a good boss in a bad company can make a great environment within his own department. If you want to do good things, sky is the limit. If you want to screw up things, again, sky is the limit.

If you are managing a large department with sub-departments, then ensure that heads of sub-departments also breed in a healthy culture. If someone is nasty with his team, you as the bosses boss must correct bad bosses under you. This will help preserving a good environment. Certifications can be copied or can be obtained, but culture has to be cultivated, always top down. Once in place, your competition cannot copy your culture and that is the best part of it.

Professional Competence

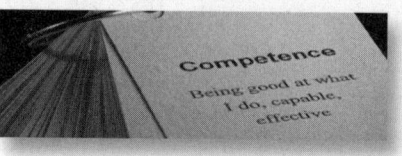

No one wants to work under an incompetent boss who is a nincompoop. It is frustrating for team members whose boss is calm, cool but clueless. Creating a great culture built on trust, respect and being good-hearted is not enough. A boss needs to be competent too.

I feel knowing your job is extremely important if you are heading a group of people to accomplish a defined task. On the face of it, this seems trivial and may sound contradictory to the definition or existence of bossism. But the fact is there are many people in high ranks who do not know their job well. Such people are seldom respected by their subordinates. Therefore, one has to make efforts to learn each aspect of one's job thoroughly. Whether you are incharge of operations, logistics, planning or execution, you must completely understand the functioning of your department. The best way is on taking charge of your new job, the first thing you must do is to put yourself in the learning mode. Ask people to brief you about the organisation, read old correspondence, look into the technical aspects, read official literature and get a hold of your department As Soon As Possible (ASAP).

Once you become familiar, it is time to act. Once you are firmly placed in the saddle, ensure that for every major briefing or action thereafter you must do your homework. Preparing for discussions in advance, having facts and figures ready beforehand, going through notes and relevant documents, and having your approach clear in your mind can give spectacular results every time. As a boss you should appear to be incharge and in-know of things. Nothing can be more effective than doing your work in advance.

A boss must remain up to date. In today's environment, not only technology but business environment and market dynamics also change quickly. A good professional boss makes efforts to read papers, magazines and professional journals as well as books on a regular basis. This automatically gives you the ability to mentor your team and guide them if they need assistance. This also gives you the ability to ask meaningful questions from your subordinates. By this, you not only demonstrate that you know your job well, but are able to make your team think on their feet and ensure that they deliver their best. When you ask questions, the team is forced to find the right answers, and that is how it finds the solution.

A good professional boss always thinks ahead. In fact, a boss is paid to think. Mental gymnastics is therefore important and a boss must keep flexing his mental muscles all the time. Clarity of thought is very important. Some people are born with a gift of a clear mind. Even if one is not gifted, hard work and thorough preparation can make you feel confident and clear headed. You should know exactly what you want and be able to articulate in the simplest way in front of your team.

This can be linked to strategic thinking as well, which is also a part of a top management's job. I feel good bosses are great simplifiers. They can break down a

BEING RESPONSIVE

complex problem into a few simple sentences or pointers. If you can weave strategy and simplicity together, it becomes an effective combination.

Being responsive is one of the most important traits of a good manager. Remember, a bottleneck is always at the top of the bottle. If you as a boss do not respond to your team on time, then how do you expect the work to go on smoothly? Holding up files, holding up mails, not responding to calls or urgent short messages can frustrate your team. I have seen this becoming a major hurdle in day-to-day operations when employees keep writing for direction, clarity or go-ahead from a boss for days together without getting an appropriate or a timely response. This way the whole chain gets affected and work comes to a halt.

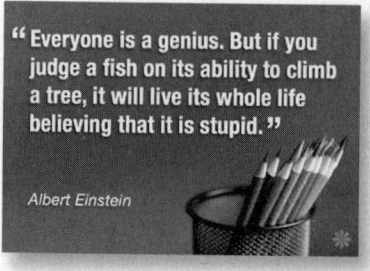

" Everyone is a genius. But if you judge a fish on its ability to climb a tree, it will live its whole life believing that it is stupid. "

Albert Einstein

Delaying things happens due to two reasons. First, the boss could be in the habit of procrastination. He or she, due to shear laziness or habit, postpones things. The second is that the person is indecisive, may be incompetent or confused, and cannot take a quick decision. Both the reasons are not acceptable to a team because it eventually affects their efficiency and output. It is therefore important to clear your desk or your mails in your inbox at the earliest.

Ability to judge is an important professional trait. In fact, top jobs carry a fat package, a major part of it is for making sound judgment.

In the Armed Forces, Judging Distance is an important ability of a Field Commander. You do not have the luxury of a range-finding equipment every time. Establishing distance of an enemy location, a bunker or a target becomes important because that determines which weapon could be used effectively, as weapons have different ranges.

In a job scenario, it is important for a manager to know his priorities. You may have ten jobs at hand but you must decide at the beginning which one would be done first and which can wait. Judging people is also very important; you must be able to make out the character, major characteristics and intentions of everybody in the team.

Ability to judge people's ability is yet another important skill to have. When you put people through a selection process, you expect a guy to be fit for the job. At some point in time later, you get to know that person a little better and you can learn much more about him or her if you are observant.

In this way good bosses get to know even the latent strengths of their people. Armed with this knowledge a boss must ensure he deploys the right person for the right job and according to his skills and abilities. If he is not aware of the ability of each member, he may end up trying to push a round peg into a square hole. It causes frustration for the team members and also affects the overall performance of the organisation.

Judging the business environment and picking up the right opportunity is close to an art. Some people have that gift to discern the right options out of a sketchy scenario. This also comes with experience where one can go by one's gut feeling and make the right decision. This is close to the sixth sense which many people display on occasions. Looking at it in another way, a person incharge must learn to deal with ambiguity because many times it is not possible to get all the facts and data for making decisions.

Every employee needs his or her Job Description (JD). Though it is mandatory to have a JD in most good organisations, in certain cases the jobs are defined rather loosely. A boss must ensure that every employee under him is clear about his or her role, responsibilities and reporting patterns. There should be no ambiguity in this. Related to this is the idea of load balancing. A boss must load people with tasks very appropriately. It should not happen that a few people are overloaded with work and the remaining people have little work to do.

Another important technique is to practice moving between macro-management and micro-management with ease. A boss should oversee the entire functioning and must always have a clear bird's eye view. He or she defines roles, tasks and sets

targets at regular intervals to monitor the progress. This is managing things at a macro level. However, there would be times when a boss needs to roll up his or her sleeves and get into some action at a micro level. These are the times to dirty one's hands and get the bull by the horns. But once the bull has come under control it is time to let go of the horns! Many bosses don't do this, once stuck with the bull they won't let go. It is important to micro manage for a while if the situation demands and then quickly and effortlessly move to the macro level.

It is also important to utilise all the expertise that one has while hiring a team. You always try to have a mixed bag of skills. You will have analysts, finance wizards, IT guys, or certain specific domain experts in your team. Whenever there is a need to take a decision and you find you need some more clarity on a certain issue, you must consult experts available within your team. As you go higher, you become more of a generalist, but you are still responsible for what happens at every level below you.

A boss cannot possibly have subject or domain knowledge of each function. Therefore, banking on experts is essential. You must take advice, discuss, and deliberate, but at the end execute your decision. If you look at the way the President of the United States operates, it will be clear as to how expert opinion matters and plays a major role in decision-making. If there is a situation, the President consults all the appropriate functional heads and keeping all the pros and cons in mind he takes a decision.

Contingency planning is an important aspect of management. As a person incharge, one makes a detailed plan for accomplishing a task. One makes sure that the plan is foolproof. But there are always unforeseen problems which can crop up while you are executing your plan. A good manager always keeps an ace up his sleeve—an alternate plan. It is good to have a detailed back-up plan which can be set into motion if the main plan fails due to reasons beyond one's control.

Putting things in writing and flawless documentation is something every manager must give priority to. Make it a habit and part of the system to put things in writing. Minutes of meetings, SOPs, routine orders and employee instructions must be available in written form. Wherever possible all actionable points must be run through the concerned person in writing so that

at some point of time in future it can be referred to, if required.

Creative Minded Boss?

A boss has to be competent because he is responsible for deliverables—end to end. This means as a manager, he should be able to visualise, then be able to nurture and develop the concept, and then deliver the results as per the given timelines. Great bosses conceive, nurture and deliver—on time. A creative streak can therefore be a great asset for a manager.

An Emotionally Intelligent Boss

It has now been well established that Emotional Intelligence (EI) plays an important part in the success of an individual. Great leaders, successful entrepreneurs or movers and shakers may not have been great academic wizards or brilliant engineers,

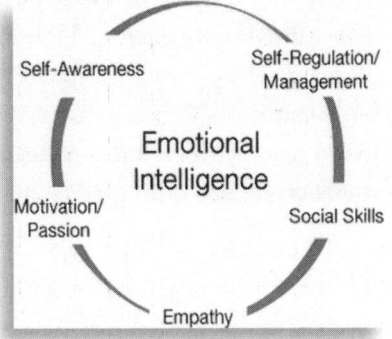

but all of them displayed qualities like bouncing back after a failure, empathy towards their people, ability to work under pressure, compassion and commitment to a cause. As one grows in stature and takes up larger roles in life, these aspects of human abilities keep becoming more and more relevant to success.

Broadly speaking, EI is the skill of knowing your own emotions and being able to handle your emotions effectively. It also takes into account the ability to understand emotions of other people and handling them accordingly. Therefore, apart from managing your own emotions, a lot of it is focused towards handling relationships based on emotions.

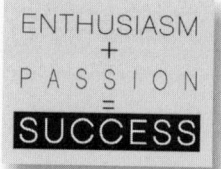

For a manager, a person in-charge or a boss, EI becomes particularly important as he or she has to deal with people on a daily basis. Let us look at some of the most important EI skills a manager should develop in order to become more effective.

Let us first deal with aspects which are internal to an individual and connected with one's own emotional stance.

Enthusiasm and passion are a state of mind and are very strong emotions. If a boss is passionate about his mission, objectives and job, he will display great enthusiasm at work. He will display unflinching commitment towards every job or task related to the ultimate goal. I feel enthusiasm and display of positive energy is extremely important for the person who has to motivate others to work for a cause or for achieving something. If a boss looks demoralised or disinterested then it will have a rippling effect on his team. This is not only applicable to a boss in a corporate role but is equally applicable to a captain of a cricket team, an actor who has to work with co-actors or even a teacher who has to keep the students engaged during a lecture.

Enthusiasm has another corollary to it and that is a sense of involvement. People who are enthusiastic in general, get naturally involved in their work or any challenge that is posed to them. Enthusiasm rubs off positively on people who work around enthusiastic persons. This becomes an important trait for an effective boss.

Drive, determination, grit and dogged persuasion are much related qualities. Can you have a boss who is effective without having and displaying drive and determination? At work, emotions play an important part. When you see your manager having no drive or persuasive abilities, you will never get pepped up to work hard. Bosses must display the ability to peruse objectives all the time.

Delayed gratification is something which lets you work extremely hard in order to achieve your goals. People seeking instant gratification tend to take shortcuts and can seldom set high benchmarks for themselves and their subordinates. Putting it in another way, some people have the patience to wait for rewards. They can work hard and sweat hard in a sustained manner till they finally achieve what they wanted to.

Taking failure in one's stride is an important quality which a manager must have. During work, things cannot be going right all the time. While you attain success, there will be a fair share of failure and frustration also coming your way. For instance, if you launch six new products  over a year with equal enthusiasm, due diligence and enough product research, you cannot expect all of these launches ending up with spectacular results. Success also may be in grades, a few great, some average and, may be, one odd failure. Good managers take failures without getting too upset or worried. Bosses are indirect mood managers for their teams; if a boss gets down and under because of a failure it will negatively impact the morale of his workforce.

Closely related to the ability of accepting failure without much fuss or remorse is the ability to bounce back after a failure. In this case you not only accept the failure without negatively reacting to it, but also take failure as a challenge and you re-launch yourself with more vigour than before. This not only happens in corporate life but also to authors, actors and singers. In most cases, creative people don't succeed in the first venture. Authors write several books to get this first big hit. Great actors are rejected by their audience in their first few performances, only to find success after many years of hard work and several flops.

Actors and authors are individuals, whereas a manager is responsible for a collective success of the team. To keep the organisation on an even keel, it is important for a manager to demonstrate enough resilience to bounce back after failure his or her team had faced.

In the life cycle of a manager, there are many occasions where he or she needs to take unemotional decisions. While dealing with people on most occasions, it is good to take unemotional decisions from the heart rather than the head. Caring for your team is usually wrapped in emotions. In some cases, while dealing with people or business one has to become emotionally detached. Therefore, even the kindest hearted bosses, sometimes have to change their emotional stance and be prepared to take unemotional decisions. There would be occasions, for instance, where you need to take a call to downsize or restructure the organisation and have to order retrenchment.

This is a hard business decision but in the interest of the organisation you have to take a surgical approach and fire some people. Certain business decisions can also weigh heavily on our emotions. For instance, due to the changing market scenario you may have to shift a product line. Products are like our own babies and letting one go can hurt us emotionally. In such cases, a manager must rise to the occasion and be able to take an unemotional decision to abandon a product or a person who may be very close to his heart.

Despite all the planning, necessary briefings and decisions for an impending task, it may happen that on several occasions the outcome may not be to the mark or may be below one's expectations. Things can go wrong because of poor performance of a few individuals or due to some unavoidable external reasons, or both. It is a challenge for managers to maintain their cool while dealing with situations and circumstances that are not fully under their control. Anger is one emotion which is difficult to manage. But for a manager it is extremely important to manage his anger.

Some people are lucky to have a cool disposition and not loose their temper quickly. This is a great quality to have. Temper is an evil that gets the better of us on several unpleasant occasions. For a boss, or a person incharge, it is important to maintain an equanimous mind despite pulls and pressures from outside or from within his or her own team. Bosses should refrain from displaying anger. It does two things, first it makes your subordinates feel that you are not in control of yourself and second, while you are angry you may take certain actions which you may regret later.

I have seen several people who hit the panic button too soon and too often. You may need to punch the panic button when the situation demands and this should be on rare occasions. The idea is not to create an emergency when none exists. Bosses who often create emergency situations and create smoke without fire end up putting their teams on tenterhooks all the time. In such cases subordinates get exhausted as their energy gets diverted towards unproductive activity and sometimes they stop reacting to actual emergency situations, thinking it could yet be one of the bosses over reactions. This is akin to creating a cry wolf situation.

These were some of the major intrapersonal emotional skills which a manager or a good boss must possess.

Now let me bring out several interpersonal emotional intelligence traits that a good manager must develop. These are not difficult to learn and can be cultivated over time. These are important and effective because without these no boss can survive. No one is bothered about your vision or mission if you behave inappropriately.

Being humane is something that is essential to building a good trust based relationship. Managing people is an art because you are dealing with individuals who understand emotions well. People have a strong ability to differentiate between a false and a genuine display of emotion. It is therefore important to be genuinely concerned about your team members. It is not enough to care for people but, over and above that, you must display and demonstrate that you are concerned about your team members.

Here, I would like to clarify one important point. It should not be misunderstood that a humane boss is always sugar and honey and cannot take people to task. On the contrary, a humane boss is kind to people when the occasion demands, and can be tough and demanding when it comes to deliverables. Bosses must therefore learn to be compassionate, but at the same time they must never forget that they are duty bound to get the task done.

Great people are humble and down to earth. They have no airs about themselves. Bosses who are humble are liked and respected by their team members. Being arrogant and conceited doesn't get you anywhere. Your deeds and abilities should speak for you and you must build your image based on your competence rather than bragging about your capabilities. To remain grounded in a position of power is quiet difficult. As a boss, since you have your way in almost everything, it requires a conscious effort to keep yourself from boasting about yourself.

One must be sensitive to the problems of the people who work with you and look up to you as their boss. The best way to deal with people is to keep the principle of compassion in mind, which is do unto others what you would have them do to you. This seems simple enough but is difficult to practice in a day's work. The other simpler way to look at it is, "Try to put oneself in the other person's shoes."

As a boss you may have great passion for your job, or for achieving targets, but do you have a heart to treat your subordinates well and also have consideration for them as fellow human beings? Many people feel that as a boss, who has to get work done from people, it is impossible to be compassionate. There seems to be a cognitive dissonance in our minds between being a hard task master and being compassionate to subordinates at the same time. This is far from true.

First, compassion does not mean being weak hearted or being a weak boss. As a boss you should be tough and demanding so the work gets done on time and to your satisfaction. But when an employee is in need of some help or assistance, you must help him out. If you analyse it critically, the requirements of employees are mostly small and many times appear to be insignificant. But when someone is in an emotional distress that problem seems to be huge, something like the end of the world for him. For instance, if your subordinate has a sick puppy at home and he or she needs to take the pup to a veterinary doctor, it becomes a big issue for him or her. If you are not a dog lover, you may not realise his or her mental agony and how desperate he or she is to take the pup to the doctor at the earliest. Heavens won't fall if you let that person leave office an hour earlier. In such a situation if you do not understand the mental agony of your subordinates, the consequences can be disastrous.

Sometimes as a boss you start comparing employees with each other or worse, with yourself. You would turn around and say, "Oh, I would never have taken leave if my dog was unwell." We make policies and often feel one policy should be applied across the board. When you go as per the book, you may go wrong. In certain cases you need to bend rules to accommodate specific situations. If everything is to run by the book, then the book should become the boss. Bosses are paid to interpret the rules given in the book and implement them in the best possible manner, keeping the larger interest of the organisation and also keeping the interest of individuals for whom the rules have been framed.

Close on the heels of compassion is empathy. While sympathy means is I know how you are feeling, empathy means I feel how you are feeling. In fact, empathy is the starting point and compassion is the point of delivery. Once you empathise with a person, you will always show compassion towards him or her. Therefore, to be successful it is not necessary to be harsh.

Ego and pride are very closely related emotions. While pride makes a person work with honour, ego works like a booster pump. An experienced boss should be able to identify who works for pride and who works for ego. If you can manage the egos of your egoistical team players, they will score the maximum goals for you! This is a positive way of looking at ego, after all we all have it.

Another important rule of thumb is to ensure that you never hurt people emotionally. This usually happens when you play with people's self-esteem. Insulting someone in front of others, comparing one employee with the other members of the team, or making a person feel small in front of his subordinates or colleagues are some of the worst practices that a boss can employ. While being harsh to someone and laughing at somebody at his weakness or helplessness is easy, helping a person with what he needs most is difficult but rewarding.

One day a group of students were going for a trek with their teacher. On their way they found a pair of old shoes which they believed belonged to a poor man who worked as a labourer in the nearby field. It was evening and they assumed the poor owner of the shoes would be back to pickup his shoes soon. The students, who were rich, wanted to play a prank and told their teacher, "Let us hide the shoes and hide behind a bush and wait to see his perplexity and helplessness when he returns and fails to find the shoes."

The teacher said, "You people are from rich families but he is poor, so don't do something that will hurt him. We should never laugh at someone else's cost, especially the needy ones. Since you are rich it is better to get greater pleasure by giving him something. Put one gold coin in each of his shoes and wait behind the bush to watch how this affects the poor man when he is back."

DIPLOMACY -
The art of letting someone have it your way

The students did exactly as told by their teacher and went and hid behind a bush. The poor man came back to the spot after a day's work and slipped his right foot into the shoe. He found something hurting the sole of his foot and examined the shoe; he was overjoyed to see a gold coin. He had a similar experience with his left foot too. Having two gold coins in his hands was something that he could never imagine. He fell upon his knees and said, "Oh God thank you for saving me and my family from starvation and sickness. I would also thank the person who has done this for me. Lords, please bless him!"

Students were moved with this incident and thanked the teacher for showing them the right path.

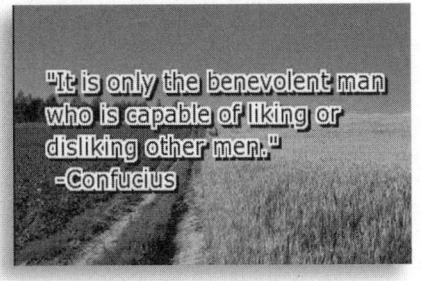

"It is only the benevolent man who is capable of liking or disliking other men."
-Confucius

As a boss or a manager you must always keep one thing in mind, that you have enough power, authority and resources to help your subordinates. If God has put you in a position of authority, never leave an opportunity to be good to people. Be big hearted, and benevolent whenever you can. It is important to understand that being benevolent does not mean being weak. You can be a hard task master and yet be a good hearted person.

Diplomacy is another skill which every manager must possess. In simple words, diplomacy is the art of letting someone have your way! Diplomacy is not only required in international relations or in politics, but is equally important for building and maintaining cordial relations with your colleagues and peers.

For instance, it is good to be open and forthright, but it is stupid to be blunt and invasive. I feel it is more to do with the choice of words and to some extent your tone and body language. Sometimes you can put across even a radical thought or an unpleasant message in a sugar quoted way which becomes palatable for the people. You learn, just as you learn good manners, how to approach things with a certain amount of democracy and take people along. Many times keeping quite on certain occasions itself can save a situation. As Will Durant says, "To say nothing, especially when speaking, is half the diplomacy." Diplomacy and tact go hand-in-hand. If one is tactful, one can handle the most difficult and complex interpersonal issues. The main idea of tact and diplomacy is to create a win-win situation for everyone in such a manner that everybody is satisfied and happy. Manager's work with teams and team members may have different views on an issue that comes up for discussion. One of the critical tasks of a manager is to build a consensus and take in every suggestion. Eventually, the discussions must culminate into an actionable idea. A manager has to use tact to get inputs from every member of the team, avoid conflict, and yet come up with a concrete proposal or an actionable idea.

All the interpersonal skills are ultimately aimed at making and maintaining good relations with people. As you build relations with individuals, you slowly build a small network of people who get along well with you. These are the people who listen to you and you can trust. Every organisation or group of people you work with is a potential network of human resource. Every manager must build a strong network of people and should never miss an opportunity to connect with them. Well connected managers are able to get a lot more information from their contacts and are able to accomplish much more than others and in a much shorter time frame.

Connecting with people is one aspect, but remaining connected with many people constantly is a bigger challenge. Effective managers spend a substantial amount of time everyday to stay connected.

Bosses who have a good network of friends, professionals and associates, do exceedingly well. Such bosses have readymade connections which can be used to get the most complex tasks executed easily. A well networked boss is not only a boon for the organisation but also for his subordinates who can rely on him for getting appropriate business connects.

Charismatic Bosses with that Oomph Factor

A boss must inspire confidence in his team. Therefore, in addition to professional knowledge and emotional intelligence, a boss must have certain qualities that make him charismatic. These are those brownie points that allow a boss in exercising a compelling charm which inspires devotion in the people he deals with. These are those oomph factors which, if demonstrated, can make people look up to their bosses. These make a huge difference in the way people perceive a boss.

Dr A.P.J. Abdul Kalam narrates an incident, which illustrates one great charismatic quality of a leader or a boss.

In 1973, Professor Satish Dhawan, Chairman of Indian Space Research Organisation (ISRO), gave a task to Dr Abdul Kalam to develop the first satellite launch vehicle SLV-3, to put ROHINI into earth's orbit. This was one of the largest and expensive space programme undertaken in 1973. Thousands of scientists and engineers worked on this project. Six years later, on 10 August 1979, SLV-3 took off, the first stage worked well, but after the second stage it developed a snag and the mission failed. Abdul Kalam was disappointed and sat in his office pondering over the failure. Professor Satish Dhawan walked in and took him by his arm and said, "There is a press conference, let us attend it." The reporters obviously asked awkward questions and wanted to know why care was not taken to ensure that mission succeeded. Professor Dhawan took the centre stage and took the entire responsibility for the failure of the mission even though Abdul Kalam was the Project Director and the Mission Director.

Satish Dhawan again chose Abdul Kalam to be the Project Director and on 18 July 1980, almost a year later, when SLV-3 successfully launched ROHINI Satellite in to the orbit, making India a space power. Again there was a press conference and this time also Professor Dhawan took him along. But this time he put Dr Abdul Kalam in the front and asked him to share the success story with the press. Professor Dhawan said, "Today it is your day and you must be on the front page of every newspaper tomorrow."

This is something which leaders, managers and bosses do rarely. To take the blame for failure as a boss and give credit to the subordinates for success is the ultimate gesture that a boss can demonstrate. Such an act puts a boss on a pedestal and raises his or her respect in the eyes of their team.

Another important trait of a leader which is appreciated by his team is to interpret rules in a way it helps the organisation and the team mates. As long as one doesn't have a personal axe to grind or a hidden agenda, bending rules at times not only can give spectacular results but also positions the boss as a go getter, a gutsy boss. As General Douglas Macarthur said, "Rules are mostly made to be broken and are too often for the lazy to hide behind." Why is bureaucracy always blamed for inefficiency? This is often due to the fact that a clerical minded person will always be able to tell you how or why a job should not be done. Bosses are there to tell you, despite rules and the rule book, that there are ways and means to get the job done.

It is easier to get forgiveness than permission. Good bosses don't wait for official blessings to try things out, yet they are careful and not reckless. There is also a bit of risk involved in such cases but effective bosses are paid for the risks they take.

I vividly recollect an incidence, when I was posted in the north eastern part of the country. This part of the Himalayan range has porous mountains and prone to sudden flash floods due to heavy and sometimes unpredictable rain. Troops in such terrain are deployed in far flung areas as small self-contained detachments, consisting of ten to fifteen men.

During the rainy season, there was a long spell of rain and it poured heavily for several days, filling up all the rivers and lakes around. One day, late evening, I got a call from a Detachment Commander, who was reporting a sudden build-up of water in the nearby river. This detachment was located more than hundred kilometres from the headquarters where I was stationed.

I knew the exact location and topology of that area and was aware there was high ground up north of that picket. "Sir, the water is rising fast, I don't think this will hold for too long, what should we do?" There was panic in his voice. I could sense that the situation was serious and if these guys didn't move immediately, things could get out of hand.

"Abandon post immediately, all of you run up north and get on the high ground," I said. "But what about our equipment, we can't leave it." I knew how unpredictable and dangerous flash floods are and how in minutes they can wipe out an entire village. "Forget the equipment, just run, all of you, don't leave anyone at the Picket," was my last order to the Detachment Commander.

This one decision saved fifteen lives as minutes after they abandoned the site and reached high ground, a powerful flood hit that picket area washing off the entire hutment. Had they tried taking the equipment along, there would have been a catastrophe on our hands. When I told this to my boss he said, "Good, I think it was the right call."

This was a split second decision with a larger interest in mind and probably not following the book. But I was happy and satisfied with what I had done. We lost some stores but could save our men. There can be nothing more precious than human life.

Calm and Composed

Bosses must remain calm and composed under trying circumstances. A boss should never look as if he is not in control of himself; a quality which very few have. Whatever the situation, a boss should never look helpless. Remember, in a crisis, the whole team is looking up to you. If you lose your nerve, the team's morale is shattered. There will be setbacks and defeats coming your way. Bosses, who can remain cool and composed during crisis, earn respect of their subordinates.

Ability to handle external pressure is something which is required of every boss. In any working environment there are powers and forces which many times work at cross purposes. There are interdepartmental pulls and pressures. There are pressures from the top which could negatively affect your team's performance or impact their morale. A boss has to act like a shock absorber or act as a shield so that the outside pressures do not impact or hinder with the team's performance. You may be a hard task master and create work pressure within, but you must not succumb to external pressure, such that it shows you in poor light in front of your subordinates.

Showing grace under pressure is not only a princely trait but can also be practiced by ordinary mortals. For ordinary mortals, ordinary things build extraordinary pressures. Board meetings, critical presentations, deadlines, submissions, conference calls, environmental fluctuations, and multi-tasking build stress for people in charge. The bottom line, we want everything to go right. Before for every situation you say, "This is important, I can't mess it up. My team must get it right all the way." High stakes, in your perception trigger fear of failure. Instead of pushing you to new heights, it is likely to increase anxiety.

One of the ways to calm you down is to underplay the importance of such events. Reminding yourself how unimportant each event individually is within the larger scheme of things, can get you back that sense of well-being and composure. Sometimes, under pressure, it is good to tell yourself, "Oh! So bloody what?" and then move on as usual. I have worked with bosses who displayed this trait all the time. Sometimes I wondered how they did it. But, perhaps, that is what one has to learn over time. I feel nothing is impossible.

Meticulous, tidy, well-organised, efficient, and spic and span are the qualities that everyone who deals with you will admire. Nobody would like to work with a boss who is forgetful, disorganised, always looking disheveled, ill clad, and untidy. This is not an earth shattering requirement that needs much effort to acquire. This is a habit which can be taught and learnt. But its impact on your team and your boss is tremendous. It not only improves your aesthetic value but also greatly contributes to your overall efficiency. I feel Business Schools who groom managers must teach students to be organised and methodical.

I have worked with more than two dozen bosses over a span of forty years. I had the greatest respect for those who made me feel comfortable and confident in their presence. When you walk into your superior's office, you should feel that the person is superior. You must feel that he or she is better informed than you, is more knowledgeable, more experienced and hence will be able to give you solutions to your problems.

This is a two way street. Bosses mostly think, "I hire people to solve my problems. If I have to solve their problems then what  are they paid for?" This is fine. But the other way to look at it is from the subordinate's view who says, "If I have a genuine problem and need guidance, who should I go to? If he is the boss, he should try to help me out."

If you want to earn respect, this is the best way to do it. As a boss, never duck nor pass the buck. You must inspire confidence in a way so that your subordinates feel that when they come to you they are in safe hands. No one will escalate the matter to you until and unless he or she has not been able to get it right himself or herself.

In addition to being a mentor and a problem solver, a boss must be a patient listener. You must hear out what others have to say. Give people a chance to explain their views. The worst bosses are those who interrupt when others are speaking. This not only disturbs the other person's chain of thought but also discourages him or her to speak.

Conflict resolution and creating a win-win situation is one quality which can earn a boss his or her brownie points easily. I feel one of the primary tasks of a boss is to resolve conflicts between employees or groups of people. As a boss you should not be seen as one who takes sides.

Bosses must be ambitious, should set steep targets but must never be unrealistic. People in charge who are unrealistic in their expectations are seen as wafflers who say a lot but lack substance and hencem do not merit to be considered seriously. The worst thing for a boss is when his team sees him as someone who should not be taken seriously.

Mistakes Are The Stepping Stones To Learning!

I have worked with bosses who had the courage to accept their mistakes. There are no perfect bosses and it is natural they can also occasionally commit a mistake. One requires great courage to take the blame or accept a mistake at a personal level. But this sort of down-to-earth approach can really earn you respect as a boss. If required, on certain specific occasions, bosses must display courage to accept their mistakes publicly.

Any setback or defeat should never be taken on personally. If a business plan fails, it is a business plan failure and should not be taken as a personal failure. Moreover, bosses who bury the past and move on with business earn more respect than those who let the emotional hangover prevail in the team for a considerable amount of time. Analyse a failure, learn from it but thereafter, move on.

Another very important quality of impactful bosses is their ability to remember faces and names. This, to an extent, is God's gift. I have seen some bosses who can recall a person's name after fifteen to twenty years. When you meet a person who worked with you ten years ago, he or she feels great if you recall his or her name and address him or her accordingly. There are people who remember names of employees' spouses' and even their children. If you have this quality then you must use it. If you lack this ability, make efforts to remember names. This becomes important when your span of control becomes larger and you have a large number of people working under you. In such circumstances, if a boss can address people by their names, he is bound to earn respect.

Bosses are great facilitators; they act as lubricating agents for the organisation. They are there to expedite things. If they themselves become an object of hindrance, then their existence is counterproductive. Therefore, bosses must cut redtapism and demonstrate a sense of urgency while dealing with issues.

People's Science

For those who deal with people, the aspect of people's science becomes one of the most important areas to improve upon. To be an effective boss there are some cardinal principles which need to be followed all the time.

You are a good manager if your people do not find it difficult to deal with you. This is a personality based issue and needs consistent efforts to make any worthwhile amends. Bosses who are abrupt, rude, conceited, unaccommodating, rigid and self-centred, overbearing and arrogant are the ones people find most difficult to deal with. People avoid such bosses or even such colleagues at the work place. In contrast, it is much easier to deal with those bosses who are gentlemanly, courteous and a bit flexible while dealing with situations and subordinates. Those in a position of authority must strive to acquire a pleasant disposition so their subordinates feel like meeting them. Keep your antennas up, observe how people react while dealing with you and you will get to know whether people like your company or not.

A Wonderful Loveable Boss

I had an opportunity to work for Dr S.B. Mujumdar at Symbiosis International University. He was the one who started Symbiosis almost forty years back as a small education initiative. Today, he presides over this vast organisation as the Chancellor of the university.

As a Director of one of the prestigious management institute under the Symbiosis umbrella, I had a lot to learn, especially from Dr. Mujumdar who was my boss for close to ten years. I can never forget his one liner, which he once told me about how to handle people. He said, "Best way to handle people is not to handle them!" The best part is, he lives by every word of this statement till date.

He gave directors total autonomy and freedom to work. In the course of ten years with him, I never found him ever to interfere in any professional matter. At the same time, he was always available for any advice one sought from him. The freedom to work was so much that at times you felt that you literally owned the institute. I feel this was one major reason for the success of this wonderful organisation created by a wonderful man. I also realised that directors enjoy total autonomy and yet, because of maturity, they seldom misuse this freedom. I recollect a very important saying in the armed forces, A senior should always forget that he is a senior, but a junior should never forget that he is his junior." If this equation can be balanced out, life can be great, productive, rewarding and memorable professionally.

Another very important quality of Dr. Mujumdar is being humble and very respectful, especially to his subordinates. I remember one incidence where I had invited him for our institute's seminar. Chief guest for this function was a very senior person from the Industry as that is the norm at Symbiosis. The event was to start at 9.30 am and the chief guest had arrived by 9.20 am as expected. Dr. Mujumdar who is extremely punctual (many times he reaches before time), had not arrived by then. I reached him on the mobile phone to inform him that the chief guest had already arrived and I was told by him that he was on his way but was held up because of a traffic jam. Within the next ten minutes he had arrived at the venue and the first thing he told me was that he was feeling extremely embarrassed getting late. It was not what he said but how he said it that made the difference. I could really see that he was not comfortable with the idea of getting late. I don't know how many of us in positions of authority will have the decency of saying sorry on being late. On the contrary, I have seen people deliberately coming late to show their authority.

He has a very large number of institutes to give direction to and therefore he has a lot of people to meet in a day. One very important thing I learnt from him is how not to look busy as a boss. Even if there are five people sitting with him and you are the sixth person, he will never make you feel as if he is busy and you are not important. I never found him ruffled up or appear to be under stress and, even if he was, it never showed on his face. He demonstrated that bosses show grace even under pressure.

This is a part of a great culture. I am myself a proponent of a culture of comfort and respect for all and working with Dr. Mujumdar firmed up my convictions further. I refer to Dr. Mujumdar's style of functioning as style M—M standing for the first letter of his name.

The man still uses a white Ambassador car, which has become his trademark. When I asked him why he uses this particular make when so many cars are now available which he can easily afford, he said, "If government of India is using it, there must be something good in it. Besides, I find it to have enough leg space and very comfortable." I can write a lot more about style M, but I would sum up by saying he is a wonderful and loveable boss.

On the flip side, bosses must never expect to have 'perfect' subordinates. If there can be no perfect bosses then how can one expect perfect subordinates. As managers, you must accept team mates with a pinch of salt. The earlier you accept it, the better it will be for you. People at the helm of affairs are responsible to deliver results. Their best bet is a good team. Hence, every manager wants a perfect team. Taking the earlier argument further, if there are no perfect individuals, there are no perfect teams. Despite the best selection process and great HR practices, it is next to impossible to get a team that can satisfy you across all parameters. Good managers make the best of what they have. They look at the strengths of people and deploy them according to the best they have in them.

It is pertinent to mention that all team members are equal but they are not identical in their temperament. A good manager should understand those fine emotional strands of individuals who work with him or her to the extent that he or she can differentiate between each member clearly. Having understood this, a great boss knows how to deal with each person individually and tactfully changing his or her style as and when required. For instance, there are people who are sensitive and get hurt easily. A good manager deals with them a little differently than with those who have a thicker skin.

Managers are also directly responsible for grooming their subordinates. Acting like a coach to the inexperienced can be a rewarding experience in itself. It is important to train the team so their skills remain updated. Sending people to attend training sessions and seminars is a good practice. Many managers, due to operational pressure, seldom spare their team members to attend training. This is good neither for the individual nor for the organisation.

Effective managers are good at convincing people. If they have a task at hand, they can convince their team to put their entire might behind a particular project. It is essential for every boss to develop the art of persuasion. You require reasoning, logic and motivation to convince and persuade people to give their best. Sponsoring your team mates for bigger roles is like being a good parent. Good managers expose their subordinates to challenging tasks. For instance, if the corporate office requires a specialist to do a turnkey job, then it is good to nominate one of your best guys to do it. This way you are giving a chance to a team member to work on a larger assignment and demonstrate his competence.

Indirectly, it earns your department some additional brownie points and boosts the morale of an individual as well. It is a good practice to expose your team to competition. Let them know the best practices of other departments through experiential learning. Seminars, workshops and symposiums are opportunities where you get to know what others are doing. One should never let go of such opportunities. Even in Business schools, good institutions encourage students to participate in intercollegiate festivals so that their students get to know the standards and practices of other rival institutes.

It is a good practice, not to compare subordinates with each other.

You should look at a team as a bouquet of flowers. Don't compare a rose with a lilly. A rose has its own qualities and a lilly has its own. Comparisons seldom help. Many times comparisons generate jealousy and breed bad blood among people.

Having favourites is something you can do without. Having blue eyed boys or favourites is the beginning of politics in an organisation. Bosses must never allow politics and favouritism within their teams. If you want peace and professional prosperity, stay away from politics. In fact, bosses are the ones who start and encourage politics and mostly themselves get entangled in their own web and regret. It starts multiple power centres, bickering and back biting which is the unhealthiest practice for any organisation.

Another closely related aspect to politics is dealing with the organisational hierarchy. There are certain reporting patterns in every organisation. A boss while playing out a larger role has to deal with different layers of hierarchy. In such a case maintaining mutual respect becomes important. This is a sensitive issue and if one is not careful it can upset the entire apple cart. You have to maintain harmony across the organisation. One major mistake which managers make is to let one person criticise the other and mostly in absentia. It gets worse if you allow a subordinate to criticise his or her immediate boss. Some bosses, who want to play politics, encourage this practice. This is the sign of an ill-mannered boss who has not had good upbringing.

Simpler expression for empowerment is freedom. I have learnt from experience that the moment you give freedom people become responsible. When you tell someone, "This is your baby," you are sure to get great results. Let people find ways and means to solve problems. Yet you need to guide or correct people occasionally. Linked with this is the review process. I have seen bosses springing a surprise only during annual appraisals. This can be a jarring experience for your subordinates. I had a boss who gave a lot of freedom and was also approachable and pleasant to deal with. He never gave any feedback during numerous interactions one had with him during the year.

One felt nice and reassured that one was on the right track and the boss was happy. It was during the appraisal session, he came up with his true colours. He started with something that happened nine months back and moved up chronologically. Most of his observations and suggestions were right, but I could not understand why he did not tell me all that earlier. Had he mentioned this earlier, I would have made amends. Was his aim only to remain secretive and devastate me in the end at a time when a written appraisal was to be made by him? I feel these kind of bosses are dangerous and surreptitiously damaging. The job of a boss is not only to observe and report but it is to observe, correct and if still not corrected, then report.

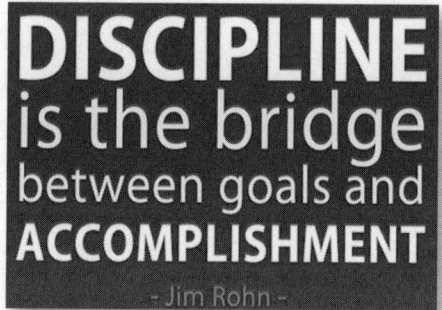

DISCIPLINE is the bridge between goals and ACCOMPLISHMENT
- Jim Rohn -

Discipline is one issue that needs to be handled on a priority and taken seriously. I look at discipline as now or never. If there is a case of poor discipline, a boss must deal with it immediately. An issue as serious as discipline must be nipped in the bud. A punishment, reprimand or a warning must be delivered at the earliest. Many bosses delay it, for two reasons. The first reason is they do not accord discipline a high priority on their agenda, the second is the lack of courage to take action. Both these reasons are manageable and are excuses which could later prove to be costly for a boss and the organisation.

Another time tested dictum which every boss must understand is do not give orders that cannot be obeyed. More of a British Army rule book matter, it has a hard meaning behind it when it comes to maintaining respect and decorum. When you pass orders that are unreasonable or are not doable, your subordinates, even if they want to comply, will not be able to comply. At the end of it, this looks like disobedience in the face of the boss. In such a situation, either a boss looks like a fool or it appears his orders are not taken seriously. This puts a boss in an awkward situation. In my experience people give unreasonable orders due to inexperience or immaturity. Both these are a recipe for a disaster.

A boss must manage perceptions. In other words it is self image management. People must perceive you to be good besides your being actually good. People must perceive you to be honest, straight forward, gentlemanly, and high on integrity. You should be clear as to how people must perceive you and ensure your image management efforts are made towards building that perception. Do not project a false image as this is the most dangerous ground to tread on. False images can neither be created nor be sustained in the eyes of the people you deal with.

Supporting your subordinates is another aspect of people management. When you give freedom, you need to give a little freedom for failure as well. If a mistake is not deliberate or is not due to negligence, it is pardonable. But act of pardoning has to be prudently decided. Ultimately, a boss must appear to be supportive and large hearted.

Nobody is indispensable is what one of my bosses had taught me. This implies having backup plans for every critical human resource that you have. If someone falls sick, what will I do? If a woman wants maternity leave who would replace her? You must plan a backup in mind. Bosses are paid for this. Plan the leave meticulously. Making an elaborate leave plan at the beginning of the year is a great practice and it should be executed effectively. You can go wrong by 10 percent but cannot go beyond this acceptable limit of tolerance.

It is a good practice to ensure every individual gets his share of leave in a year. Some good organisations make it mandatory for the entire staff to avail their entitled leave quota. This ensures every individual gets a break from work. Even if there is no such rule in the organisation, as a departmental head, you can always ensure it for each of your teammates. Work hard and play hard should be the spirit of every manager.

If you are emotionally caring and understand what people require, you will earn everyone's respect. I have seen bosses who have been difficult with their subordinates, and created unnecessary pain and bad taste for people who worked with them. Such bosses are not only hated during their career but people hold bad blood in their hearts for the rest of their lives against such guys.

It is difficult to understand why bosses don't make little changes in their behaviour to earn respect and love from their colleagues. Being a good person in no way compromises on the efficiency and output of the organisations they run. In return, they get a lifetime achievement award and blessings of many people for the rest of their lives.

I remember one retired senior officer sending a written complaint to the Army Headquarters regarding how other retired officers staying in the same colony treated him. His complaint was that most of the people avoided him, so much so that when they saw him walking on the road they would cross over to the other side. This gentleman had been nasty to people during his career and had earned a reputation of being a heartless guy. Now, how on earth could such a man expect people to give him any respect later in life?

Bosses in the Armed Forces

Work and life in the armed forces are different from what they are like in the civil street, specially the corporate world. Change of scene every two to three years is something inescapable for the entire rank and file. Therefore, transfer to different locations, different job roles, and working with different teams and tasks comes naturally to those who have ever been in uniform. In addition, the transfer system is centralised and there is no choice but to move to the location and organisation that one has been posted to.

It goes without saying that one meets a new boss every two to three years. Unlike the corporate world, you do not have an option or luxury of leaving a boss in case you get a nasty one. If you are posted under someone, you remain under him or her till he or she himself or herself moves out after his or her own two to three years long tenure. Therefore, there is no choice but to manage yourself with whosoever is your boss; this comes as a blessing in disguise because one has to learn to put up with different types of bosses. The flip side is that if you get a boss who is nasty, he or she can make your life miserable for three years which maximises your helplessness.

In the Armed Forces a boss has a tremendous influence and control over a subordinate's life. There are several reasons for it.

The first reason for a stranglehold a boss has on his subordinates is the promotion system within the armed forces which is a highly pyramidal organisation having limited room at the top. Due to this fact, the promotion system becomes stringent. As one goes higher up the ladder, number of vacancies becomes lesser. Unfortunately, the rejection rate for promotion is very high. The promotion system is based on the confidential reports of individuals known as annual confidential reports (ACRs). Here, the immediate boss writes a report for a yearlong performance for all the subordinates. This is similar to performance appraisal in the corporate world, though the format is different. In a twenty years long career, even one or two poor appraisals can seal one's fate forever. This happens because it is more of a rejection system than a selection system, which becomes highly competitive. If one is overlooked for promotion, there is no other recourse till one retires from the service at the same rank. This is a stiff price to pay.

In contrast, in the civil street if one boss does not appreciate your work, he can harm your promotions or increments within that organisation alone. If you decide to move on or take up a job elsewhere in another organisation of your choice, it is possible to leave your negative baggage behind and start afresh with a clean slate.

Such a tight leash promotion system of the armed forces does two things. First, it leaves you with no choice but to put up with a boss, who has been assigned to you. Second, because of fear of jeopardising your career at one stroke of the pen of your boss, the system promotes sycophancy. One gets used to dealing with the good, the bad and the ugly with tact and diplomacy.

In the Armed Forces a boss not only has a hold on one's next promotion but can make his subordinates life miserable because a lot of things are in his hands. On the other hand, a good boss, if he wants can create heaven for his team. The Armed Forces a self-contained organisation and person incharge has huge resources at his disposal. Bosses therefore enjoy enough autonomy to swing your life between heaven and hell. I have seen bosses who created a wonderful environment even in small stations located in wilderness. On the other hand, I have seen bosses who could make life difficult for people in the best of the locations, even exotic hill stations.

On a professional level I have seen bosses who were on a shaky wicket and inspired no confidence in their subordinates. There were professional people who could guide and lead their teams effectively and, simultaneously, be gentlemen all the time. Such bosses would be remembered for a lifetime by those who served with them.

One typical trait of a boss in the Armed Forces is being large hearted. One would meet many with swollen heads but few with a large heart. Large hearted bosses display valour in decision-making and also while dealing with situations. They don't bother about small things; an error here or a mistake there. Such valorous behaviour is on the decline though. The reason is, earlier people joined the armed forces for prestige rather than money. People took decisions from the gut and not in a calculative way. Such bosses also displayed valour in war.

In contrast, one would also bump into those meek people who are over- cautious and have a limited risk taking capability. I have worked under such bosses and found it difficult to give my best. Even though professionally competent, such people never inspired confidence in their subordinates. Instead of feeling motivated, you feel some discomfort and suffocation when you are with such people. The basic survival principle under these circumstances is, "If your boss is weak you cannot be aggressive."

While in the corporate world big money is at stake, in a war scenario more than money, many lives are at risk. In battle situations there is much at stake and there is a lot of ambiguity in assessing situations and passing orders. Many times the orders are verbal and it is difficult to keep track of what was said by whom and at what time. Therefore, trust becomes the fulcrum for working in such a fluid situation. Subordinates need to have 100 percent trust in their Field Commanders in order to carry out orders.

I have seen bosses giving orders to do something specific and later denying having said anything like that to save their own skin. This is nothing short of failing in integrity. There are bravehearts too, the people you can blindly trust and even bet your life on. Over the years this breed has dwindled in numbers. This has happened primarily because the top brass no more act as professionals who are responsible to the public and the nation. Instead, they started looking after their own interests. During the Second World War, many General Officers were relieved of their commands because of incompetence, cowardice or both. Such a thing rarely happens now, the trend has taken form after the 1960s.

Being a Field Commander in a combat is extra ordinarily difficult and many capable officers fail. During the Second World War, the US Army played a major role and a large American army, Air Force and Naval Forces were deployed in operations. Senior American Commanders of the rank of General were given a few months to prove themselves. If found lacking, they would be replaced by someone more capable. A pretty substantial number of senior officers were relieved of their command for unacceptable performance, some of them being Corps Commanders.

Scenario in the US Army itself has changed since the Second World War. The US troops have been in action in Vietnam as well as in the Gulf. Though these have been long drawn wars, not a single General has been sacked by the US Army. Lt. Col. Paul Yinghing noted that relief of Generals became so rare that a private who loses his rifle is now punished more than a general, who loses his part of the war. In a book *Crisis in Command*, the authors Richard Gabriel and Paul Savage argue that United States military force has been weakened by the members of the officer cadre who have abandoned honour and integrity to further their individual careers.

They further conclude that the armed forces have adopted a corporate culture and hence lost the cutting edge. If one goes into military history, one would not be surprised to discover several blunders committed by the military top brass, or bosses across nations. Many due to external factors and mostly because of incompetence of the people on top. They were responsible for hundreds of lives perishing and equipment worth millions. Professional competence of a boss therefore becomes a vital factor for him or her to earn respect of his or her subordinates. Not surprisingly, the ACRs written for service period in battle field, commonly termed as war reports, become extremely important for promotion in the armed forces.

Talking of confidential reports, during peace time a boss who sees a promising person writes a citation in the report saying, "I would like to take him to war with me". Such an expression becomes something extraordinary and is given huge weightage for promotions.

In the armed forces there are no 360 degree appraisals, otherwise many subordinates would write, "I would never like to go to war under this bum", for their bosses.

Battle honours may sometimes get biased because of blue eyed-ism. It depends on how the citation is written. Therefore, your valour in war is proportional to the power of the pen which writes the report. Behind the pen is the hand and the hand belongs to your boss.

Mostly in the British parlance Order of the British Empire (OBE) was in a lighter vein called 'other bugger's effort'.

I earlier mentioned that bosses in the armies have tremendous power over the subordinates which actually stems out of the military law and army acts. If a situation demands (which has to be justified), a superior officer can even place a subordinate under arrest. The person incharge or, as in military parlance person in command is vested with a lot of authority over his subordinates because of the nature of the job. The Commanding Officer in most cases becomes a one man jury with immense powers to pass a verdict. Most orders and laws are framed for war like situations. Many times bosses exploit this and keep the entire control with them, leaving little elbow space for others to take decisions.

In the Armed Forces, there is a great concept of Second-in-Command, in every sub organisation. The Second-in-Command is meant to be a hot standby for the person incharge. In all fairness, the Second-in-Command must be given sufficient freedom and respect by the person in command. In most cases, unfortunately, this does not happen. It is difficult to pin point whether this is due to the skewed military psyche or due to individual authoritative style of leadership acquired by many military bosses. Surprisingly, the Second-in-Command is required to behave in a subservient manner in front of the number one in command. If he or she does not behave as desired, he or she could miss his next promotion.

Therefore, more often than not, the Second-in-Command behaves like a lamb in front of his boss who acts like a tiger. I call this a 'tiger-lamb syndrome' because the moment a Second-in-Command takes charge as number one after his promotion; he starts roaring like a tiger. Therefore, a tiger becomes a lamb and a lamb becomes a tiger with equal ease, as and when the situation demands. It could be a coincidence that the official nick names for appointments in the army are also tiger and lamb for the officer in command and the Second-in-Command, respectively.

It would be much better for individuals serving as number two in the organisation and for the establishment if the person in command gives some freedom and respect to him. In the Armed Forces, I have seen a tendency of zero error tolerance. Officers are sometimes myopic and judge a person on one incident, one mistake, or even an accident. How can you pass judgments on somebody's capabilities based on one event? I have seen people getting a rap on the knuckles just because a car did not reach on time to pick up a General.

On the other hand, I have seen one-job-heroes as well. In this diametrically opposite scenario, if a person does a great job once, which impresses the boss immensely, he is upgraded to the blue eyed boy category forever. Such behaviour is more whimsical than rational. When you judge a person for one year, you must look at all his achievements and underperformances in totality, rather than basing your judgment on one incident. This could happen in other professions also, but in the Armed Forces many senior officers often get swayed by one good or one bad deed alone. Such bosses always keep a negatively charged atmosphere, where people are always on tenter hooks, ever ready to please their boss, lest he feels otherwise. Obviously, this promotes sycophancy across the organisation.

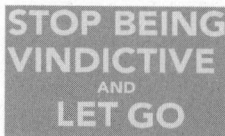 There are some great souls in the Armed Forces too, who one could revere. I have had the opportunity to work with some great bosses, who could be taken as a role model by anyone. Majority of the people are honest and I have had people on top who were caring and would go to any length to help and support their subordinates.

There are many vindictive bosses who take things to heart, striking a venomous punch whenever they get an opportunity. These are like green snakes in green grass. I actually had one. This vindictive attitude is a result of ego which bosses tend to have. More often than not, these things that hurt bosses are not based on professional issues. Sometimes these are frivolous occurrences for which people are superceded for life. One wonders why people have such small egos and get hurt so easily. More importantly, how do such bosses have the heart to ruin somebody's career based on flimsy reasons.

Armed Forces provide enough opportunities for interaction among families of their personnel. Army wives participate in many semi-official activities. This is done to promote camaraderie and brotherhood. While it works well on most occasions, I have seen wives' ego clashes creating major problems among the officers. Mostly, you need to not only manage your boss but also his wife! The best way is to keep wives away from the official side of the profession. A difficult order, only few can manage to implement it in its practical sense. I have seen careers being ruined based on just one argument or a professional disagreement between a boss and a subordinate. In contrast, having also worked in the civil outfit, I have realised that people do want to follow the policy of let's agree to disagree. This stems out of the fact that many such bosses expect healthy discussions and arguments to throw up great ideas which can be beneficial for the organisation.

I have also observed that the armed forces officers take a long time to destarch themselves when they move to civil street to take up a second career. They carry their old mindset and do not venture into discussions or arguments with their newly found civilian bosses. Most of them have great potential and can contribute immensely to the civilian organisation if they can change their outlook and start speaking their mind, which is appreciated in a business environment.

The Armed Forces as an organisation makes people conformists— people who should obey and not argue. This being a part of military training gets embedded into people's mind forever. As a result, those who do not manage their bosses by toeing their line or want to become non-conformists, often do not rise up the ladder.

This teaches adaptability, but at a heavy cost to the establishment and to those who are professionally competent and speak their mind—at times. A very popular and often used term to manoeuvre well up the ranks is to know the boss' mind! Once you know the boss' mind then the best way out is to tune your mind with the boss' mind. So 'go along to get along' is the

ADAPTABILITY
You can't direct the wind, but you can adjust your sails.

success mantra. This happens in highly professional armies all the time. Colonel Douglas Macgregor, as an author blames sycophantic culture for failures in Iraq. The biggest problem, according to him, is within the department of Defence at the senior level as the officer corps there brooks no arguments. Arguments are seen as sign of dissent which is equated to disloyalty. This loyalty, albeit, is to the person and not the organisation. The question is, "Should a subordinate be loyal to his superiors or to the establishment in the largest interest of the organisation?" Unfortunately, bosses see a suggestion, a discussion or an argument as a threat to their being superior, a word which sometimes itself is demeaning.

A whistle blower or a person who stands up for what is right can save millions of dollars and thousands of lives but, more often than not, the army bureaucracy can retaliate harshly through the appraisal system, unreasonable work schedules, and harassment through frequent moves, inflicting thousand cuts.

Sycophants encourage sycophants. The top brass becomes full of spineless guys, who can neither say 'No' to their bosses, nor can they take a 'No' from their juniors. People who criticise or even suggest the right things are labelled cribbers and complainers, and weeded out early in their career. As they say, "With such state of affairs, things are all going haywaire."

Sycophancy is not confined to the armed forces alone, though more visible, but is quite prevalent in bureaucracy and the political class across the world. Not surprising then that Lyndon Johnson, former President of the United Sates, said, "Yes I want loyalty and absolute devotion," declaring, "I want someone who will kiss my behind and say it smells like roses."

Impeccably above Board

Bosses who have impeccable morals and behaviour are the most respected lot. In fact, every boss should have and display high moral standards and this is required 24 × 7.

To earn respect, a manager, a boss or a leader, whichever hat he wears, has to ensure that he lives with honesty, courage and strength of character. In today's turbulent times, when we witness scams, cheating and deceit all around us, we still expect people in power to have a strong moral fibre. Here I am going to discuss those attributes that collectively make a strong character.

A boss, however competent or accomplished he may be, will not be able to survive long if he lacks integrity. There are many examples where many prominent leaders did well and rose to great heights, but fell with a severe thud because they acted out of self-interest and were labelled dishonest. Rajat Gupta is a case in point. Gupta, an Indian American businessman who was the Managing Director of Mckinsey and Company for almost a decade and also a board member of many prestigious corporations, was convicted for insider trading charges. A man of that stature had to resign from all his prestigious positions to undergo a couple of years of imprisonment.

Alan Simpson an American politician said, "If you have Integrity, nothing else matters. If you don't have integrity, nothing else matters." This is all the more true for people in positions of power. Those who fell on this account failed to understand that the more authority we are vested with, the more accountable we are. People in positions of power are responsible to the establishment, to the law and to the people they manage.

I feel integrity, ethics and morals have a direct relation with honour, shame and pride. In earlier days, people lived for honour and pride and hence, almost clamoured for it. So much so that a person would prefer losing his life rather than his honour. People took pride in being upright and honest. Unfortunately today, bureaucrats, politicians, policemen, industrialists and even corporate honchos having been exposed by media, caught by the law or even jailed show no remorse or regret, which is a very serious flaw in the society today.

People earlier lived by a code of conduct and demonstrated integrity so that they could hold their heads high with pride. They did this, so that nobody could point an accusing finger at them. Today a majority of people care more for money than morals and it is difficult to find people who are high on integrity. This is more to do with the society than the corporate environment.

Another important aspect of appropriate behaviour is being

politically correct. People in responsible positions must speak responsibly while dealing with others. They should not offend either the society or the institution they belong to in the context of gender, race, culture or even religion. This is now becoming increasingly important for bosses or leaders in the corporate arena because of globalisation where people from different countries, religions and ideologies work together.

To be politically correct, choice of words becomes important. For instance, instead of calling someone a Negro or Black, the Americans now address them as African Americans. Disabled or physically handicapped are addressed as physically challenged. Dignity is in words.

People who are downright straightforward usually walk the talk. In simple terms, bosses must do exactly what they say. Bosses are put under the scanner by their subordinates if they say something and do something diametrically opposite. Such bosses are also seen as promise breakers, downright liars and at worst, labelled as frauds. For a boss to earn respect and keep it intact, it is important to do things in accordance with what he has been saying to his people. For instance, if you promise that you will give a certain percentage bonus to all employees, then it is better to ensure that the promise is fulfilled in letter and spirit.

Closely related to this is word of honour. What good is a boss, if you cannot believe in what he says? Even thieves have a code of honour. In better days if someone of stature said, "You have my word for this," it meant a lot and people took things for granted thereafter. For earning respect it is important for people in power to demonstrate that once they give their word, they honour it.

we all deserve happiness. sometimes its just takes a painful journey to help you find it, so that you can then truly cherish and appreciate it.

Be fair and show that you are fair. People must perceive you to be fair. My boss is absolutely fair at all times is a great compliment from a subordinate that a boss can expect. In fact, being fair to all across the board is something a boss must always follow.

Courage and Conviction

To have courage and conviction is something a boss expects from his subordinates and subordinates expect from their boss in equal measure.

What you believe in strongly is what your values or beliefs are. But do you have the courage to stand by your values or beliefs? It is important to spell out your conviction, value system or professional stance to everyone around you. It is probably more important to demonstrate courage and speak your mind out when somebody challenges your convictions.

Another important factor to earn respect is to always conduct yourself with grace. A boss who tries to curry favour from his superiors is never respected by his subordinates. Bosses, who are too obsequious towards their bosses, demonstrate a servile behaviour. I feel it is more to do with one's personal respect and therefore, people in power must behave appropriately by maintaining a certain level of decorum while dealing with their bosses.

Politicians are examples of servile behaviour, where some of them shamelessly lie prostrate in public to demonstrate respect and submissiveness to their supreme leaders. Therefore, it is of utmost importance that a boss conducts himself or herself properly in front of his or her team and otherwise, in a dignified manner.

Another important trait that subordinates appreciate and expect in their bosses is straightforwardness and to be someone who accepts no nonsense from any one regardless of whoever he may be. Bosses are supposed to protect their teams from the political pressures and the usual heat and dust of the organisational hierarchy. Many bosses succumb to the outside and inside pressures and fail to dig in their heels. They need to deal with subordinates firmly whenever required because bosses should never tolerate disrespect from subordinates.

A boss is as good as his team perceives him to be. All the earlier factors matter in building an impression and perception in front of your own team. In a way, perception is like demonstrated credibility. Every boss must pay attention to building up his credibility and reputation in front of his subordinates, in particular, and rest of the organisation, in general.

Creativity and Common Sense

When I look for creativity in a boss, I am looking for a person who can think out of the box and who is prepared to experiment. Ability to take risks and experiment with new ideas, suggestions and situations is one of those top-end qualities that one expects of a leader or a boss. I have also worked with many rulebook bosses who are sticklers for regulations. You need to sometimes move out of the rule book to think out of the box.

Usually people relate creativity to art and music alone. This is far from true as creative thinking can do wonders in business, problem-solving, and handling situations while dealing with people. Bosses face extraordinary challenges daily. Many of them have no past precedence. None of the daily problems have bookish solutions. Therefore, a creative mind for a boss is a boon.

Bosses, apart from domain knowhow, must have common sense so they can deal with situations effectively. A common sense approach sometimes can get you out of the trickiest of situations. I look at the science of management as a science of common sense or as a science whose base is common sense. Ralph Waldo Emerson said, "Common sense is as rare as a genius—is the basis of genius."

Our education system and training makes our thinking process cluttered, complicated and cramped. We, therefore, sometimes take complex routes to solve simple problems. Common sense indicates a basic level of intelligence and that is why we all have it in us—which we never use mostly. It is like an animal's instinct, I call it horse sense. Horses seldom fall, even in the toughest of terrains because they can sense danger instinctively. Several scientists, engineers and managers have used their raw common sense to solve complex problems.

When Thomas Edison called people for an interview he used to ask taking a bulb in his hand, "What is the volume of the bulb?" Most of them, who were brilliant engineers, used to take the dimensions with vernier calipers, do some complex calculations and came up with the answer. One odd person would fill it up with water and pour the water in a measuring flask to tell the exact volume and he got the job!

I sometimes feel we feed too much analysis into our students in business schools and make them numb to common sense. It is better to have common sense without education than to have education without common sense.

A situation was given to a group of job applicants. The situation was, you are driving a car during a heavy downpour and see three people at a bus stop who are drenched and are shivering in the cold. One is an old friend who once saved your life. The other is a beautiful woman and the third is a sick lady who is old and needs medical care. You can take only one passenger in your car, so whom would you take and why?

Your heart says you must save the old lady; your head says you must not leave your friend whom you owe your life to. But you have fallen for the girl and you would not like to let this opportunity slip out of your hands.

The candidate who got the job said that he would ask his friend to take the car and escort the old lady to the hospital, while he would wait at the bus stop with the pretty woman and give her his coat to keep her warm. Only one out of hundred candidates came up with this idea!

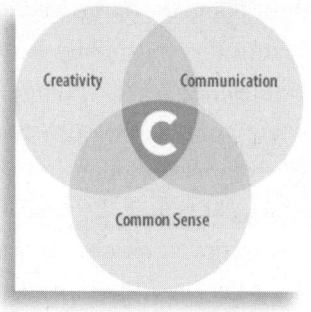

To bring creativity and common sense in your life, one should start thinking metaphorically. When you create an analogy between ideas and objects by use of words, it becomes a metaphor. He or she is at the peak of his or her performance, or he or she slept like a log are metaphors. Being able to create metaphors out of situations and using them to explain your point during professional communication is an art worth acquiring.

To be creative you must do two things. First, don't worry about being right or wrong and second, break rules if required. How can you break barriers of human thinking without breaking rules which have been made by humans? As Steve Jobs said, "Innovation distinguishes between a leader and a follower."

You need to be ahead of the problem in every way. Another aspect about creativity is, to be creative your new ideas are never fully clear. There is always a sense of clutter or smoke around those ideas. This smokescreen gets lifted gradually, as you keep refining your ideas about your idea. It is like a peeling process, layer by layer. As Albert Einstein said, "Problems cannot be solved by the same level of thinking that created them."

Creativity is also linked to simplicity as it is to common sense. "Simplicity is the ultimate sophistication," said Leonardo Da Vinci. As bosses or leaders, you must make your plans, simple and workable. Too complicated a plan will be difficult to execute and may not work.

Even technology that succeeds is simple. "Too many screws," was what Henry Ford commented about the carburettor design of his most popular car, the Model T car. Facebook is a simple idea, but beautifully and boldly executed and made a twenty-year-old a billionaire. Project Iridium was a complex system of 66 satellites going around the earth providing worldwide telecom coverage between 1996–98, providing calls at Rs. 150 per minute. It failed as a business venture because at that time GSM networks had already started operations, but at the centre of the failure was the complex design of the Iridium system as compared to the landbased GSM mobile systems.

I feel that as bosses, people must question complexity and favour simplicity. With this rule of thumb a lot can be saved in terms of money, time and effort.

As someone said, "You have achieved perfection in design, not when you have nothing more to add, but when you have nothing more to take away." As a boss, always ask a question, "Is there any simpler way to do it?"

Some Quintessentials for Bosses

One of the most essential requirements of a good workforce is discipline. I see many senior members of management of large corporations struggling to handle this issue. Some of them are very confused as they are constantly bombarded with words or concepts like empowerment, fun at work, freedom is essential for creativity, flexible timings, and combating stress at work, which they can neither comprehend fully nor do they know how to actually have these, if at all, alongside discipline within the workplace.

My experience tells me that creativity and empowerment as well as flexibility have nothing to do with discipline. You can implement discipline and yet retain freedom, if your people understand that freedom comes with responsibility. This is a typical problem with companies operating in India. Indian workforce wants everything as a right, but does not want to demonstrate responsibility.

To set things right, the top management must make it clear to every employee that the company they work for holds discipline as one of the most important performance attributes for employees, right from the top to the bottom. Bosses who take charge of undisciplined organisations have a tough task at hand. To rein in discipline, they need to be very focused, committed, and be prepared to take a bit of flak from all quarters. When you enforce discipline, you are moving people out of their complacent attitude, their comfort zone. Who wants to work out of their comfort zone? Hence, there is resistance. Best way is to move top down. This way you sort out the top brass and then gradually move downwards till you reach the lowest denominator in the organisational hierarchy. It requires huge efforts, sometimes at the cost of firing a few who become obstacles to this change. Someone said, "Sometimes in order to cleanup, it is necessary to make a mess." At the end of it, it pays rich dividends.

The Indian education system must make all efforts to make students responsive and responsible. This is one thing which we lack as a nation and there is no better vehicle than educational institutes to bring discipline in the society.

A boss decides how to run his organisation. Discipline within an organisation is seen in the context of the rules and regulations laid down by him. As far as possible, bosses must spell out their code of conduct and what they expect from employees, clearly and in writing.

> **Maturity is not when we start speaking BIG things, it is when we start understanding small things.**

One of the most practical ways of getting into the saddle is to take some time to settle down. I have seen bosses who are in a hurry to change things without getting to know the people and the problems. If you kick the horse, the moment you sit on it you may either scare the horse, who could buck and throw you off its back or it may gallop so fast that you may lose control over the horse. Riding an organisation is no different. I learnt this from my first boss. When he joined the organisation he never commented on anything for almost a month. He just observed, observed and observed. He listened to everyone, read all the files, policies and asked the department heads to make presentations. He got into every detail and knew exactly what was wrong and where. In almost two to three months he had drawn up his entire blueprint for the change he wanted to bring about. He got into a discussion after almost a month and soon he was in full form. I feel every boss must do this. You must tighten the screw slowly so you do not cause any damage to the wood. Remember, the screw has to be screwed in and not hammered in like a nail. If you nail a screw, you will surely go wrong.

Grace

Once you observe, digest and then act, you are less likely to make costly mistakes which you may regret later. Don't hit the ground while running, you may hurt yourself. Be patient, results will be there for you to see but only after some time. Therefore, understand your role fully, learn your responsibilities, and don't hesitate to ask your subordinate if you have a query. This requires maturity and grace.

I learnt some great things from my bosses. One of my mentors told me that certain management principles can be learnt straight from our home. Do we give in to all the demands and tantrums of our children? We listen to them, we agree to certain things and to certain things it is a No. As a person in charge, one must learn to say 'No' at the work place too. Some of us find it difficult to say No to clients, subordinates, and peers. It is important to learn how to say no.

The fundamental stance for this is be polite and yet be firm. A good boss does not mean being good all the time or accepting every proposal or request that comes up to you. Listen to things up to a point, but be sure to learn how to draw a line without being rude or discourteous. At the same time, a boss should never look as if he is pleading. You can urge people to agree, but should never plead.

Giving orders or instructions is also an art. Another of my mentors once said, "My instructions are so clear that if a person still cannot carry out my orders, he should hang himself rather than come back to me."

Articulation is an art which can be learnt. I have seen some senior people giving instructions that are confusing and often contradicting to the spirit of the problem at hand. Why do some people in authority not give clear orders? There are several reasons for it. The first one is they themselves are not clear about what exactly they want. The second is that they purposely don't give clear orders and want to leave some ambiguity so that a person makes a mistake and they then can take credit by giving the right solution. The third is they lack expressivity or articulation, and are unable to explain what needs to be done. Bosses who are clear headed give precise instructions and are respected by everyone.

Post mortems are sticky affairs. When things go wrong, people huddle up to find an escape goat. Somebody is looking for somebody's scalp. "Heads must roll, someone has to pay," people exclaim. Mistakes are a part of work. As a person incharge one must ensure your people do not make the same mistake again. In addition, you must find out how it happened and who was responsible. Once it is done, the organisation must move on. Don't get emotionally tied down to goof ups. These can drain your energy and also bog down a lot many other guys, hampering their work. Bosses must take goof ups matter-of-factly. It is a good idea for the team which made a mess to find out and let you know what happened, instead of appointing an outside committee. This is a much neater arrangement which gets you the results without letting any garbage fly all over.

Decision-making is a major part of a top guns job. People at the top have the privilege of having many experts and specialists under them who are easily accessible to them. This privilege has certain advantages and disadvantages.

One must take advantage of experts by consulting them; after all they are specialists in their field. It would be wrong to underestimate their valuable inputs. But having consulted the domain experts, the person incharge has to finally use his judgment to take the final decision. It often happens that experts have a myopic or a limited view, whereas the person in charge has an overall or macro view of the situation and hence, is in a better position to take a final call. The observation of a successful General of the US Army said, "The elites can become so inbred that they produce haemophiliacs, who bleed to death as soon as they are nicked by the real worlds."

Being a boss is a tough job, especially when it comes to keeping people happy all the time. And worse, if you are able to do it then something is grossly wrong somewhere. The reason for this is simple. Bosses are accountable first to themselves and then to the organisation they work for. For this reason alone, they often have to take tough decisions which go well with some and are not appreciated by others in the organisation. If you take decisions based on the premise that hope it will keep everyone happy, then you can never take decisions which are good in the larger interest of the organisation. If you are in for meaningful decisions then be prepared to piss-off a few people in the organisation. Remember, you are not paid to keep everyone happy.

Even appraisals cannot be great for everyone. As a boss you give a raise or promotion to some, while others don't get it. So there are mixed reactions to every action of a boss. But you have to be impartial and judicious so that no one should feel that he has been victimised or cheated. Similarly, policy decisions also affect some people adversely while benefitting others. You don't have to be ruthless or a dictator to get the job done, but must have enough courage of conviction to take some unpopular decisions, which could annoy a section of people. Therefore, don't stay in the middle of the road, you may get run over.

I will not be wrong if I say an idea is money. Living in a knowledge economy, one has to understand the value of an idea. In fact, ideas build knowledge. In technology space, killer applications begin with an idea. On the face of it and in the beginning, an idea may not look very spectacular. Most ideas when presented get rejected only because they don't appeal to decision-makers or bosses. This is a trap which needs to be avoided by the bosses. In a way, bosses are paid to identify talent and a worthwhile talent has great ideas buzzing in his or her head. As great film makers spot good talent, great bosses must be able to spot great ideas within their organisation. Bosses must have the risk taking ability so that they are prepared to experiment with new suggestions, ideas and avenues. I feel this is another important quality of a great boss or a manager. As Oscar Wilde said, "An idea that is not dangerous is unworthy of being called an idea."

Last of these quintessentials is the art of getting things done, in one word, execution. The problem is that everybody wants to be a strategist, a planner, a consultant, or a director while nobody wants to dirty his or her hands by actually doing it. This is a typical top management syndrome, where there are more Generals than foot soldiers.

For execution, a sound detailed planning is a must. Having done that, job allocation, responsibilities, monitoring, and feedback mechanism must be put

in place. It is important to have the required resources, manpower, equipments, and material before hand so that you do not create bottlenecks which could have been avoided. As far as possible, a boss must participate in the execution of the plans. If you have too many projects running under you, then be sure to keep a track of each project by some means of communication. Bosses must remain updated and should be in touch with every team or project at regular intervals.

Execution also implies a good responsive culture. Now, this is very important for a boss to build. If your team and individuals are responsive to every call, every challenge or every requirement that comes their way, you can rest assured that your projects will never be delayed. Therefore, execution is a function of organisational culture which takes years to build.

If not God, be a King—A Blue Blooded Boss

Has it ever crossed your mind that a boss can even behave like a king? Can he sometimes display a royal attitude? Can he let go of trivialities? Can he rise above the ordinary?

Now I am talking of the ultimate in bossism.

I feel every boss worth his salt must attempt to achieve this.

Chanakya, a 4th BC scholar, who was a mentor to emperor Chandragupta Maurya, defines the qualities of a good king very well. According to Chanakya, a king must possess certain traits and qualities for him to be effective. To be an affective boss, these qualities, if imbibed, can go a long way.

- A king must have self-control and must demonstrate this all the time. In the modern management parlance this is an important trait within the Emotional Intelligence Continuum.
- He must cultivate intellect by association with elders and the

noble. This would be akin to getting coached by mentors and coaches.

- A king must be disciplined and must demonstrate self-discipline. He goes to say that a king, therefore, keeps away from another's wife, practices non-violence (ahimsa) and avoids day dreaming, capriciousness and falsehood.
- An emperor must always keep his promise. This is extremely important for a king's credibility.
- A royal attitude is full of gratitude. Kings seldom keep any debt and tend to repay and reward with grace.
- Royals think big, they do things king size.
- Kings are neither dilatory nor do they procrastinate. If there is problem, they act immediately to solve it.
- Great kings are amenable to guidance. They listen to the wise as well as ordinary people, and that is how they are remembered by their subjects and the nobility.
- A king or a queen is always valorous, especially during a crisis.
- They are dignified, sophisticated and display a sense of royalty in their behaviour.
- Kings are large hearted and show mercy appropriately when the occasion demands. They rise above the ordinary in certain trying circumstances and are willing to pardon.
- A good king is always just in giving reward and punishment. According to Chanakya, a king acts according to Dharma which directs him to be just, compassionate, and impartial in all his dealings.
- Kings and queens are good with words. They choose the right words for the occasion, appropriately.
- Royalty has a charm; with their confidence, apt behaviour and poise they command respect.
- Successful kings do not fall prey to back biting.
- They resist greed and control their anger.
- Kings are decisive and seldom fickle minded.

The following is true for a virtuous king.

In the happiness of his subjects lays the kings happiness, in their welfare is his welfare. He shall not consider as good only that pleases him but treat as beneficial to him whatever pleases his subjects.

Come to think of it, it is not difficult to behave like a royal. You need not have blue blood running in your veins to be like a king.

I have had the pleasure of working with some good people who had a tinge of royalty in them. But that breed is almost extinct now. I am certain that with a little conscious effort an ordinary person can transform himself or herself into a blue blooded boss. That I feel should be the ultimate objective of every man or woman in power.

To behave like a king, there is a price to be paid. This is best summed up by Field Marshal Philip Chetwode, Commander-in-Chief, India, who during his inaugural address to the cadets of the Indian Military Academy in 1932 said, "The safety, honour and welfare of your country comes first, always and every time. The honour, welfare and comfort of the men you command come next. Your own ease, comfort and safety come last, always and every time."

There is a glaring similarity between nobility and the officers of the Armed Forces. In both the cases the welfare of the people they deal with comes first.

If every boss, regardless of the profession, can keep this in mind, he or she can bring a huge value addition to the organisation and his or her people. Most importantly, he or she would earn the respect and trust of his people and that too for a lifetime.

Don't Be a "Banana Boss"

Banana republic is a pejorative Political Science term for a politically and socially unstable country whose economy is largely dependent on the export of one product such as bananas. In such a scenario, the plutocracy that rules the country comprising the rich businessmen, politicians and military, exploits the country's economy.

When a country is ruled by a group of people who exercise power and influence by virtue of their wealth, it results in exploitation of people. Similarly, bosses, who are in power due to their position in the hierarchy and refuse to look after the interest of their people, end up exploiting the organisation they work for.

With such banana bosses at the helm of affairs, the organisation is bound to doom, largely due to the mass exodus of good people from the organisation. Collateral damage is far larger in terms of poor productivity resulting in lower profits and huge loss of organisational credibility in the marketplace.

Organisations, therefore, must ensure they appoint bosses at all levels who work towards building a cultural stability in the organisation, so that people stick to the organisation for larger periods, deliver optimum output and remain happy.

Bossism like leadership is not a science, but it is an art.

THE VERY GOOD BAD BOSS

Ibrahim Ahmad
Group Editor
Cyber Media

> *One needs to learn to work with his boss. Why do we think only*
> *the boss has some shortcomings? I am sure there are*
> *a few things you can improve too!*
> It was a meaningful statement that brought a big change in me.

I would start my story with my first job related meeting with a gentleman who later became my boss.

For a kid, it is said that school is the second home. Then for the next 35–40 years, the office is the second home. In most organisations, the boss plays a big role in making or breaking his team and the team members. So, before I start the story, it is fair that I share a bit about myself—my background, my upbringing, my parents and others. I am sure a lot of those experiences got imbibed in my value system and it is possible that I view and narrate my experiences with my bosses, past and present, from that prism.

Being born and brought up in Aligarh (of the Aligarh Muslim University fame) has moulded the fundamentals of my personality in a certain way. Aligarh was then (in the late 1970s to mid-1980s) a small town and there was nothing there besides the University. It was relaxed, idyllic, and an everybody knows everybody kind of a town. One had to greet and get up whenever a senior relative, family friend or the class teacher arrived. Everybody aspired to be either a doctor or an engineer. I don't remember anybody wanting to be a professor, even though we lived in the middle of the university campus. The bright ones would be aiming for the Civil Services. Like many of my friends, I had no clue about what I wanted to be when I grew up. I loved jungles, wildlife, and envied the life of wildlife wardens. Maybe that is what I should have been.

Our Lady of Fatima, my first school, was run by missionaries and besides education and sports, they focused on discipline. Caning was not unusual, and parents would be summoned if required without much fuss. My next two schools—Minto Circle and City High School—had their own unique character. Run by the University administration, here I was introduced to life beyond classroom education.

Bunking classes to spend the day chatting at tea joints or running off for morning show movies was the first step. Later I became part of student gangs that were mostly involved in stealing mangoes from the school orchard, puncturing the unpopular teacher's bicycle, and bullying and thrashing up students who were trying to be smart. Our teachers thought these were useless and anti-social activities, but we were proud of them. Our teachers in these two schools never cared to bother our parents. All my schools had huge playgrounds, sports facilities like swimming, tennis and horse riding. I will not be incorrect if I say life in school was one of opulence.

Life at home was simpler and humbler. My father being a professor of Political Science was a cool yet very different person. He never tried to influence what career his children should pursue, though he always said, "Get what you like otherwise you will have to like what you get." He was mostly busy preparing for his classes, often telling us that he must do his job for which he is paid, sincerely and well. He spent most of his time reading philosophy and poetry, which I always tried to run away from. He loved gardening, and insisted there must be space for weeds and other unwanted shrubs as well in the small lawn in the front or our kitchen garden at the back.

My mom was a housewife, who wanted to ensure that we (me and my younger brother and sister) were fed properly, did well in studies and sports, and did not lie. A woman of grit and determination, she had married my dad just after doing a post high school professional diploma. She then did her pre-university course ten years after marriage, and ten years later attempted to do her B.Sc Hons. She always told us to keep trying, and believed that saying no to elder's wishes was showing disrespect. One thing my parents always preached as well practiced was equal treatment towards their children.

By the time I finished my graduation and MBA, I had got addicted to the lazy life at Aligarh. I did not want to leave Aligarh and that is maybe why I decided to join a group of friends in their fish farming venture. The venture failed and I was given marching orders, 'Go and get a job.'

No to Not Know

Coming back to the story of my chance meeting with the future boss. My first job interview was for a Market Research Executive in an organisation called IDC. They dealt primarily in the ICT space and no wonder the small test they asked me to take had questions about computers. One will laugh at those questions today and I am sure a kindergarten child will answer them without even blinking. "Name three Indian and three foreign computer companies." I was stumped. I had never even seen a PC in my life. The only Indian name I knew was Hindustan Computers Limited (now known as HCL) and the foreign names I had heard was Apple Macintosh and IBM.

I was cursing my luck when a man with a smiling face peeped in. He was looking for someone, but when he saw a young puzzled man inside staring at the ceiling, he asked, "What's up?" I told him I was taking a recruitment test. He looked at my vexed face again, glanced at the question sheet, and said, "Don't worry; the answers are all around you." True, a little later I discovered that there were some old cardboard boxes lying in a corner, with words like Wipro and Zenith written on top. I wrote them down as my answer to questions. I somehow managed to get selected.

Shortly after I joined IDC (now re-christened as Cyber Media Research), I found the man who had helped me was Raju Chellam, the Editor of Dataquest. Just a few days later I bumped into him and he asked me if I liked Market Research. I said I wanted to be a journalist. "PCWorld needs a reporter. Go and talk to them," he gave me a lead. Since I had given a test for PCWorld also, I was shifted there.

Raju Chellam had the reputation of a jolly good fellow. I always saw him smiling, cool amid any crisis, and always going out of his way to help others. Later, when I was working for him, I asked him why he gave me a hint that day and he said, "After I spoke to you that day, I instantly  knew you did not keep yourself abreast of business news, so there was no point testing you further on that. By giving you a hint I wanted to test how smart you were at working on hints and you did a decent job."

I must say that I learned a lesson of my life. I always found Raju endlessly encouraging his team members and getting the best out of their strength areas. It was he who later told me that choosing the right team members is the first and the most important step for an organisation. One way to hire good people is to test them on what they know and not on what they don't know. With him work was always fun. While working on articles or going for interviews with us, he would crack jokes, laugh at silly mistakes, and take us out to the nearby *dhaba* for tea. By leading from the front, he made work easy and, in the process, made sure our learning was faster and as per his requirement. The first experience can also be the last experience. By giving us freshers, there were two of us in the team then, a good experience at the beginning of our career, he also made sure he was developing two young men who would be passionate and ambitious about their profession.

The Good Side

The Good Side From the time when I started my career in 1989, the world has changed and so have its people. In 1989, I could not think of sitting down when my senior or my boss was present. We would stand respectfully or wait for her or him to ask us to sit down. Today, many of my juniors would think that their boss is a useless person. I am sure. I remember one of my earlier bosses, L. Subramanian (popularly called Subu in the office), who gave me a useful secret. Unhappy with the ad-hoc method of my supervisor, a snooty News Editor who never moved out of office but would send me from one assignment to another, I decided to escalate the matter.

Making sure this person was not around (he was not very popular with others too), I sneaked into Subu's cabin and complained to him. He first offered me a cup of coffee and then slowly encouraged me to vent everything out. When I had finished, he asked me, "You find many problems with your boss. I can see you are a observant chap. Can you also tell me what you think are one or two good things in the man. Things you could respect him for."

I was a taken aback, but anyway reluctantly listed down some of his strengths. It was then I suddenly realised he has many good things which I had perhaps shut my eyes to. My supervisor might have been a man of his own whims and fancies, but he did bring many values to the table. For one, he had excellent contacts and I don't remember not getting news wherever he sent me. He was also fast at rewriting news and reports the team of reporters filed. Some of my reporter colleagues were not too eloquent with their English and their piece could have devastating consequences if it had gone without sharp rewriting. Thanks to our News Editor we were saved from many serious embarrassments and possible legal wrangling. There was once news of a local dealer in Delhi involved in software piracy. But the proposed headline indicated that the CEO of Microsoft in India was the one involved. We would have landed in a major soup had the news piece been printed.

During a visit to Mumbai, where I was doing a survey on challenges before young software professionals, I ran into a person called Hoshiedar Ghaswalla who looked after Western Region operations. We were discussing my meetings and I told him that many software people have problems with their boss. "*Yaar*, one needs to learn to work with his boss," Hoshie later told me. "Why do we think only the boss has some shortcomings? I am sure there are a few things you can improve too", he said pointing at me. It was quite a meaningful and perhaps philosophical statement that set me thinking. The big change in me after that was my problematic News Editor and I were soon bum chums. I would not bother about his working style but focus on getting him to share his news leads and story ideas, often offbeat and with a new twist, and get his contacts. I was filing one great story after another and in the process pleasing my boss to no end.

Once I had to do a story on UNIX, an emerging operating system for enterprise computing, which had just started getting noticed by the CIO (Chief Information Officer). The report had to be filed by the end of the day and I was in a panic. My boss said, if you try and talk to people who are indifferent to UNIX, it will be tough to get a response. Go after CIOs who either hate or love UNIX. He also advised that I should not attempt to go and personally meet the people. "Simply pick up the phone (there were no mobile phones, not even pagers back then), call them up and just ask one question," he ordered. I must have spoken to about twenty five CIOs across the country and got answers from about eighteen CIOs, and my story was ready.

The big lesson for me from my bad boss was significant. Thanks to my boss, I learnt that support (in this case  quotes for the story I was doing) comes easy and fast when there is an emotional connect. These CIOs had strong views, either positive or negative, about UNIX and wanted to share them with their peers. I had not thought on these lines, which my "Snooty" boss was able to. I also learnt that a telephone is a great means of communication and getting information. I was foolish to assume that my boss was lazy and did not want to go out of office. I could have continued my disliking for my boss, but a small lesson made me respect him.

The Goal is God

When I was doing an MBA at Aligarh, we were made to believe that we just had to learn and remember these principles of management and go out and conquer the world. But the real world out there was so different. No plan was perfect, even good plans could run into problems because the situation changed. Or, if the situation did not change, the people who had to implement the plan changed. It was all so complex and dynamic.

While Subu was a great boss and friend, there was one big problem I had with his style of work. His decisions seemed to be ad-hoc. He would decide something in the morning and then change that in the evening. Once we were working on DQ Top 20, the 3 volume annual survey and report that Dataquest magazine does to estimate Indian IT industry's performance in the fiscal year. Those were times when there used to be a big tussle between HCL and Wipro, the biggest giants of Indian IT. To be one up on each other, both these

 companies would refuse to share their sales figures with us until and unless we could assure them the other one had shared their figures. In this running around game, often the magazine pack-up and printing would get delayed.

Subu would have none of this. He decided to swap the magazine issue which ranked Indian IT companies with the issue where IT industry's segmentwise performance is covered. The result would have been that the cover of the most coveted DQ Top 20 issue, instead of crying out "Wipro #1 Indian company, and HCL #2 company" or "HCL #1 Indian company, and Wipro #2 company", it would now say "HP India's top printer company and TCS India's top software exporter". The thought that instead of coming out as leaders of Indian IT industry, the warring HCL and Wipro would appear as smaller players or leaders in some segments and losers in some was not a great one.

Their corporate communication managers quickly advised the CEOs that they should share data with us without any conditions. And we were able to pack the issue without much delay. When I now think back, I realise I was a plan-oriented person that is, make a plan and then act as per those plans. Anything outside the plan would make me uncomfortable. While Subu's adhoc style often put me and other team members, and people outside too, under undue stress, the big learning was Change plans but not the target.

Let me share with you my experience with another gentleman who I would think had a great impact on how I think and work today. Shyam Malhotra, our Editor in Chief, was my boss' boss, but often worked directly with us. The only (but a big one) problem most of us had with him was that he would ask too many questions. One often wondered whether he is helping us or trying to delay or completely jettison the plan. More often than not, we would avoid going to him for any help. I remember an incident when I and my team were working on a plan where we were given a target to meet hundred CIOs and IT company CEOs to get their inputs for our next year's editorial planning.

We had one month to finish this exercise and Shyam was to review this with us every week. After we had given him a brief on the first week's action (where we claimed we had made good progress), his first question was like a bomb. "I am happy to hear that you have started well, but can I look at that list  of hundred CIOs and CEOs that you're contacting for feedback." We looked at each other. Someone said he had the list in his mind, someone said he had it on his computer, and someone said he had stuck the list on his desk board. Shyam said, "How can we claim to have made progress or how can we review our progress when we do not know our target, and the list is not in front of us."

As he started asking more questions, we realised that there were many gaps. For instance, a few of us said we had been trying to contact but the person is not picking up the phone. Shyam amusingly asked us why we are assuming the person has no other work but is waiting for our call. He suggested we do not intrude by repeated calling and just drop an SMS. "Try a fax. People often respond to a fax." We got practical and common sense solutions to a result of his questioning. We discovered that sometimes there were small problems coming in the way. The lesson for us was that his probing questions were actually useful, cleared cobwebs, gave us solutions and, most importantly, gave us an idea of our actual progress.

What Shyam was doing with his small but incisive questions was making us realise the task before us was not huge. All that was required were simple, systematic steps and that we should be able to meet those hundred people in just 15 days and not one month. His way of questioning and discussing was such that instead of coming out of the meeting dejected and depressed for failing in our job, we came out wiser and charged up. In reality, Shyam might have been unhappy with what we had achieved so far and would have liked to dismiss the meeting. But what he did was to make sure that when we left the meeting, we knew how to do our job better and were motivated, and not demotivated.

I am sure that we knew there will be similar questions in the next review meeting also and hence, worked on the project harder and smarter to be better prepared for the next review meeting with

Shyam. I have often heard and seen people avoiding bosses who ask questions, and bosses completely shattering their team's confidence with their questions (interrogation and intimidation), but here was one boss who helped motivate us and grow with his questions.

A story on bosses would not be complete if I do not narrate experiences with perfectionist bosses. Mine was Prasanto Kumar Roy, popularly known as PKR. A thorough tech journalist whom many of us avoided because he would always be looking for perfection and completeness in whatever he did, and that would put us in trouble in terms of more work, that too unexpected God forbid, if you ask for his opinion or help for some story. He would call for a short meeting that could go on for hours, upsetting your other plans. In that meeting he would surf the net for more and latest information, call up some experts for expert views, and call for earlier issues of the magazine to check out what we have written in the past. After a lengthy and a gruelling meeting, we would discover that it is a different story that we need to write, and, therefore, a different set of information has to be gathered.

I remember once we were working on a long report on structured cabling (cables used for building networks) and to our misery ran into PKR. He called for a short meeting, where he searched the net, spoke to experts and got to know that how real estate builders, both commercial and residential, were now tying up with structured cabling vendors for smart building. While checking out previous issues of Voice&Data, we discovered that we had done similar reports in the past too, and it was likely there would be nothing significant to add this time. The final output (after a lot of heartburns though) was a landmark story where Dataquest built up and catalysed smart building concepts in India.

Similarly, once while trying to do a story to celebrate the much-hyped "India has 900 hundred million mobile users" story, one correspondent, who did not know about the hazards of working with PKR, sought his help. The

correspondent cried and moaned and must have cursed his luck, but what appeared was another landmark report where Voice&Data proved that 900 million was the number of SIM cards sold in the market, which included inactive, duplicate, and triplicate cards. The actual number of mobile users were nowhere near 900 but around 650 million. Thanks to PKR, we were always thinking about perfection to be a no mean achievement by itself.

Fortunately, PKR had a passionate interest in other things in life too. He was a foodie, and I am reasonably confident that there would be no restaurant or eating place in Delhi or, for that matter, any other metro in India that he would not have tested out. The other passion in his life was green technologies for green environment. He was rebuilding his Delhi home as a 100 percent green home. He loved to talk about these things. He was always ready to help people with information, be it airline fares, movie ticket booking, or road routes to hill stations. So, the moment any of us saw that there was a chance of getting caught up with PKR for some story, a good escape route was to bring up a discussion on any of the above.

Bosses who review work at short intervals are not always popular. Everybody wants the boss to assign work and then forget about it. If he or she wants to see a regular progress report, that is seen as meddling and interference. When I was posted in Bangalore, my boss Abraham Mathew had a reputation of being very meticulous and systematic. He always maintained a diary where each conversation in the meeting was noted. And in the next meeting he would just open his notes and it was like an uninterrupted continuation of the last meeting. Most of us were caught off-guard because half the decisions from the previous meeting we either did not remember or had deliberately forgotten. Even if there was no review meeting, his notes helped him follow up on each action point. That is what was often disliked by us.

I remember an incident which could have been a big embarrassment had we not had an interfering boss who insisted on regular reviews. I was the lone Dataquest reporter in Bangalore and was working on a story about foreign CEOs in Bangalore. One specific person was a Frenchman, who headed a large software house (I think they are no more around) was not very conversant in English. During the interview he said, "I am alone in India and miss my family and that hardly gives me time for working" (what he meant was that since he did not have his family with him, he had all the time to focus on work). While transcribing the interview, I had given the header as "I am hardly working," which I planned to change in the final draft. During the review, Abey reminded me twice that I should change the header, otherwise I might forget. I kept on ignoring his advice thinking it is a small thing he is getting worried about. I will make the change before I send it to my editor. All was forgotten, but a few days later I got a call from my printing press executive praising me for the hilarious interview headline, "I am hardly working." I was shocked and stunned, and I alone know what all had to be done to change the printing plates, change the headline, make new plates, and waste all the forms which had already got printed. I would have lost my job if the interview had got published.

Finally

Later, when a few of my MBA batchmates and I were trying to put together some Urdu couplets that had a message for the corporate world, I found the following one so apt.

Har aadmi mein hotey hain dus-bees aadmi; jis ko bhi dekhna ho kai baar dekhna (every person has got many facets; evaluate the person many times before you decide whether he is useful or useless).

Getting the best out of a person's strengths, whether he is your boss or subordinate rather than brooding over his weaknesses, in my opinion is the best way to handle tough bosses. I think this can be perfected into a management art. It gets the best out of people, reduces conflicts, and can be a great source for putting together best practices.

As I write this piece to share my experiences, I realise that those who I considered as bad or unnecessarily tough feel good bosses, have taught me much more in life compared to the feel good ones. I should now remember them as normal bosses who took tough or unusual decisions to get the work done. I might have found those decisions as strange and uncomfortable hence started believing that my boss was bad.

There are all types of bosses whether you like them or dislike them depends on your own personality, rather than the boss's. I have known slave driver bosses, whom some team members like, and some hate. My take on difficult and tough bosses is that if you can identify their strengths and try to imbibe some of them, you can take your mind away from the bad side of your boss and focus on your work and life.

If nothing else works, there is always an option of a coup to overcome your boss . . . we will talk about it some other day.

"A good boss asks meaningful questions. My boss, the way he asked questions and discussed them was such that instead of coming out of the meeting dejected and depressed, we came out wiser and charged up."

2

EVERY BOSS CAN BE YOUR HERO: IF YOU WANT HIM TO BE ONE

Vinay Agarwal
Managing Partner
PGT Partners
Consultants for Profit and
Growth Transformation

In fact this was a great quality of my boss, Mr Rajgopal. His people worked for him to make him happy and not for rewards or from fear of consequences. This was the level of motivation he could foster.

A Great Beginning

Jayprakash Vinayak Wagh, a suitably weighty name of my first boss. Mr. Wagh was the Vice President (Diversification) of Blow Plast Limited, the Mumbai based manufacturer of VIP luggage, Moderna furniture, and Leo toys.

I joined Blow Plast in 1980 as a Management Trainee after graduating from IIT Kanpur and IIM Calcutta with no work experience. I was brought up in a family of civil servants and doctors where no one was remotely connected to the business world. Mr. Wagh and my senior colleagues kick started my carrier in the business world in my two year tenure at Blow Plast.

I finished a ten day induction programme and presented myself in Mr. Wagh's office. I was immediately given three assignments. The company was discussing a venture to manufacture leather luggage in Sri Lanka with a Canadian firm to feed the North American market. I was asked to study how to establish the venture in Sri Lanka and make a project report. The other two projects were equally onerous; to study and work on a proposal prepared by a consultant to establish a 300 room 5-star hotel and prepare a concept note on the potential of entering the retail sector. All came with deadlines from two to four weeks. Was it Mr. Wagh's naiveté or his trust in his people? He was focussed on what he wanted, expected results and was willing to trust his team's abilities. I did not realise it then, but I learnt that young people have a lot to give and also how to create expectations from them, delegate to them and yet give them the necessary direction.

Under Mr. Wagh I did a number of meaty assignments during my first year, namely studying the feasibility for soft luggage, market research for plastic consumer goods, market study for plastic industrial goods, market study for plastic corrugated sheets, and market study for the existing business of blow moulded industrial containers. Not only this, I got two operational assignments in parallel:

- Taking over procurement of leather luggage from two vendors, establishing a small leather luggage manufacturing unit and disengaging with the vendors without causing supply disruptions.

- Taking over marketing of the industrial container business which was to be closed, based on my recommendations, with the aim of collecting the 90 days outstanding from our customers, a tough task when going out of business; but it also gave me my first opportunity to supervise another colleague.

During this stint, my learning curve was extremely steep as I was fortunate to have a boss like Mr. Wagh and many other wonderful supervisors and seniors. The President, Mr. Shashi Dash, a charismatic person, had piloted the management trainee scheme at Blow Plast and hence had recruited me in the company. He would stop by at my desk, park himself on its edge and informally chat on what I was doing. It was a lesson in the virtues of managing by walking about. By observing Mr. Athalye, Executive Director, and a leading Plastics Technologist of the time, I saw the power of being humble while being accomplished. Mr. Dabholkar, General Manager, my boss for a while, was always happy and jovial, and I understood how to be friendly while still keeping one's distance.

Mr. Suresh Ghai, who was also my boss for a while, showed me how a boss transitions to a friend for life. There was my senior, Vivek Datye, from whom I learnt how to detail out my work, especially on the technical side. My senior and mentor was the dapper and dashing Rahul Tandon from whom I learnt to be focussed on results and by emulating whom I got the courage to take on so many weighty assignments as a rookie entering the business world at the young age of 24; for this I will be forever grateful to him.

And last, but not the least, to our young Chairman, Mr. Dilip Piramal, who with his wife made it a point to host an annual event for all the managers. He had the company organise an annual one night trip for all employees and participated in it with enthusiasm. His approach exemplified to me my school's motto Noblesse Oblige, nobility has its own obligations. I felt so good about Mr. Piramal's conduct that I have always participated in every event organised for or by the staff I have had. Many years later when I was the Managing Director of RPG Cables, he was on our board and I was happy to have a chance to acknowledge his contribution to my learning.

My stint at Blow Plast was not yet over. I was offered two choices, to become the number two in the company's largest branch in Mumbai or to go to New Delhi as the site incharge for the prestigious contract for providing and installing the seating in the Indraprastha Indoor Stadium being readied at breakneck speed for the Asian Games of 1982. The latter, a typical civil engineering job, which constituted five per cent of the company's turnover for that year, was being offered on a political platform. I was the only engineer in marketing at the Head Office and the concerned managers in furniture marketing did not want to let the factory people into the contract as then they would have little say in it. The first job was a great move both internally and from a career standpoint. But I had ideas of teaming up with friends in Lucknow to become an entrepreneur. So I chose the second option to move to the right geography and be in touch with my potential partner even though it was a dead end assignment which did not do anything for my career. But it did teach me a host of things as I got thrown into the deep end of things.

The Janta Party Government had dithered from 1977 to 1980 on whether to hold the games or not. When the government changed in 1980, Mrs. Indira Gandhi decided to go ahead and hold the games in November 1982. Left with only two and a half years, all the projects were on shorter timelines, and we were given only four months against our tendered quote of nine months. The site was full of contractors, the site managers of all the other thirty contractors being over forty years old. Tough civil contracting people, and here was I, yours truly, new to both contracting and civil engineering with less than two years of work experience to boast about.

The company had appointed Mr. K.B. Oberoi, furniture manufacturer, as our prime sub-contractor. While Mr. Oberoi's position was below me in the business, he was accomplished, pleasant and worldlywise. He was a fatherly figure. So I immediately adopted him as a mentor. The assignment taught me how one can accomplish something large and difficult. Mr. Oberoi taught me how to be fearless in business as well as to be street smart without compromising on basics.

I also learnt how to control and deliver a large project from the project bosses who were officers of the Delhi Development Authority. Yes, DDA! They held a review meeting every Wednesday morning where the Member DDA would review the Chief Engineer of the project, Mr. Chetal, and his team. As each subject came up, the relevant contractor would be called in and reviewed against a Gantt chart provided at the start of the project. This review would be for about two minutes, and if the contactor was not on schedule, he would have to say how he would make up, else the concerned Executive Engineer would be reprimanded.

Any delay of over a week or two would lead to the contract being immediately handed over to another contractor. If the contractor had a difficulty, it was instantaneously removed. For example, we were

having difficulties in getting the electrical connection for our equipment and lighting on site. The concerned department was making us chase them for over a week. In the next Wednesday review, I cited the cause of delays due to lack of electrical connection. The reviewers were furious, and within minutes of my exit from the meeting the electricity department was after me to take the connection and they established it in two hours flat! The total review of thirty contracts lasted only 90 minutes, and the eventual project was delivered on time and, till date, stands as a national asset.

The indoor stadium project was controlled by our furniture division at the Head Office (HO) where everybody was experienced in the consumer durables business, but had no knowledge or understanding of the contracting business. So they dumped me on the local office head, who had zero interest in the project. As problems cropped up, I created solutions, but many of them needed approvals from the HO. There were no response from them. The client started threatening to cancel the contract, but all my requests were cries in the wilderness. Then I turned to an experienced and savvy relative from the private sector, Naresh K. Jain, on how to get the HO to move. There were no e-mails then; so I started putting the issues on record through a daily letter made in triplicate, one copy for my boss and one for his boss and one for me. As these letters reached the HO, it put pressure on them and we were able to save the situation at the last moment. This taught me lessons on the criticality of backing one's staff in the field and the importance of written communication.

Entrepreneurship

entrepreneurship

In the last two years at IIT, my friend, Himanshu Rastogi and I had been dreaming of becoming IT entrepreneurs. We made all sorts of plans and did few crazy things like travelling to Delhi to meet a visiting business delegation from the European Union. The fire remained alive even though I went for management studies and Himanshu went to Lucknow to resolve matters related to his recently closed factory. He soon started to work on an IT venture and teamed up with a local Chartered Accountant, Vinay Krishna, to incorporate Prime Consultants Private Limited to take up IT processing as outsourced projects for the corporate sector. The business was launched in 1981 in the early days of the Indian IT industry when, out of the big five IT companies, TCS was king, HCL was a hardware company, Wipro was about to enter the field of hardware, Infosys was incorporated in parallel somewhere in the country just like us, and Satyam was nowhere on the horizon.

The next year, in 1982, myself and Sanjay Bhargava, my close friend from school and IIT, joined the business as partners and directors. Sanjay soon left to take over his family's publishing business due to the untimely demise of his father. Another lesson was learnt on how fate can play a huge role in one's career.

The business was a huge challenge. They were such early days of IT in India that most companies had to be convinced of its utility. Even large companies did not own computers and the IBM PC had just been launched abroad. In this environment, I landed straight into a crisis on joining Prime Consultants in August 1982.

The UP Pre-Medical Test (PMT) conducted for admissions to all medical colleges in the state was being conducted by Kanpur University. The PMT results had been prone to litigation resulting in admission delays. The Vice Chancellor took three decisions to ensure that the year's PMT passed off uneventfully. She centralised all matters with a few people to avoid leaks, offered candidates to take a carbon copy of their answers to the multiple-choice question paper and published the correct choices in the papers. She also decided to outsource processing of the answer sheets on a computer. Our company had done the data entry and preliminary work at Lucknow and then taken the data to Delhi to process it on a bigger and faster computer. The final scores were printed on cards to be sent to the candidates when I landed in the company. Himanshu, a stickler for systems, insisted that at least 1,000 of the 40,000 results be manually checked to ensure there were no errors. And, all hell broke loose.

The day we had to go to Kanpur to hand over the results, we discovered that many results did not tally. On investigating, we found that wherever we had a problem, the discrepancy was four marks; obviously a bit-error in the data transfer on the Delhi computer. So we had to hang our heads and meet the Vice Chancellor and her team with the bad news. We met them at her house at 10 pm. In the meeting, we proposed a solution that in five days we would reprocess the top 8,000 results on our computer in Lucknow against the 1,600 seats on offer and let the rest remain. This was an audacious tactic on the assumption that the rest who were well below the cut-off would not bother if their score card had an error of four marks. The Vice Chancellor was waiting to announce the results and had given the date to the press. It took her just five minutes to assess the situation and take a decision despite a lot of apprehension in her team. She told us to go ahead! She inspired me to develop nerves of steel and keep myself calm in a crisis.

We were facing business pressures. We were the first in the field in Lucknow. Later entrants managed to buy their equipment at one third the cost and it ran three times faster. So, we had a cost-disadvantage of nine times on the equipment cost and three times on the running cost. Hence, we looked for value added assignments. In the process we became highly profitable, and learned some more management lessons.

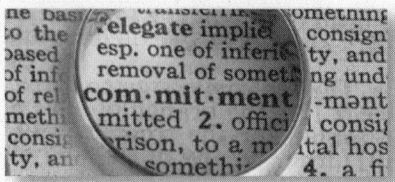

We made a presentation in a gathering of Chairmen of Regional Rural Banks (RRBs). The Chairman of Bank of Azamgarh and Ballia immediately gave us a problem to solve. RRBs operated at the district or division level, and had to employ people based on public exams. These exams were conducted by the National Institute of Banking Management (NIBM) in Pune, who also conducted the exams for all the other public sector banks. The problem for the RRBs was in getting dates from NIBM and also that NIBM conducted exams only in English while the candidates' proficiency in English was low. We offered an end to end processing – advertisement, applications, exam fee payments, conduct of exam, evaluation of results, and invitation to candidates for personal interview. The Chairman agreed. If we had failed, he would surely have lost his position, but he did it for his organisation. A great lesson learnt about commitment.

The other grand lesson came from Mr. Brijesh Kumar, Managing Director, of Pradeshiya Cooperative Dairy Federation (PCDF). To replicate the success of the Anand model, the Central Government had formed the National Dairy Development Board (NDDB) which, in turn, launched Operation Flood to take the model countrywide. NDDB was wary of launching the model in Uttar Pradesh fearing that they would not be able to deliver. Mr. Brijesh Kumar with his minister made a commitment to them and Operation Flood was launched in the state.

PCDF had eight dairies with twelve more in the pipeline, but faced an acute problem of credibility with milk supplying villages due to PCDF's past track record of delayed payment for the milk supplied.

So he came up with the idea of insulating the entire payment accounting from the normal bureaucratic processes and delays. He appointed our company to process the purchase accounting. He took keen interest at each stage of the application development and implementation lasting a few months. During this project, he was available to us within a short notice of 24 hours. Once the system was implemented and was running smoothly, we could not even get time to meet him for Diwali greetings! We often talk about strategic focus. Here we saw it in resplendent action.

We could deliver critical assignments with success because of my partner, Himanshu Rastogi. He handled the operations while I handled the software development. We had many challenges. As the pioneer in the city and with the industry as a nascent one, we could only get graduates with medium or low academic accomplishments to work for us. On the other hand, our operations were critical to our customers and involved our staff working independently. For instance, the PCDF processing for the twenty dairies was done four times a month. The input documents flowed in by messenger from all over the state and had to be entered manually and processed with a turnaround time for each dairy of two to twelve hours; leading to a 24x365 operation for us. This could only happen due to Himanshu's skills in organisation. Without ever having heard the term Standard Operating Procedures (SOPs), he devised foolproof procedures which delivered on time, every time—a record which the best of organisations could feel proud of. Since then, I have always insisted on SOPs to manage operations.

A Long Inning

In 1986, the partnership in Prime Consultants started fraying at the edges on the issue of longterm direction. Since Himanshu and I could not put together the finances to buy the company, we exited. I held two assignments for about a year each in New Delhi, but ones which had lessons to learn in them.

At Usha RKKR group, my boss was Mr. Vinay Rai, Vice Chairman. He was an astute businessman, but also possessed a humane touch.

My father, who was only sixty, fell ill suddenly and I rushed to his side in Lucknow. Unfortunately he passed away. I remember Mr. Vinay Rai calling me to his office as soon as I returned from my father's cremation in Lucknow. He spent half an hour with me, and shared with me as an equal about his own struggles with his father's health, and discreetly enquired if I needed help to manage my family after the sudden loss. I still get goose pimples at the thought of this interaction even though twenty five years have passed. I have always endeavoured to achieve this ideal.

I had a stint with the Management Consultancy division of Tata Consultancy Services (TCS). At TCS, every communication to clients was peer-reviewed. This stint helped me learn the nuances of working as a management consultant. In addition, I learnt the art of making presentations from our senior, Mr. Batra. Most of the things I learnt at TCS are invaluable to me in my present work.

After TCS, I joined Shri Ram Fibres Limited (SRF) in 1989, where I spent eleven years of my career.

At SRF, we had a set of accomplished people, and I learnt from every boss I had. My first learning was from the Vice Chairman, Mr. Arun Bharat Ram. We had a strategic planning meeting of DCM Data Products at Agra. Mr. Arun Bharat Ram joined us at lunch on the final day, and made it a point to move from table to table to ensure he spoke to each manager. His ability to make people comfortable and an inherent gentleman spirit is something I have always sought to emulate as I rose higher.

The person who recruited me into SRF was Devraj Singh. He was intelligent and possessed razor sharp analytical skills. He had the ability to express his conclusions straight and to the point with an intellectual honesty. He always reposed his faith in his team members. I learnt these things from him and am happy to say he has become a friend for life.

I had joined SRF in the Strategic Planning function under Devraj, whose boss was Mr. Ravi Sinha, Senior Vice President. After a year of my joining, there was an internal reorganisation and Mr. Sinha took additional charge of the company's two bearing manufacturing companies with plants in Ranchi. Both companies were ailing and needed to be turned around. I assisted him in strategic planning and became a multi-faceted General Management Assistant for the bearings businesses.

Mr. Sinha was a master strategist, the best I have seen. He could also articulate visions as wll as formulate and execute plans to achieve them. The world declared war on refrigerant gases as these could deplete the earth's ozone layer. Just a few years before that, SRF had entered the field and had quickly established market leadership in India under Mr. Sinha's guidance. He took up the challenge of working with the government to secure India's national interest in the ensuing Montreal Protocol negotiations and helped create a bright future for the industry and the country in this area. I learnt valuable lessons in strategic action from observing Mr. Sinha and interacting with him, which greatly helped me in my career as a CEO.

Mr. Sinha was also a great communicator at every level. I have seen him interact at the board level as well as with his workmen. I particularly recall his meetings with the union leaders at Shriram Bearings and with the general body of workers at Shriram Needle Bearings. He had both groups eating out of his hands. In Shriram Needle Bearings, he gave the group a goal larger than themselves which they could believe in. He challenged the team to beat our main competitor, who was then six times our size. When I became CEO of the company, I could capitalise on this thought and unleash the creative energies of the team to turn it around and improve the turnover ratio with the competitor to about half.

After three years in planning, in 1992 Mr. Sinha asked me what I wanted to do next. He was keen on me taking up the Corporate Systems and IT role for the SRF group which was one of the areas under him. But, I bluntly told him that I did not see much scope since Indian organisations were personality centric and not systems driven, and would not become so till many had failed under the newly launched liberalisation in India (Yes, one could talk to him like that on strategic issues). So I requested for an operational assignment, and landed up as the Marketing Head of Shriram Needle Bearing, an ailing company. This was once again under Devraj, who had become the CEO a few months earlier. Then there was a twist of fate through a corporate reshuffle. The bearing companies were brought under the charge of our group's Head of Human Resources, Mr. R.M. Rajgopal. And I met the boss under whom I have worked for the longest period.

My first real opportunity to spend time with Mr. Rajgopal was on a trip to our collaborator in Germany where we were on a mission to convince them to let us export some of our products to South East Asia. They continued raising objections as their master distributor in Singapore was uncomfortable, though he had no sales for the two wheeler bearings we wanted to export.

Suddenly they agreed, and we were jubilant. I was puzzled by the change in their stance and discussed it with Mr. Rajgopal conjecturing on what I thought could have prompted the change. He asked me to stop and said that he saw their body language change when I told Mr. Alt, the German Export Head, that I could empathise with him as he was a father of two sons and had to decide between them. Mr. Alt was then forced to do justice between the Singapore distributor and us, and, in the event, allowed us to export with certain riders to appease his distributor. This was an invaluable lesson on observing people and their reactions in meetings.

When I read the book, *The One Minute Manager*, such a possibility seemed like a fairy tale. That is, till Devraj moved on to a bigger assignment in another corporate reshuffle and I was appointed the CEO of Shriram Needle Bearing in 1994. Till then, I was used to doing a large amount of paperwork with my earlier bosses, and meetings which would go into issues in depth. So when Mr. Rajgopal invited me for my first monthly chat on the company's performance, I was well prepared and armed. I went to his room, and after a minute of preliminaries, he asked me a couple of key questions on performance. As soon as I stated the key point, he moved on to the next question. After a minute of this, he moved off into some pleasantries and visit schedules etc., and I was out of his office in less than five minutes. To say that I was unnerved would be an understatement. Over the next few meetings, I did learn that one does not have to spend a large amount of time on meetings if you know how to ask the right questions and let people do their best.

Mr. Rajgopal was a true delegator. The whole industry had payment problems with one of our customers, and everyone was supplying them only on letter of credit. One day, just after I had joined as Marketing Head, we were summoned to a meeting with the customer's new Head of Materials. My people had indications that he would perhaps ask us to supply on direct credit. I did some homework on the personality of the customer's new Purchase Head and the pros and cons of the proposition. My team advised against change and Mr. Rajgopal asked me to be careful. In the meeting, the customer did ask for the change but explained his need to ramp up his output due to success in the market and his lack of LCs to fund this growth.

I had to take a quick decision as the potential business was large enough to stop our company from bleeding and it all hinged on my judgement of their sincerity. I decided to supply on open credit. When I reported to Mr. Rajgopal, all he told me was that it was up to me to ensure that the outstanding with the customer did not increase. He checked with me once a month and let me handle things my way. I had to take varied measures to honour my commitment to Mr. Rajgopal and I did honour it. I set up an internal credit limit for the customer and controlled the supplies and payments within that. Thus, we did roaring business, started breaking even and still kept our business risk in control. I was very happy to have kept my commitment to Mr. Rajgopal.

Motivation

In fact, this was a great aspect of Mr. Rajgopal. His people worked to make him happy, and not for rewards or from fear of consequences. This is the quality of motivation he could foster. If this makes you

feel that he was a person who developed a cult following around him, nothing could be farther from the truth. Mr. Rajgopal was a simple person and completely people focused manager. He let his people do their jobs, was always available to help and took responsibility for their failures. He always had a good word for people and was empathetic while keeping his distance. More than that, he was a simple person and always taught that we should not fantasise we have two personas, a work persona and an out of office persona. To quote, "You cannot just leave a part of you on a ledge at home, and go back in the evening and pick it up again." I still remember his visit to my office a few days after the untimely death of a colleague and friend of his. He broke down and sobbed uncontrollably, then gracefully apologised to me for his show of emotion.

I learnt from Mr. Rajgopal what is meant by true support from a boss. Our sister company, Shriram Bearing had turned around just like Shriram Needle Bearing, but had again slipped into problems. So the company was added to my responsibilities. There were improvements to be made in the plant and a large amount in overdue payments had to be collected to keep the cash flow going. Mr. Rajgopal offered to go and sit in the factory in Ranchi so I could deal with the collections and sales issues. I felt otherwise and said I would handle all my old and new responsibilities and asked him to help me only with the collections in the new company. He went after this with gusto. Even though he was my boss, he would report his progress to me daily as I still had the accountability for the results while he had taken responsibility for the actions. Needless to say, he did a fantastic job, and we got the breather we were looking for.

As a group, SRF had by then gone into a deep financial crisis due to one particular acquisition decision taking up more cash than was available with the company. This warranted restructuring and hiving off all non-core businesses which included the bearing companies. Mr. Rajgopal had moved out of the group. I was offered the position of group HR head, but declined as the line management bug was a strong influence in me. I joined BPL Mobile, the country's largest mobile services operator then, as their Chief Operating Officer for Maharashtra and Goa Circle.

The Birth of an Industry

The mobile service industry had started in the four metros in late 1995 and in the state circles in late 1996. In 2000, we were at the forefront of a revolution which was waiting to happen. Under the guidance of its young and charismatic Chairman, Rajeev Chandrasekhar, BPL mobile was exploring new frontiers. It was organised as two companies, one for Mumbai and one handling Maharashtra and Goa, Tamilnadu and Kerala circles. Mr. Fausto B. Cardoso was the CEO of the latter and my boss.

A new industry was being built and that too with multiple sources causing disruptive change—technology, customer preferences and government regulation. Just one of these would have kept most industries on their toes and we had three! More importantly, drastic changes took place in six months on each of the three fronts. For example, SMS services used to be free and then we started charging for this service in March. Volumes plummeted to one third, and we worked hard with the consumers and the original volumes were far exceeded by November.

One fine day we got an innocuous fax from the regulator, Telecom Regulatory Authority of India, that effective midnight the roaming charges would be slashed by 70 per cent. We immediately went into a frenzy to stop billing, modify all the programs, deal with its effects on credit control, while worrying about the 10 per cent loss on our total monthly revenue that this entailed. On the technology front, we had countless presentations from foreign vendors peddling IT based tools, but found we had little to learn, as our group already had the same or better, or was close to having them from in-house sources.

The pace of work was frenetic and excitement was always around the corridor. In such an environment, it was Mr. Chandrasekhar's focus on technology development and fresh ideas on customer connect combined with Mr. Cardoso's tenacity and systems implementation skills that led us to achieve and sustain market leadership in our circles till our funding problems led to a decline, but that's another story. I did not work directly with Mr. Chandrasekhar, but I learnt to admire Mr. Cardoso's ability to get things done without curbing the creativity and frenetic pace our work required. That too without any direct exposure to telecom operations as our head office was in Bangalore, far away from each of the three circles.

Learning Never Ceases

As BPL Mobile became a prime candidate for takeover by Hutchison Max, I moved to RPG group, first as Managing Director of RPG Cellular and later of RPG Cables. I had wonderful people as my bosses, Mr. Harsh Goenka, Chairman, and Mr. P.K. Mahapatra, Business Sector Head. Mr. Harsh Goenka was soft spoken and courteous to a fault. He left such an imprint on me that I still remember most of my interactions with him. I particularly remember my interview in his office where at the end he walked me to the lift, summoned it and waited till I had left. Mr. Mahapatra was a master of the art of combining seriousness in business with a down to earth and open style. He is also the most networked person I have come across. After my short stint at RPG, in 2004, I moved to Grindwell Norton Limited, a subsidiary of the *Compagnie de Saint-Gobain* of France.

Saint-Gobain was founded in 1665 and by 2004 was a 50 billion dollar company, perhaps the largest industrial company in France and a full-blown multinational with over 1000 factories around the world. Just getting to know the history of the company and seeing its results was a lesson in itself. After a brief stint of nationalisation in the early 1980s, Saint-Gobain was re-privatised in 1986 with Mr. Jean-Louis Beffa as its CEO. Till then the company was a manufacturer of glass and glass products of various types. Mr. Beffa wanted the company to stand on more than one leg and went about it systematically and created two new business lines of engineered materials and manufacture plus distribution of construction products. The result was a stable and growing company with a global presence and leadership in its chosen fields.

When Saint-Gobain acquired Norton of USA in the early nineties, it also became the owner of Norton's minority stake in Grindwell Norton. Grindwell Norton was led by Anand Mahajan from the Grindwell family. Then Saint-Gobain decided to take majority control in the late nineties, Anand stayed in his role in Grindwell Norton and also became the General Delegate (read Country Manager) for Saint-Gobain. In this new role he established a clutch of new companies in India representing many diversified activities of Saint-Gobain worldwide. Each of these businesses are now number one or two in India. This was a remarkable metamorphosis from a Family Manager to a Leader within a giant multinational.

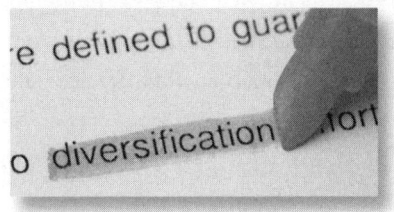 

The Saint-Gobain growth and diversification story worldwide and in India holds lessons for all. I got to learn the spirit of it when working with Anand, my boss, and the various global managers of Saint-Gobain. The success I saw was a result of ensuring the company had deep knowledge of the market, keeping tremendous focus on financial results, and repeatedly making bold moves, despite its inherently conservative culture. I also learnt about a multinational's mindset and methods from myriad interactions with my local and international colleagues.

I briefly joined Dish TV as CEO in 2008 and then worked with TVS Interconnect Systems till my last assignment at Samtel Color. In each company, I had a remarkable boss. Mr. Jawahar Goel of Dish TV had an ability to keep a detailed grip over a vast number of things, Mr. R. Haresh at TVS was the most gentlemanly boss I have had, and Mr. Satish Kaura at Samtel was the most intelligent and open.

I had the consultancy bug in me ever since my days at Prime Consultants. In 2011 end, I decided to take the plunge and form PGT Partners. A dear friend, Ravi Gilani, had introduced Dr. Goldratt's Theory of Constraints (TOC) in India in 1998. Ravi had become a TOC guru (called a "Jonah") and his results were nothing short of astounding. He had used TOC techniques to help companies multiply their profits several folds in one to two years, make dramatic improvements in their ontime delivery performance and release cash from inventories and receivables.

As an executive I too had led quantum leaps in results in diverse businesses as well as done successful turnarounds. In addition, I had been associated with Ravi in his TOC journey in many different ways, and was quite enamoured of the methods and the results they were delivering. So I found a great fit in what Ravi was doing and decided to associate with him at Goldratt India. It is proving to be an enjoyable journey working with companies from diverse fields and adding value to them.

There are two things I have learnt in this short time with Ravi. First is, how getting more and more clarity about the operational dynamics is critical to make large improvements at small costs. The other is from a personal trait of Ravi. Ravi always operates from a space of abundance rather than a space of shortage. He is willing to openly share knowledge, contacts and all other things consultants typically guard zealously.

Apart from my professional career, there were other people from whom I learnt a lot. My father, Mr. K.P. Agarwal, was a stickler for punctuality, self discipline and integrity. As a top level police officer, he had his office at home in some of his postings. But we were never allowed to even get a sheet of paper from his office as it was government property. Along with his strictness, he was also very tactful. On assessing my rebellious streak, he got family members to talk to me at my level and discourage me from my idea of becoming a history professor to taking admission in IIT, and from doing a masters in systems engineering to joining IIM Calcutta for which he had quietly paid the fee, despite my insisting on following the other admission I had.

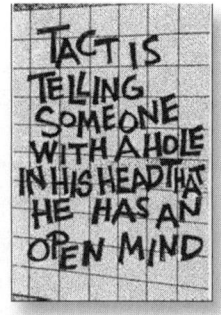

Integrity and tact were his gifts to me. My mother, in contrast, has always been a happy and a relaxed person. I learned how to be easy going and not take people's shenanigans to heart.

My friend and roommate in school hostel, Vinay Kumar, was a confident and determined individual, and I was an introvert and a shy person. As school kids we did some remarkable things like setting up a photography lab for the school, calling in local light vendors for functions created by us and so on. In all this, Vinay demonstrated that if we put our hearts into it and get into action, we can easily do things which look too big and scary at first. Another person who helped to draw me out was Mr. S.M. Adukia, President of one of the group companies in my first job.

He shared his transformation through undergoing the *est* training (Latin for the English verb, is). I learnt the value of sharing from him as well when I did the training. The *est* training was a large group interaction workshop which operated through sharing by the trainees. It helped me make a huge personality shift towards dealing with my introvert nature and thereby setting the foundation for my achievements. The *est* training was subsequently closed by its founder, Werner Erhard, and was later reinvented by others in the form of the Landmark Forum.

Most people are quite focused on themselves and what they want out of life. However, my wife, Bandana, has an amazing ability to focus on other people. She is able to give unconditional love and support to all her colleagues, friends and family. She is vivacious and combined with her ability to give, she brings sparkling sunshine to any group she engages with. I have been able to imbibe in whole or part many of the lessons I learnt from people in my life, but the ability to give unconditionally has proven to be the hardest, and will remain work in progress for the rest of my life.

Looking back at my experiences, I would say that being a good boss is all about people and how one holds them in one's own consciousness. To get the best out of a team, we need to set clear tasks, motivate individual team members and give them our support, especially when things are not going right. All this is possible if we have genuine respect for people which comes from one's own sense of humility and ability to engage with people. Both are traits which can be learnt. The learning can happen formally through training or informally through observing people in one's life. One can learn something from each person. It is up to oneself to cultivate the art of observing, finding the good in people and adopting that which works best, and that can be a very exciting journey!

"My father Mr. K.P. Agarwal was a stickler for punctuality, self discipline and integrity. As a top level police officer, he had his office at home in some of his postings. But we were never allowed to get even a sheet of paper from his office as it was government property."

3

A GENUINE AND AN EFFECTIVE BOSS

Raju Bhatnagar
Partner–ITI Consultants

If there is a reassurance given or a promise made to a subordinate, don't betray it. If you are not sure of being able to deliver on it, then don't promise.

One of the first thoughts that crossed my mind when I decided to write this piece was to check what the dictionary cited as a meaning for the term Boss. As expected some of the meanings were a person in charge of a worker or organisation; control; command; authority; administer; govern; oversee; supervise, etc. All these suggested that the boss is a person in a command and control structure who is mainly responsible for ensuring that his or her subordinates work. Intuitively, this flies in the face of the expectation that a boss can also be a wonderful person to work for.

Frankly, each one of us, irrespective of the seniority of positions, would have been a boss at some time or the other. Middle Management is Boss for junior management as is senior management for middle management. The boss is not necessarily someone who occupies the corner room.

Each one has a choice of how we behave as a boss and how we would like to be remembered by people who have worked for us. Would we, for example, like to be remembered as being:

- *Benevolent*
- *Objective and Open*
- *Supportive and Mentoring*
- *Straightforward and Skilled*

Or, do we end up being remembered as:

- *Boorish and Biased*
- *Overbearing, Opinionated and Offensive*
- *Supercilious*
- *Specious or Phony*

But I am getting ahead of myself.

My personal preference is to refer to a boss as a manager, which is what I shall do throughout this article. Through my professional journey, like most of us, I encountered several Managers, some good, some bad and some who didn't leave any impression at all!

My take on this chapter is to share some of my experiences and learning's about my relations with my managers at various stages in my career. The flip side to this, regarding the impressions and views about my role as a manager, from people who reported to me over the years, would not be covered at all. I will, however, briefly capture some generic thoughts about what a manager would like to see in a subordinate. You might find this article staccato, but that is by design and to keep this article from meandering with inane details which are not relevant to the thoughts being captured.

I have pleasant recollections of my first manager, or should I say Super Manager, when I joined Grindlays Bank in 1980. I had joined as a Management Trainee, the lowest slot on the totem pole and had heard rumours about how the High and Mighty, the senior officers in the bank, were. I spent the first day completing the joining formalities. I had to report to the Officer-in-Charge (OIC) of Current Accounts Department, at the 19 N S Road branch, in Kolkata on the following morning.

The next morning, on reaching the branch I walked up and introduced myself to the OIC as I had been instructed. I was given a couple of sheets of paper which outlined my training schedule over the next few months. The OIC spent some time giving me a quick review before the bank opened its doors for its customers at 10 am. At about 11 am the OIC came to me looking flustered and said *Boro Saheb* (Big Boss) wants to meet you. I too was taken aback because according to the rumours that I had heard, such High and Mighty senior officers were not supposed to be aware, let alone meet, a small-fry like me.

In any event, I walked up to the mezzanine floor where my Super Manager, Mr. Raghu Raj Bahadur, had his office. To my surprise, I was warmly welcomed, asked to sit down and served a cup of tea as well. Mr. Bahadur, spent the next 30 to 40 minutes talking to me about the bank, eliciting reactions from me, giving me advice and making me feel at ease in the new environment. He came across as humane, and not high and mighty at all. When our meeting ended, he reiterated that in case I needed advice or help in my work, I should feel free to reach out to him. Over the next few months that I trained at the 19 N S Road branch, I realised that Mr. Bahadur's statement was not just empty words, he meant it.

The subliminal message that was passed on, and which I must admit crystallised much later in my career, was that all employees, irrespective of seniority, need fair treatment and respect. Employees come to an organisation to work towards a common goal of furthering the growth and expanding the sphere of influence of the organisation in the firm belief that as the organisation grows, so will the employees.

Sometime later, shortly after I got confirmed as a Junior Officer with Grindlays Bank, I was posted back to 19 N S Road branch in Kolkata, as the Foreign Exchange Dealer. The Regional Head for Eastern India was a charismatic personality.

One afternoon, his Secretary called me and said that he would like me to come across to his cabin since he was having a small gathering of Junior Officers who were posted in Kolkata. By now, I had seen and experienced enough to realise that many pre-joining rumours that I had heard were baseless. So we trooped into his office and sat down for a chitchat session, which we were assured, would be between *Us and the Four Walls*.

During the session, which I might add was pleasant, I was asked about my typical day's routine, which I outlined. During our interaction he enquired whether I got time to go through business papers, etc., since it had a significant impact on my job because I needed to keep myself up-to-date. I confirmed that I did spend sometime in the afternoons glancing through business dailies. Imagine my surprise, when the following day, I was summoned by my manager, who asked me why I had to complain to his manager that I did not have enough work to do and spent time in the afternoons reading newspapers! Possibly, the disbelief and shock showed on my face because he asked me for further details.

On recounting the events of the previous day, my Manager just smiled at me and said it was alright. This learning did not have to wait for me to mature further—if there is a reassurance given or a promise made to a subordinate, don't betray it. If you are not sure about being able to deliver on it, then don't promise!

Some years later, I managed a branch of Grindlays Bank, on 31 Chowringhee Road in Kolkata. In those days, having branches with an "open plan" was in vogue. This meant that except for the cash counters there were no partitions or cabins in the branch. This provided an informal and friendly atmosphere in which banking transactions could be conducted and better relationships forged with customers. One of my customers was a senior officer of the bank who had retired and his pension account was maintained at my Branch.

It was an experience to witness the staff's behaviour every time this senior officer walked into the branch for his banking transactions. Everyone in the branch would suddenly be seized with urgent work and would start diligently carrying out their task. All heads would be bent low and the entire staff would appear to be in deep concentration with whatever they were doing. It wasn't that they continued to be in awe of this senior officer, but my staff and officers just did not want to have anything to do with him. They wanted to avoid him and were reluctant even to wish him a good day. I learnt later that he had been a terror while he was working. Hardly anyone had a pleasant memory of their dealings with him.

The treatment meted out to this gentleman reminded me of a children's novel set in Victorian England, written in 1862, by Reverend Charles Kingsley, titled *The Water-Babies*. One of the characters was a stern, bespectacled, unbending spinster called Mrs Be-Done-By-As-You-Did. She behaved towards the water babies as they behaved towards others, making sure their actions came back to bite them, until they gradually learnt the golden rule of civilisation: *if you don't like it yourself, then best not do it to someone else.*

One should introspect whether the respect being shown is because of the position occupied or is it because of the individual and the position occupied is secondary. If it is the latter, this is what one should strive for. Instead of being shunned the individual will always be welcomed even when he or she has moved on. It is a sad and mortifying sight to see people who once ruled the corridors of power being reduced to non-entities after they leave office.

This reminds me of a song *Foot of Pride* by Bob Dylan, which was sung in 1983 and forms part of the classic collection *The Bootleg Series*.

Parts of the lyrics are as follows:

You know what they say about being nice to people on the way up,
Sooner or later you're gonna meet them coming down.
Yeah there ain't no goin' back,
When that foot of pride comes down,
Ain't no goin' back.

In the 1980s, Kolkata had a tradition of having sports competitions among mercantile firms also dubbed as the Merchant's Cup. On these occasions teams would be put together by various commercial organisations to compete against each other and provided cause for bonhomie and celebrations. This served as an opportunity to meet and get to know a multitude of people in the same age group, from different organisations and widen one's social circle. It was during one such gathering that I met an expatriate who had a superb sense of humour. He had a manager who was a wimp, always kowtowing to his manager and was a Yes-Man, much to the chagrin of his subordinates.

One evening, after we had quaffed several beers, he described his manager hilariously by saying, "His boss had given automobile accident victims new hope for recovery because he walks, talks and performs rudimentary tasks, all without the benefit of a Spine." While we rolled on the floor hysterical with laughter, on reflection one realised the real meaning of his comment.

As a manager one should be decisive and take responsibility for their actions. The person taking a decision should be accountable and responsible for the decisions taken.

Many a times, managers take the easy way out by giving an explanation like he or she has tried his or her best, but senior management refused to budge or the company policy did not allow, etc. While the manager might gain a temporary reprieve from his subordinate, in the long run the standing and authority of the manager gets eroded. It culminates and forms an impression about the individual that he or she doesn't fight for his or her team or worse he or she won't argue our case at all .

Some years later, in the early 1990s, I was posted to Cochin (now Kochi). During my stint in Cochin, two existing branches in the city were merged, because of which there was a delay in completing the Inter-Branch Reconciliation. The issue escalated and my Manager from Madras (now Chennai) flew down to Kochi, to understand the problem and help address and resolve the issue. The big worry was that because of backlog in the inter-branch reconciliation, the Bank could end up facing a monetary loss, as which I tried to explain just could not happen.

The details of why I believed that is not relevant to this story. However, when this matter reached the Country Head for Retail Bank, Mr. Nani Javeri, I was labelled as one of the poor performers. This moniker stuck even though I was able to prove on completion that there was no financial loss suffered by the Bank. I am recounting this instance because it lays the ground for my next two experiences with my managers that left a lasting impression on me.

About a year after the event took place, the Executive Leadership Team in Retail Banking met for an off-site. It was early 1993. One item on the agenda was to decide on the future postings and promotions of a legion of officers in Retail Banking. At that time I was still under a cloud because of the issue that I just recounted. When the discussions on postings and promotions began, the Regional Head of Retail Bank for Northern India expressed his keenness to have me as his Regional Head for Operations. The Country Head, Mr. Javeri, responded to his request with words to the effect, "You are aware of what Raju was responsible for in Cochin. Do you still want to have him in your Region, and that too as the Regional Head of Operations?"

The Regional Head of Retail Bank for Northern India baulked and backed off from his preference of selecting me. During this discussion, Mr. Soumen Basu, who was then the Country Head for Operations, expressed his desire to have me on his team in the Corporate Head Office. Mr. Javeri made a similar remark to which Soumen responded with words to the effect, "I have known Raju for some time and I am willing to take the risk." So while I was blissfully unaware, my fate was decided and I had to move from Cochin to Mumbai as part of the Country Operations Team.

Over the next 6 months or so, the Regional Head for Northern India told me about this incident and confessed that he did not have the courage or conviction to push his desire through. After narrating this incident, he apologised to me. Soumen also recounted the incident, which more or less tallied with what I had heard first, which lent further credence to the likelihood the incident had taken place.

One fine morning, Soumen called me and told me that Mr. Javeri would like to see me in his office. Off I trotted across to his office, where I was warmly welcomed, offered a chair and tea. Nani (as most of us called him) came straight to the point. He recounted the sequence of events that took place during the off-site and mentioned more than once that he had written me off as a non-performer who would not achieve much in his career.

He went on to tell me the reason he had called me to his office was firstly to tell me that he had been wrong and secondly that he was sorry for having jumped to a conclusion based on incomplete information. He told me that I had rehabilitated myself and congratulated me for having weathered the storm. Finally, he told me that he had suggested my name as one of the top five officers in the bank for a coveted assignment and that I would shortly be hearing further on that front.

This sequence of events, though spread over a year and a half, forcefully drove a few points home, namely:

- Anyone can make mistakes – but there is no shame in admitting that mistake, if need be to the face of the affected person even if he or she is a subordinate.
- One should have a belief in one's convictions and stand by them even in the face of adversity.
- No harm is ever done in appreciating good work. Delay in appreciating is better than not appreciating at all. It always works wonders for the morale of the person who is appreciated.
- The Buck stops with me – whoever that me is and at whatever level the me is at.

Looking back, even then I did not feel any bitterness for Nani at all, but on the contrary, my respect for him soared. I felt that he need not have called me to bare his heart and apologise, he could quietly have given me the reward that he planned to give, congratulated me and moved on. The fact that he chose not to take the easy way out but admit that he had erred, had an impact that no apology could ever have had.

This incident had a lasting impact on me. Even today I reach out to Soumen to bounce off thoughts and look on him as a mentor. After nearly two decades of working with Grindlays Bank, I moved out to Times Bank mainly because Nani was the CEO and he invited me to join his team. In my career, this was an instance where I joined an organisation because of a manager, contrary to the often repeated cliché of quitting an organisation because of one.

Often there are instances when a manager is privy to some information about his or her subordinates and the rumour mill starts working overtime increasing levels of stress. In such scenarios, the manager is always approached by his team members seeking some sign or reassurance that everything will be fine. A poor manager, with his or her hands tied, is not able to provide even an inkling of things to come. He or she takes refuge with time honoured statements like believe me, I don't know about it. If I knew I would tell you about it.

I have often wondered why are managers reluctant to say, "I am aware of the decision taken, but I am not in a position to share it with you. You will just have to wait till the announcement is made." By taking the I-don't-know-about-it route managers invariably strain credibility and credulity. It makes life so much easier just by being honest and straightforward.

There are times when a manager lets you down. You are left holding the can, even though the action was taken after a discussion with the manager. This could (and often does) happen when there is a risk of a decision going awry. Like in the instance when one of my managers during my banking career turned round and said, "Surely, Raju, I could not have said such a thing" on hearing that bewildering remark – you could have knocked me down with a feather.

At a total loss for words, I literally stumbled back to my desk and tried to figure out how I was going to extricate myself from the predicament that I had been placed in. However, after that incident, at least with that particular gentleman, I was cautious about ensuring that I acted only on unambiguous and written instructions.

Then there was a gentleman, a senior officer in a large bank, who was successful because he always exceeded his targets, but he treated his subordinates like dirt. He used foul language and often would

deliberately leave the door to his cabin open when he planned to give a dressing down to a subordinate. Often this would be with theatrical gestures which included flinging sheaves of papers which the hapless employee had been asked to bring to the cabin of the manager.

The reputation of such managers precedes them and they are feared even by employees who haven't worked for such a manager or don't even know them, but they know of him. Subordinates fear and possibly loathe interacting with such managers.

After my stint in banking I moved to a different sector, i.e., Business Process Outsourcing (BPO).

One aspect that remained consistent between Banking and the BPOs was the approach of managers. I continued to have some managers who were good and others . . . ! Let me just say, say that some managers continued to provide opportunities to better understand human behaviour and the psyche of Managers.

I will share my experiences with two of my managers from this industry.

My manager in the first organisation that I joined, eFunds International, was Pradeep Saxena, who was the CEO. Both Pradeep and I came from a banking background and were new to the BPO industry. Both of us were trying to learn the ropes while trying to make sure that things did not go out of control. My journey into this new industry became easier. In Pradeep I found a manager who would give space to his subordinates to perform and deliver, but would support them to the hilt if a decision was sub-optimal. He would support his team while interacting with Board Members, but later reprimand them if they had been at fault or been negligent. But this happened only in the privacy of his office and never publicly. It was done with the intent to drive a point home and not to humiliate.

Pradeep was well networked within the business community.

However, he never hesitated to introduce and open doors when any one of us (his reportees) needed to reach out to someone for either information or support. In Pradeep I found another mentor on whom I have continued to lean from time to time.

- Publicly accept the brickbats but publicly pass on the bouquets to the employee concerned. In essence, this is taking responsibility for the actions of the team the manager leads. Simultaneously, give the team its place in the sun when something the team did turns out to be right, even though the Manager could legitimately take credit for it.

- However, poor performance should neither be ignored nor should mistakes be allowed to be swept under the carpet. The errant employee must be pulled up and/or given a dressing down, but without destroying his self-respect or standing in the eyes of his peers.

Obviously, the rest of the team will get to know that their colleague was reprimanded for a poorly carried out task. The fallout is important because while the team realises that shoddy work will not be tolerated by their manager, their self-esteem will also not be impaired. More often than not, the team members are not really interested in the details of what transpired during the reprimand, but what the take away from the experience is.

The other manager that I thought I would like to share my experiences is a sharp contrast to Pradeep. This person was not only impatient but would refuse to listen to what is being said, constantly interrupting. As a result, there were instances when I would fail to communicate, leading to all sorts of complications. On one occasion, I was outlining an issue and a solution that I felt might be the most suitable approach to resolve it. I got an absent minded acknowledgment and a vague sign that I could go ahead.

A couple of weeks later when I was giving him (my manager) an update, I was told that he would have much preferred if I had run the approach past him. I reminded him, testily, that I had discussed the approach with him, to which he responded that while I may have briefed him orally about intended plans for action, it might be better if I also left a note with him for him to read. I felt it was a strange thing to say the least and I voiced my view; to which I was told that I was being difficult.

The other odd trait of this person was that he believed that it was a good strategy to put the employee on the defensive when an interaction started. This meant that as soon as a conversation started, the opening gambit was to highlight some issues that hadn't been completed. Once the employee was on the defensive, then the rest of the conversation would continue.

Often the issue raised to put the employee on the defensive had nothing to do with the agenda for discussion. Sometimes one wonders what is achieved by chastising employees at every opportunity and to watch them break down piece by piece.

Finally, the icing on the cake was that this person also played favourites. As is usual in such cases, favourites could seldom do wrong and the others were seldom right. This had a devastating impact on the team as a whole, which was bereft of team spirit. It reminded me of a wisecrack an HR head once made to drive home the point about being biased. He once famously remarked, "We're only hiring one summer intern this year and we won't start interviewing candidates for that position until the boss' daughter finishes her summer classes."

As I mentioned earlier, this was also one of the persons who provided me with some learning:

- Be open minded and an effective listener.
- Let go of problems and mistakes and don't hold them against the employee forever. Once suitably punished, reprimanded or pulled up, it is time to move on.

I had stated in the first part of this article that I would take a shot at outlining some generic thoughts about what a manager would typically like to see in his/her subordinate. After giving it much thought, I feel that as a manager there are only a handful of traits that I would like to see in a subordinate of mine. In order of priority these are:

1. Bring Professional Competence and Knowledge to the job. There is nothing as annoying and time consuming when you have a team member who is not sure of what the job requirements are and how to deliver on them.

2. *Be Brave and Willing to Challenge the Manager*. While this is a two-way street, a member of the team should feel comfortable in disagreeing with his or her manager. A small word of caution, the disagreement should not be for the sake of it. Normally, it should have been thought through so, it is possible to put forward the alternate suggestion and where necessary, citing reasons one believes the manager's approach may not work. Also, once a decision has been taken (even if it is not something that a team member agrees with) the team should work towards implementing it, instead of constantly sniping at the progress being made or repeating *I told you so*. It is good to remember that one should feel free to disagree but avoid being disagreeable.

3. *Work as a Team*. It is important that every member of the team should be a team player and not an individual achiever. The often repeated acronym for a Team is worth repeating: Together Everyone Achieves More.

4. Finally, a *Committed Hard Worker*. This is a two-fold need. One of course is the ability to work hard and the other is a commitment to organisational goals.

There is a well-known American Comedienne Anita Renfroe, who has sung an acclaimed song called "The Mom Song" (set to Rossini's "William Tell Overture" and is available on You Tube). This song is all about the advice that mothers constantly give their children. The song, lyrics and its rendition is hilarious.

The common thread is that across cultures mothers usually give similar advice to their offspring. There is so much that has been written about being a bad manager and it has so much of commonality. I sometimes wonder whether one of these days some

comedian will pen and sing "*The Boss Song*" and render it like Anita Renfroe.

But, coming back to this article, let me try to summarise what I think are some qualities that a manager should exercise which would at least set him or her on the path to becoming a wonderful manager.

I believe there are 11 qualities a manager should have or be able to display during his work which would go a long way towards making him or her a wonderful manager.

The primary, and possibly sole, objective of a manager is to consistently improve the performance of his or her team. If a Manager can manage to do this effectively, then he or she would automatically become a wonderful manager. So the first question that arises in everyone's mind is how does one improve performance and do it consistently?

My 11-point mantra is as follows: (I am expanding each of the 11 points to give a complete picture of what each of them entails).

1. Perform

It is essential that the manager should perform and deliver results and targets that he or she is responsible for. If the manager is *laissez-faire* and not committed to the goals that have been set for him or her, invariably the team that works for him or her will not perform either.

Inevitably, the thought that crosses one's mind is how a manager can keep himself or herself abreast of all developments taking place in their field, to effectively guide their team in doing the right thing? My personal belief is that a manager does not have to know everything or be a technical expert. Let me cite two examples to back this belief.

A. Tony Hayward, ex CEO of BP, had to resign on 1st October, 2010 following the Deepwater Horizon Oil Spill. As the CEO, he was not expected to be aware of the technical details of reasons the Oil Rig exploded on 20th April, 2010. But he failed on two counts namely:

(a) A cardinal mistake was in not ensuring that he was adequately briefed before making statements in public, and

(b) Making a series of public gaffes which sounded his death knell. For example

    (i) He claimed on 17 May 2010 that the Oil Spill was "Very very tiny" but contradicted himself on 27 May 2010 when he described the Oil Spill as an Environmental Catastrophe barely 10 days later; or

    (ii) At the height of the crisis and unprecedented disastrous environmental damage when he told a reporter, on 30th May, 2010, that "He would like his life back", or

    (iii) Even worse, when on 19th June, 2010, he took a day off to take part in the JP Morgan Asset Management *Round the Island Yacht Race* off the Isle of Wight in his co-owned boat.

After all these gaffes, President Obama, in an interview on NBC, said, Hayward wouldn't be working for me after any of those statements.

B. J Robert Oppenheimer led Project Manhattan which produced the first atomic bomb. No doubt that Oppenheimer was intelligent and had made fundamental contributions to the fields of atomic structure and astrophysics. But if he had tried to create the A-Bomb on his own, it is unlikely that he would have succeeded.

So how much do managers need to know?

I think managers should know Enough.

- *Enough* to understand the work being done;
- *Enough* to make good judgements about decisions being taken;
- *Enough* to coach their team when they encounter problems;
- *Enough* to create conditions in which their team is able to find the answers.

2. Empower and Don't Micromanage

There is often a misunderstanding about what empowerment really is? Delegation is not empowerment.

Empowerment consists of:

a. *Assigning responsibilities*
b. *Delegating suitable authority and decision making power and*
c. *Most importantly, holding the employee accountable for the results.*

It is a package deal if it has to work effectively. Empowerment allows a manager to give an employee tasks and responsibility so that the manager, can focus on other jobs. The essence of empowerment is to release, rather than ignore or underutilise an employees' experience, initiative, knowledge and wisdom.

3. Relationship

There is an often repeated truism, "People don't leave organisations, they leave their Managers". If one was to try and peel the onion, one would realise that in the hustle and bustle of today's world, we are losing the human touch. Stiffer targets and Key Performance Indicators (KPIs) are adding to the pressures on each one of us. Today, managers neither have the time nor the inclination to build relationships with their teams nor do they interact with them as humans, but just subordinates (as numbers or statistics) tasked with carrying out a job. Absence of such a relationship often results in employees feeling that their managers don't value them or their contribution, and the alienation deepens.

It is important that managers should try to make an effort to reach out to their team members on issues other than work, however, without becoming too intrusive. It is a fine line, but if handled well it can foster team spirit.

4. Flexibility

Being flexible does not mean allowing anarchy to prevail nor does it mean adoption of a regimented approach like it's my way or the highway. There could be some justification in reduced levels of flexibility at lower or junior levels. However, as managers move up the corporate ladder, they handle more complex issues and regimentation necessarily needs to take a back seat. He or she needs to be open to accepting approaches suggested by their team and willing to accept flexibility in timelines, while ensuring, of course, that project time lines don't go bust. Overall, this helps in making the team interactions and the work less stressful. A direct fallout of this is a more productive team.

5. Optimal Execution

This arises from the need to perform and the need to be flexible but warrants being called out separately. While the manager needs to drive the team to be productive and result oriented, there are times when a manager needs to get down to the trenches and work with the troops shoulder to shoulder. Apart from boosting the morale of the team, it binds teams like few other things can. The reason I refer to this trait as Optimal Execution is because every manager needs to ensure the work is done properly and in time. Performing it optimally allows managers to be humane with their team.

6. Recognition and Appreciation

To some extent this is an aspect that managers in India need to make an effort to be conscious about. We often take deliverables of our teams for granted and often slip up on giving a pat on the back or a compliment. I believe that apart from recognising and complimenting a job well done, it is well worth the effort to celebrate achievements as a team.

Many organisations have documented the Reward and Recognition (R&R) programmes. However, these often degenerate into a formality and right importance is not given to it. Managers have been known to assign it the lowest priority in their tasks for the day and don't give a second thought if they miss a R&R event.

Appreciation does not always mean talking only about the good things that an employee has done. This also includes providing feedback on performance to the employee and suggestions on how things could be improved instead of waiting till the end of the year and raising it during appraisals, leading to endless angst.

7. Motivate

It has been famously said that a manager stands on the shoulders of his or her team. He or she succeeds or fails based on their team's work.

In any journey there will always be ups and downs. While it is important to celebrate when there are upswings, it is equally important to keep the morale of the team high and keep them motivated when things don't go as planned. This is a crucial role the manager needs to play.

It is the manager's responsibility to keep his eyes on the goal and get the team to refocus on the goal so the trough can be overcome and crested. This has become very important, especially over the past 5 years or so when the world has witnessed an economic downturn.

8. Authenticity

Authenticity means being genuine, honest and transparent. I am sure many of us would be able to relate instances when your manager has outrightly denied having made a commitment or leveraged semantics to get out of a tight spot.

Every person in any organisation fully accepts there is always a hierarchy of information and that every single piece of information will never be accessible to everyone across the board. However, being open about not being able to share classified information reduces the importance given to the grapevine.

Authenticity also means being frank and open enough to admit when the manager doesn't know or doesn't understand some part of the work. The respect that a manager gets by admitting his or her willingness to learn has to be experienced.

9. Nurture

A manager is like a gardener. While the seeds are sown, unless they are nurtured, the plant will wither away. This analogy applies to a manager and his or her team members. The team will face professional downturns and he or she would not able to move forward.

It can be hugely frustrating to hit a road block and not know how to proceed. It is at times like these the manager needs to don the hat of a mentor and guide the employee from the abyss he or she is stuck in and enable them to see the bright light again. These are times when it helps to have frank discussion and cover negatives (as areas for improvement) and positives (areas to be further strengthened).

10. Communicate

Communication is the lifeblood of any group. While communication is a two-way street, care must be taken that both are not approaching each other from opposite ends of the street and on the same side of the street.

While, communication usually takes place freely and openly at lower levels in an organisation, mainly because there is no leverage that one employee gains from the other. However, communication across levels and at senior levels is often guarded and Politically Correct so nothing can be held against an individual. The loser in such a scenario is, initially, the team and, eventually, the organisation. Here again, it is the manager's responsibility not only to encourage open dialogue but also to ensure that the negative fallout of such open communication is contained. Please keep in mind what I mentioned earlier – Feel free to disagree but don't be disagreeable.

11. Encourage

Lastly, the lubricant for the entire process is encouragement. The manager constantly needs to encourage his or her team to raise the bar, failing which complacency and failure set in. Some managers also take an active interest in helping their team members in their career development to its fullest extent.

My 11-point program for becoming a wonderful manager is summarised below:

P   *Perform*

E   *Empower and don't micromanage*

R   *Relationship*

F   *Flexibility*

O   *Optimal execution*

R   *Recognition and Appreciation*

M   *Motivate*

A   *Authenticity*

N   *Nurture*

C   *Communicate*

E   *Encourage*

In conclusion, at a recent Human Resource (HR) Summit, I was asked to state in one sentence what my credo, as a Manager, had been through my career of 33 years. My response to this question was, "Being honest, treating each team member with respect and calling a spade a spade."

"Anyone can make mistakes—but there is no shame in admitting that mistake, if need be to the face of the affected person even if he or she is a subordinate."

4

A GOOD BOSS IS A GREAT TEACHER

Anshoo Gaur
President and Head
Amdocs, India

> *Integrity means always doing the right thing, whatever*
> *be the consequences. It takes courage to do the right thing*
> *and that day I had the courage to take a stand for*
> *what I believed was the right thing for us.*

Early Musings

It was an interesting question posed to me by Virender Kapoor, "Would you like to contribute a chapter for a book about Wonderful Bosses?" I was initially skeptical but once Virender explained the thinking behind the endeavor, it was hard for me to say no. As he started describing what he hoped people would share with him on this topic, I found myself thinking back on my career. More often than not, life happens without us realising it, and then a simple question or a comment makes you reflect on all the water under the bridge and the path one took to be where one is today.

During our lives, we have many Events and Learnings, while the core experience itself might be forgotten (blocked from our view) the learning from those experiences becomes a part of who we are. So in some sense, they are with us and, at the same time, not with us in the present. In my case, as I am sure it is true with a lot of you, School/College/First-job get-togethers are great places for these experiences to come gushing out from a hidden vault as if the get together was a catalyst added to produce magic from a mundane chemical reaction going nowhere.

So here I was, a person interested in writing (mostly blogs!) being asked to write about wonderful boss(es), the trade-off being this would be one person get together, a get together nonetheless, and of course the added opportunity to relive Boss-Centric experiences. As you can imagine, the answer from me was, "Yes, would love to do it."

Who's the Boss? And the Word Wonderful

Well, we know the answer to the above for a married man. Clichés apart, I wanted to understand the term Boss a lot better because I, in my simplistic belief, feel a Boss is someone we look up to and, hence, I intended to share experiences about people in my life, beyond just my career. These are people who I looked up to for a variety of reasons and would like to share how and why a part of that experience has become an integral part of me today. I will add though that in some cases, there are aspects that are still under construction.

To confirm whether the approach mentioned earlier would take me way off the commonly understood meaning of Boss, like many of us, I turned to Google search and found the following:

Boss

/bôs/Noun

1. A person in charge of a worker or organisation.
2. *A round knob, stud, or other protuberance, in particular.*
3. *A cow.*

The first one is logical but the words in italics; I was not prepared for and have no way to reconcile, imagine writing about A Wonderful Knob.

Not to give up with two- third of the meaning being not what I anticipated, I continued the quest and searched Wiktionary and there I found the following:

Boss (Plural Bosses)

Noun

1. *A person who oversees and directs the work of others; a supervisor.*
2. *A person in charge of a business or company.*
3. *A leader, the head of an organised group or team.*
4. *The head of a political party in a given region or district*
5. *(Informal) A term of address to a man.*
6. *(Video games) An enemy, often at the end of a level, that is particularly challenging and must be beaten in order to progress in, or complete, the game.*
7. *(Humorous) Wife.*

Leaving aside the informal, video game, and humorous definitions this fares a lot better but I picked Etymology 3 (which already filters down) and goes as follows:

From Dutch baas, from Middle Dutch baes (Master of a household, friend) etc., originally a term of respect used to address an older relative.

Well some of the definitions can take us to different places but I simply wanted to validate whether I could go beyond career experiences as I share my view of the proposed topic. In this regard, from the definitions, one can conclude that a boss could be anyone to learn from, look-up to and respect. It can include someone who heads a team, organisation, party, etc. Needless to say, very much in sync with the range of people about whom I reminiscenced and the experiences that I plan to share with you.

Before starting to write, I still need to tackle the question of what makes a person (or boss) wonderful. My view is that what makes a Boss wonderful is the learning imparted by the boss. By the way, learning is the key, and for argument's sake the bosses may or may not be wonderful on their own (as an individual) but the learning emanating from them should be.

Now with all the definition and terms out-of-the-way, I would like to share with you stories about some wonderful bosses from whom I learnt a lot. Like I stated earlier, in many cases some of the learning from them are a part of me today and in others I continue to be in awe of these folks and aspire to adopt some of their traits as I continue to grow as an individual. Within each category, I identify the wonderful ones that stand out because of the transformational nature of learning from them. The categories I choose are:

(a) Teachers,

(b) Family and

(c) Professional bosses.

The meaning of the word Boss I shared earlier supports the approach that I take or at least have hopefully made a good case for the same.

Teacher....Teacher

Starting with the Teacher boss category, two wonderful people stand out for highlighting the role of storytelling and humour in effectiveness of learning and simplification of complex topics. Effective teaching (and hence learning) is a global challenge. We come across hundreds of teachers in our lives but I am sure that less than a handful stand out as great teachers. It is likely the traits mentioned earlier are the ones your favourite teacher had as well.

Learning from many teachers requires much filtering; two of my teachers made this filter redundant for me. A smile breaks out on my face when I think of these wonderful Bosses. Interestingly, these great teachers had a non-linear impact on learning of all students across the grade. Through stories, humour, and associations they got students involved in the discussions and deliberations, kindled the desire to learn and, in the end they left an indelible mark on me and almost the entire class. Humour somehow became a common currency, a great equaliser. Interestingly, our seniors and juniors also had a similar view. In effect their influence was across years.

The two teachers I refer to, I encountered at the opposite ends of my educational career. One was my High School teacher in the Stewart School, Bhubaneswar, and the other was a Professor at the University of Arizona (UofA), Tuscon, Arizona where I was pursuing my Master's degree. The high school teacher taught us Geography and made the class the most anticipated by one and all. He told us amazing stories as a carrot for discipline, attentiveness and focus. A two minute pin drop silence was the price to pay for an unforgettable episode from World War II (How he knew these stories, I have no idea…even to this day). Weaved into the stories were topics that were important for us, for example, he got us to learn about time zones… East Gain Add (EGA) and West Loose Subtract (WLS) through the ensuing discussions.

The love and respect the students have for him was tested not long ago when we found that he was unwell and could benefit from some support. Former students from across the world got together to offer their help and support, collectively solutions were found to provide some relief. Not surprisingly, the monetary offer was more than the need and this left us with an interesting problem that we still need to deal with.

The UofA professor taught us a complex topic like Linear Programming with an unforgettable smile and contagious humour. He made the formulation of difficult objective equations and convoluted constraints simple by using real life associations. In effect, every statement he made had an association, combined with a hint of fun and humour.

We often believe that people who bring the happy attitude to work must be lucky and happy, because they have a happy life outside of work. Hidden from view is the reality that, as with

many of us, the folks with happy attitude have their fair share of challenges in day-to-day life. In reality, happy people have decided to control the only part of their situation they had control over, their reaction to the situation. For them happiness and humour is an attitude not a conditioned response to circumstances. In both the examples that I shared, without getting into the details, their attitude was a choice.

As I write this, these wonderful bosses remind me of the reasons why *Guru* (teacher) has such an important role in the Indian tradition. The summary lesson: "There is tremendous latent potential in humans; humour, stories, associations play a key role in helping us discover what we like and what can we become, and these kindle our latent potential." Also, "Happiness is an attitude...not a conditioned response."

Everywhere, Work is Indeed Worship

The world is replete with examples, stories and quotes, movies that depict the factor that helps determine success of an individual or the accomplishment of an objective, hard work and associated perseverance. Whether it is a successful sports personality, an Olympian, distinguished businessmen, or world leaders; one common thread that binds them all is the ability to work harder than most.

Then there is the never ending debate on the role of talent or skill and luck in the success of individuals. To resolve this debate, I am reminded of two people; Gopichand – the famous Indian badminton player and coach who was with us at Amdocs India, recently. He made a profound comment stating that if you can spend 10,000 hours focused in the pursuit of your goal or passion then he believes that one would very likely achieve it. Then there is Samuel Goldwyn (American film producer) who was right on the money when stating, "The harder I work, the luckier I get."

Luckily for me, the virtue of hard work was presented to me in a way that I could absorb without having to undertake the uphill quest of finding the true meaning behind the words and actions. This virtue has been the closest to my heart, essentially because it came to me from another wonderful boss, my father, Dr. K.D. Gaur.

Growing up, it was hard for me to understand why he would be the last to go to bed and the first to rise, why he would work on books he was writing till 2 a.m. Leading

by example, he proved over and over that through hard work one could continue to overcome obstacles and accomplish ones goals. He became one of the youngest professors in the university He overcame challenges he encountered being from a different part of the country and taking on a senior role in a regional university. All this, while not knowing the local language. India was very different 35 years ago, where opportunities were few and competition severe. Elements of castesim and regionalism were prevalent and this made regional mobility difficult. My father overcame these challenges with continued hard work, dedication and focused pursuit of his objectives.

Even today, after having recovered from several illnesses, being close to 80 years, it is not surprising to see him working the same hours and with the same enthusiasm that he did 40 years ago. Work for him has been and will continue to be his worship. He epitomises what Vince Lombardi succinctly summarised as "The difference between a successful person and others is not a lack of strength, not a lack of knowledge, but rather a lack of determination." This has indeed become my most valued principle. I often joke (in reality, I mean it) that I am workaholic and I love it. "What about work-life-balance?" is the rejoinder question, I do think that it is sometimes more difficult to allocate the right amount of time to the family and this is of paramount importance. In my case, it does help that my wife grew up with her father's story being not very different from mine as far as hard work was concerned.

Business of Integrity

There is a complementary trait, virtue if you wish to call it so, that develops in parallel to hard work and that is integrity. This relationship became clearer to me because of another boss that I worked for earlier in the US. I was responsible for the global deployment of a large change management program involving process and technology. This was a program that was fundamental to the success of the company. Our teams had been working exceedingly hard on the program. Change management programs, in large corporations with more than $20 billion in revenue and over 100,000 people, are not easy and are scrutinised by the management frequently.

One such review, in hindsight, was a seminal learning moment. Our company had a new CEO and review was sought of program we were responsible for. As the review got underway, I found it surprising that my immediate boss and my peers were only answering questions asked and were not transparently sharing the plan, approach, challenges, etc. Also, no one was defending our teams who had been working hard and in fact helped cross a tipping point (over 70 percent) in the IT process and system deployment, a point from where we would not return.

I expected that my boss would proudly present the Defend the Program story while acknowledging the areas of improvement. None of that was happening, and almost involuntarily I decided to play the role. I still don't know from where I got the courage, but I was sure that it was the right thing to do. Now, I became the focal point of the discussion and transparently shared the details, positives, areas of improvement, tackling tough questions, etc. Later that evening, I spoke to my boss, asked him why he was quiet. His defence was that the review was more like an inquisition.

Funnily enough, the next day the person leading the review for the senior leadership called me to her office and I was asked to transition out of my role, handing over my responsibility to her or someone she would identify with. Well, this then was the price to pay and now I better understood the reason for silence by my boss and peers was self preservation rather than being about what was right. Integrity means always doing the right thing, whatever be the consequence. It takes courage to do the right thing and that day I had the courage to take a stand for what I believed was the right thing for us.

I know that courage came because my team and I had been working hard, our work was detailed, were open to improvement, and in the end wanted the best for the organisation. Keeping quiet would have been convenient and likely the discussion next day would not have taken place. I was the leader that day.

To make the long story short, I transitioned out of the role, took a different one in the same company (a larger impact transformation on the business side). My boss and my peers eventually left the company or took on less prominent roles. The person who was leading the review (inquisition) also left the company; our paths crossed several times but that person avoided eye contact. The IT transformation program was completed as per the plan we were on.

Several leaders responsible for deployment moved to help me with my new role and I learnt the importance of integrity. I know that  in the absence of integrity, I would not have had the courage to stand up that day. When I look back at the experience, I believe it was a wonderful boss who by his inaction helped me to learn the importance of integrity, conviction and hard work.

Summary: Anyone who is willing to work hard and persevere will eventually achieve success whatever the odds, whatever the goals; and integrity nurtures our character and gives us the courage to do what is right.

Output: Humility. Input: Trust and Respect

The debate in the corporate world about whether one earns trust or trust should be given without the need to earn it, is never ending. While the debate goes on, a few wonderful bosses helped answer this question for me. The two people who stand out are one of my earlier bosses at two different companies. Through various incidents these two wonderful people not only made it clear that trusting people was a no-brainer but also a mirror of whom one is, as a person. I recognise today the ability to trust and respect people is a reflection of who you are.

The boss that I talk about is a wonderful (I will describe why, shortly) person with whom I was associated in different roles. We were a fast growing technology company, servicing brick and mortar corporations to become efficient in a fast advancing technological world. My boss was unique in the way that her approach was never to tell one how to get something done, was available to consult and guide, and that only when someone reached out to her. She would allow different approaches to troubleshoot problems, but would not take the eye off the goal.

My boss would call on me to take on and lead complex assignments, assignments that were new to us as a company, assignments that took me to different parts of the world. At all stages, the trust placed on me was complete and this allowed me to thrive and give my best. For someone who was committed to working hard, this was a boon. When mistakes happened, my boss would back me up. Respect and care were two added aspects that I think are closely intertwined in the trust.

I remember an incident when I was on an assignment in New York for an extended period. Monica (my wife) had come along to get me settled into the service apartment I was to stay in. The next morning, the apartment complex had a fire alarm and Monica had to be evacuated (I was at work). Needless to say, we were shaken up. My boss reached out to both of us and by that evening ensured that we had moved out to a different place, much closer to work, with the rental being over twice the other place.

I do believe that humility is the outward manifestation of a person who trusts, and respects people. My boss was humble and caring and her actions were proof of her wonderful and balanced personality.

Interestingly, it is so true that the world is indeed small. After my boss left the company she joined a different company, a company closer to their home. To my surprise, my boss not only joined the company my

younger brother worked with but joined the same team. My brother did not work with my former boss for long, since he took a different role within the company soon, but while he was there, he too was full of praises for my boss's trust in people and her humility.

This attribute of trusting fully was hard (it still is, though it is getting better) for me to internalise. The struggle I faced was (and is), would the outcome be compromised with

too much trust? The person has not proven himself or herself, so how can I trust? If I let them be then how do I know if I were indeed pushing the boundary to the best possible extent? This internal conflict went on till I met another wonderful boss more recently, and this helped clarify the how and why around trust.

This boss started every relationship with 100 per cent trust and his endeavour is to continue to maintain that trust. Every time there was a deviation from the steady state of 100 per cent trust, he would strive to bring back the steady state with the opportunity given to understand the reason or logic for the deviation. Lo and behold, this approach always worked, people strived to maintain the trust that was placed in them…some kind of Pygmalion effect at work. What my boss got was a non-linear output from people and in addition, their approach demonstrated a global mindset.

Global mindset is an often talked about idea but clearly one that suffers from an individual interpretation and from an absence of implementation. For global companies, if implemented correctly, it is clear the benefit accrued to a company is non-linear. Benefit accrual for our company was clear because of this attribute of my boss.

Perhaps sharing an example could bring clarity to this demonstration of trust. Let me first share the context. As a global technology company, we had come to rely increasingly on our talent base in India. Enhancing our delivery capability from India was a challenge, expected skills and expertise were hard to find or build, and leadership gaps were real. While all this was true, the ability to solve these challenges had to be found. To digress, the funny thing about India is that we have many problems, but it is equally true that if there is a will and the willingness to work hard, there are solutions to all these problems. The solution is often uniquely Indian.

As we worked diligently and successfully to solve these challenges in India, some of the solutions that had to be applied were uniquely applicable to the context and local operating dynamics. The pursuit of the solutions attracted comments from some of my global colleagues and peers, "You are thinking about India, and not globally," in my view, the opposite was true. For any organisation to be successful globally one had to "Think global and Act global" plus "Think Local and Act local." In the thinking and acting locally, one had to apply solutions that would be effective in the operating context.

My boss would promptly highlight such concerns or comments for me, not as something that needed remediation, but for awareness; leaving it to me if I would want to do something (or nothing) differently. Further, importantly he would highlight to tell the individuals raising the concern that they likely were not thinking Global … in his view, only by the approach (Thinking and Acting Locally – in addition) we could ensure the whole was greater than the sum of the parts. I know it was not easy, but it helped others recognise and digest the perspective coming from a global mind-set. I changed my approach, becoming more respectful of other's perspectives and to provide more context and explanation while pushing for changes.

My boss in his wonderful management of this complex topic had debunked the theory that while it was easier to trust people you have been around with, people from similar cultural and behavioural traits, 100 percent trust was rare when dealing with people from other cultures and backgrounds. My boss showed me that it does not have to be as difficult and working with this boss changed my approach on how to trust people and continue building the foundation of trust as personal or professional relationship grew with a person.

As I wrap up, I wish to leave you with a thought about our belief system, every culture has this. The myths and stories that are shared with children have the cultural moral code built into them. In India, for example Dharma is central to stories and metaphors that we are brought up with the moral of the story is the wisdom embedded in the story.

Often, as we grow up we forget the Dharmic concepts which reinforce traits such as respect, courage, humility, humour and integrity. Or we start feeling that these concepts are not applicable while we pursue business or personal objectives. As our world becomes complex, the only thing I believe will redeem us is our belief system and principles. My view is that we should constantly practice and revisit our foundational belief system not to lose the acquired wisdom. If it means that we have to reread Amar Chitra Katha (Famous Indian comic books, founded in 1967) to be reminded of Birbal's wisdom, then that is Ok.

At all stages the trust placed on me was complete and this allowed me to thrive and give my best. The boss started with a hundered percent trust and every time there was a deviation from this steady state, he would strive to get back the steady state.

Kallol Hazra
Managing Director,
India
CSG International

5

BALANCED, OPTIMISTIC, SMART AND SAVVY

A quality I admired in one of my bosses was the sense of tidiness. Everything has to be spick and span, was his mantra. I appreciate this, because if this is not driven from the top, the organisation will become sloppy, lethargic and even casual.

After spending two days in my first job going through manuals of how a minicomputer operates and what commands you have to use to start and stop the system, I went to attend a customer call at a customer's premises with a colleague of mine who was an expert. When the customer explained the problem to us, the expert said we have to open the machine and replace a hardware component. Guess what, I was going round in circles around the floor mounted box to figure out how to open the damn machine. The manual

didn't mention that and it was baptism by fire for me to get on to my IT career.

It has been a long and enjoyable journey spanning multiple companies, enriching experiences and meeting some amazing people. I joined the IT industry as a rookie, straight after my engineering and have been associated with it for the last 28 years. Meanwhile, I have also dabbled in management studies to get a feel of the theories behind the real life experiences I have been living.

I started as a Field Support Engineer in Kolkata in an R&D oriented hardware and software organisation called PSI Data Systems and after a year and a half moved to Delhi to join Pertech Computers Limited (PCL) in 1987 as a Product Executive (they were launching the PC/AT and servers at that time). I did a long stint in domestic and later in International Operations in erstwhile Russia and Northern Europe. I then left Delhi for Bangalore to experience the MNC flavour when IBM returned to India through the Tata IBM joint venture and spent about 4 years in multiple roles.

The next stop was Compaq, and through various mergers and acquisitions on the way landed in HP where I ended spending 14 years in the combined entity performing several roles during my tenure. Currently, as the Managing Director, India, I head the Global Delivery Centre of a US based Telecom software and services company, CSG International, India (formerly known as Intec) for the last 3 years.

During this long and eventful journey, I have met some amazing people, peers, colleagues, bosses as well as customers, some of whom had a direct bearing of who I am today whilst there were others who helped me shape my thought process and behaviour, both at work and at home, and have had a lasting impact on my career. During all these years, I was fortunate enough to work with different bosses and colleagues.

This is an attempt to recollect some of those experiences and share with you the learning's from several leaders and game changers of the Indian IT Industry.

The first characteristic which I think is the most important quality of someone in power and who has to get the best out of a team is Integrity. I have had the opportunity of working with several colleagues with uncompromising integrity and this rubs off on the team. With integrity, you inherently associate trust and the two together become a potent combination to get the best out of your team under the most difficult circumstances.

In my earlier days, I was working with my boss in an organisation dealing with different types of computers and its associated peripherals. We had sold a large system to an educational institution and the full payment had not ben received even after 6 months of the final installation. The system wasn't being used by anyone. My boss wanted me and a colleague of mine to visit the customer who was in a faraway place on a red herring of conducting free training and bring back the printer on the pretext that it wasn't working and had to be sent to the manufacturer for repair.

This was just a way to recover the final amount which was equal to the cost of the printer which in those days was high. Ignorant of the repercussions, my colleague and I worked out a plan and got the peripheral device out in its original packing and flew out of the town to recover the money. But the manager and his team didn't get any future business in that town or in that vertical. It might have given him a short-term reprieve for that quarter, but he lost the war. I for once didn't trust his judgment from that day. Sometimes you have to learn it the hard way.

Talking of trust, I also recount another boss of mine who had nothing but the customers in mind. In the mid-eighties, there weren't any mobile phones or web based train reservation systems to be constantly connected to reach a remote place like Bilaspur where Brooke Bond, a customer's factory was located, to attend to a breakdown in the minicomputer installed there. My boss, who was the Regional Manager East, gets a call from the customer on a Wednesday evening that the Omni (the system's name) is down and the trucks will get lined up and will not be able to leave the factory if someone doesn't show up by Thursday morning.

Sensing the situation, our boss turns to one of us (the support team), fishes out Rs. 400 from his pocket and tells us to take the next train to Bilaspur and go and fix the problem. The rest of the *jugar* had to be done by the individual starting from boarding the Mumbai Howrah Mail, reaching Bilaspur and fixing the problem. He had enormous trust on the team and knew that no matter what, the work will get done and the customer will definitely call to thank him. He trusted his team to deliver the results and had nothing except his personal cash to offer. The office was a branch and I am sure all of you are familiar with the imprest cash position, especially during the middle of the month. So trust the team and be open – they will surely deliver.

As you progress in your career, handling various assignments and managing customers, the maturity you gain builds self-confidence which is accentuated by the trust your boss reposes on you. I remember a story going back to my Tata IBM days. I was incharge of support (hardware and software) for a particular product line and there were many government tenders the teams were responding to which required details of bits, bytes, and clock speeds of each component of the system.

The Product Manager and I scanned the entire IBM network to get the details and wrote to the respective experts for the data. We were 95 percent successful and the other 5 percent had to be filled in, as any blank row or column, would have nullified the entire effort of the team. We formed a small core team locally which worked overnight to work out the missing numbers based on benchmark results and other competing products and helped us to participate in those tenders. The confidence that was reposed on me and the Product Manager by the respective bosses spurred us to work on this and not give up saying that these are not published or not available which would have eliminated us from bidding.

A different quality I admired in one of my bosses was the sense of tidiness and looking at the various aspects from a customer's point

of view. With his grooming in Hindustan Lever (no guesses for some of you), "Everything has to be spick-and-span", was his mantra and I do appreciate now that if these characteristics are not driven from the top, the organisation becomes sloppy, lethargic, and sometimes too casual. I have always seen him neatly dressed, even if it is a Saturday. The way he did up the company guest houses in Bangalore and Gurgaon was something everyone speaks about, even today. He was equally vigilant about selecting the right set of people, especially for the front office.

Once I remember interviewing a senior colleague of mine and referring him to this gentleman, then CEO of the organisation, for the final interview. He spent a long time with this former colleague of mine, was impressed with his technical expertise and said everything was fine except "He *chews paan.*" This will not be good when he meets with the customers. He will be good in the backend. Later, I had to convince him that he will be absolutely fine with customers as this person chewed *paan masala* and not *paan* and he wouldn't do that when he was visiting customers. His tirade continued with another team member of mine when he noticed that he was wearing skin coloured socks with black shoes and black trousers which was a no-no. Attire and grooming are an important part of our lives, irrespective of whether it is at work or at home. I have personally learned a lot through my interactions with him.

How many of you have gone into team meetings with a critical problem and wished there was someone to go to who could think out of the box, do magic and come up with an innovative solution when the customer is breathing down your neck either for a proposal from you or solving his current problem? I am sure all of you will agree that your work style and thinking abilities are definitely influenced by the thought process of your immediate boss, especially if you happen to be working with him for a considerable period of time.

One of the greatest traits of an ideal boss, I have learnt, is to always think strategically and explore areas where no one has dared to venture. I was fortunate to work with such a person who, irrespective of what the situation was, would come up with an idea which made you think differently. Whether it was related to a pricing strategy in a large and complex bid, or solving a critical customer's delivery problem or getting a large payment (quarter ends are always bad you know) released, he always had a different approach and guided the team to get the best results.

This person had been my mentor and guide for 11 years and I learned the most during this period of my career. His creativity took charge of him after dusk. Our long meetings, both strategic and tactical, used to go on late at night till one of our wives interrupted to ask whether we were coming home for dinner. In the product business you have to always be on your toes and be ready with strategies to counter competition.

On one occasion, some of you might remember the Desktop ad war going on between Compaq and DEC in 1998 when Compaq decided to acquire Digital. Compaq first came out with advertisements showing the photograph of a computer with the monitor and a keyboard. However, a small note in fine print at the bottom of the advertisement mentioned that the offer of a PC at Rs. 39,990 was without a monitor. Some competitors quoted the advertisement did not mention whether a mouse and keyboard were inclusive, which is unethical and misleads the customer. The Digital advertisement boldly stated, "No fine print. All accessories shown and more are included in the price. Only local taxes extra." This created a stir and his brain wave was behind the Digital rebuttal.

We must remember this was in a situation where it was clear that only one of the brands of PCs would survive after the merger and the entire stock had to be cleared out before the end of life was announced officially. The lesson learnt was: whenever there is a task at hand, we need to complete it with the same passion and zeal, irrespective of what the future holds for that entity. Be tactical, play to the galleries whenever the situation demands and, at the same time, do not miss out the big picture related to long-term strategy.

He was one boss I would always like to work with, a suave performer whose every act would teach you something. He would involve himself in every major challenge his team faced and would provide innovative solutions. That is what a boss must do.

On another occasion, I remember him talking to one of our prospects (we didn't know that he had already shortlisted his choice of purchase from a competitor and not ours) about the great features and speeds the new 32CPU system would deliver for these large banking customer's solution requirements. He went to Hyderabad the next day with the Product Manager, had a daylong meeting, closed the deal and came back with the order before the competition could realise that we had eaten their lunch. Prior to this meeting, the customer had settled on a competing platform and was about to sign their purchase order when this incident happened. Our competitor's salesperson, who lost the order, was fuming as all their party plans went awry.

On yet another occasion we were supposed to put in a bid for a government project where the tender condition specified the bidders were supposed to put in the lowest per transaction cost for the project to be delivered in the Build, Own, Operate, and Transfer (BOOT) Model. The costing was worked out and since this was one of the first such business models we were working on, no one was sure what price to quote.

Further, this was being architected on a solution which was already implemented by one of the subsidiaries of HP in another country, of course in a different language (Japanese) and hence the cost of the software Intellectual Property (IP) was within control. We did a SWOT analysis of our competitors and had a gut feel of what we had to do to win the business. The team dispersed in the evening and reconvened in the morning to work out the numbers. He called our financial analyst who was working on the bid and asked him to crunch the numbers for him.

He had a keen sense of numbers and came up with a strategy of going with x paisa per transaction. All of us were taken aback as our traditional thought process didn't allow us to understand how the entire stack will be delivered and

margins made at that price point. He later told us that he thought through the night and came up with this rationale to not only outwit the competition but also to make sure the company breaks even and shows some profit in the first couple of years of the contract. The lesson learnt here was manifold, know the numbers well, think out of the box for critical problems and do not let your guard down even when you are under tremendous pressure. Last but not the least, take inputs from the domain experts available to you.

Talking about domain experts, one of the most interesting learning experiences I had was related to another project we were working together in a multispecialty hospital. We had just implemented a Hospital Management Software and asked the doctors to start using the same. What do you do when the software starts throwing up errors in Spanish, that too to a doctor attending to a patient and having no idea of the Spanish language? Well, we did learn it the hard way and came up with several solutions. Some of them worked whilst others didn't. The challenge was the error messages in Spanish were all hardcoded and were there all over the code. We got some of them translated, but as you can imagine the literal translation of some of these didn't make any sense to the doctors or nurses. Hence, we had to take the help of an IT expert specialising in medicine to retranslate all the codes to make logical sense.

His Wharton background was definitely a great help for us to learn the nuances of ethics, protocol and the 1-2-3 of business. But trust me, there cannot be any other way of learning the tricks of the trade other than slogging it out amidst competition (especially in India) and either sharing the spoils with the team with each victory or drowning the sorrows with them for every loss and thanking them for the great effort. He is and will be my favourite boss and has been a great influencer of who I am today. His much loved opening lines were "Be that as it may…" and "By the same token…" and we had all picked it up in our dialogues with customers, colleagues, and friends. I have learnt the essence of key communication skills from him and tried to pass some of it to my teams.

While covering every dimension of theories of management, one of the things we learn early in school is "Focus on the customer." Some of the managers I worked for did a great job in ensuring laser sharp focus on each interaction of every customer. There have been a couple of them who shied away and always looked for a shield when the customer called or escalated any issue. The art of staying calm and collected under these circumstances is something all of us should learn and practice. There will be situations when the customers will escalate to you and will ask for quick decisions. Knowing that some of these are dependent on others, (and you don't have a clue on the solution) how well you handle the situation mars or makes your relationship with the customer, and also becomes your leadership trait and, trust me, some managers make a mess out of this.

Every Leadership Foundation Training covers the aspects of key behaviours of leader's vis-à-vis five pillars of competency. One is Strategic Thinking and the second one on the list is Implementation. The ideal combination in any team is having persons exhuming such behavioural competencies as a group. Imagine having two masters in the same team, one a great strategic thinker and the other a master executioner. It is the most royal combination you can think of and I was fortunate to be part of such a team which tasted success in abundance and provided me with the greatest learning experience in my career.

I have covered the strategist in detail. Let me now talk about the other person who, according to me, is the master executioner par excellence I have ever seen, leaving out the Mukesh Ambani's and the Nation Builders who did amazing jobs in their own sphere. The person I am referring to has an uncanny ability to join the dots in every situation and could literally mind read the future moves of the customer and/or competitor.

When he took charge of the India Operations of Compaq and then HP (after the merger), the team was satisfied doing small projects of less than USD 70M while the transformation within our geography was going at breakneck speed. He built an A-Grade talent pool, managed it well and developed this team to handle much larger opportunities – USD 500M-plus. He brought a sense of self-belief that such things were possible with the same team. The rewards started to show in the phenomenal wins we had in the mid twenties on large scale transformational projects across industries. His rapport with customers is still discussed today, and they trusted and supported him wholeheartedly.

One of the other characteristics this person had was to understand the situation and deep dive into areas where the customer showed interest. He was one of the few people in the organisation who could explain the complex structure of HP clearly to anyone and explain the technicalities of any solution to the last feature and functionality, starting from the Pocket PC to Indigo printers (large format printing press like printers consuming litres of ink), to enterprise servers, storage and software. His attention to detail was like folklore, including usage of correct fonts, punctuations, and colour in PowerPoint slides we used to create for him.

Once, I remember we went for a customer meeting with the CTO and his team of a large organisation. This was, again, for an outsourcing opportunity worth more than half a billion dollars. There were four of us and when we started setting up the laptop with the projector, the CTO asked who will present. He stood up and said, "I will present on behalf of my team." The look on the face of the gentleman was worth capturing as he went through the technical details and financial business model with equal flair. It was a 30-page document and he had rehearsed the entire deck while we were travelling by car from our office to the customer's meeting. Lessons learnt: Focus on the details to create a lasting impression. Lead by example when the situation demands and always understand the big picture.

He had an encyclopaedic memory and treated everyone with reverence. Talking of respect; he would visit customers, have a one on one meeting with the Chairman and debrief the team about the meeting, word for word. On his visits to the customer's premises, he didn't miss a single opportunity of meeting the juniors down the hallway who were in some way connected with the project and were not necessarily high enough in rank to deserve a meeting with the Managing Director of the supplier company. We had a Steering Committee meeting with the Chairman, Executive Directors and the General Managers of a large Public Sector bank where we were delivering a transformational banking solution on an outsourced model.

The meetings normally took place on the 8th floor of the building, but he made it a point to meet the DGMs and the AGMs associated with the project by visiting the 3rd Floor first before heading for the Steering Committee meeting. This created an environment of trust between the two working teams (ours and the bank) and the congenial atmosphere didn't vitiate any situation even when there were small mistakes committed on either side. In hindsight, it looks like a simple act which he did without fail on every trip of his but in reality, while working with large teams I realise how important it is to reach out and seek out, rather than wait for someone to come and speak to you. Having spent enough time with him, it comes to me naturally and has helped me build this trait of my personal leadership style.

He had reached the pinnacle of his career by becoming the Asia-Pacific Leader of HP handling more than USD 10 billion, but his feet were firmly planted on the ground. When I pestered him to buy a large car so we could test drive a Mercedes or Jaguar, he always said he doesn't want to overburden the company with a huge cost as he feared that every day when he came to office and worked at his desk, someone would come from behind, pat him on the shoulder saying, "Your time is up buddy." Be prepared for the worst but do not lose hope and give up, that was his mantra and he lived it to the tee.

His personal leadership characteristics were something each one of us tried emulating and being in that environment day in and day out had an effect on every one of us in the team. He had the exemplary skill of binding the team together, sink or swim in success and failure, and made us see one clear vision. Everyone had his or her part to play in it and he ensured we did our acts well, like the conductor of a philharmonic orchestra, at the same time ensuring that the minutest details were taken care of. One example I can clearly remember is related to preparation of a stage for an internal leadership training event organised in the ball room of a Five Star hotel. It was 7 pm when a couple of colleagues and I got a call from him asking us how the preparation was going on for the meeting next day. When we assured him that things were fine and under control, he said he would be there in the next 90 minutes to get a firsthand feel.

Mind you this was an internal training program and all those who would be there, including the presenters, were employees of the company. As usual, he landed at the venue after two and a half hours and proceeded straight to the raised platform. He walked over it and found a small protrusion below the carpet which was barely visible. You could only feel it if you walked over that particular spot and to us it was okay. He called the Banquets incharge and told him to rectify the same. The explanation he gave to us was that it might disturb the concentration of the presenter if he inadvertently, stepped on it. Such was his eye for detail for an insignificant thing (to us) which according to him can have an effect on the program. As I mentioned earlier, he could read the situation early and prepare for the consequences.

This leads me to another aspect of his which I think is important for any boss, the humane aspect of our behaviour towards the people we manage and showing empathy.

A colleague of mine was facing a disastrous time, he lost his wife to cancer. He was one of the first to be there with him and stayed throughout the night, not only to console the family but also to ensure that the entire procedure the next day went off without any glitches.

He didn't catch a wink that night and told me that since he knew the family's background, he was apprehending some problem when the deceaseds next of kin would be there the next morning. He wanted to be there just to make sure things do not get out of hand as the blame game begun. He could have left for his home late in the night and come back the next morning but he chose to be there with the rest of us.

Amidst all this, he didn't lose his sense of humour which, I think, is one of the most important traits we sometimes bottle up while we are enamoured with our daily problems and situations. In one of our Executive meetings with a large customer, when he was the head of the Asia-Pacific business, we were sitting around a round table getting badgered by the customer's project team for many issues. This was a Hospital Management System (referred to earlier) project we were implementing for a large multi-disciplinary (Speciality) hospital, owned by one of the top 10 richest Indians. The executive sponsor was the first lady of the organisation, and she was sitting next to him and talking about possible solutions to make the system stable.

The meeting started late (usual occurrence) and there was another colleague of ours who walked out of the meeting before it could end as she had to board a flight. The customer didn't take this well and showed a lot of displeasure. He understood the situation, took charge of the meeting and ensured all the action items were driven out of his office. When we returned to our office for a debrief to the team, he told me that he had forgotten to take all the notes as he was admiring the huge diamond ring our project sponsor was wearing as he will never get an opportunity to see such a huge piece of diamond at such close quarters.

As a boss he did not want the pressure caused by displeasure of the customer to be passed on to the team, and hence this statement. He later, of course, apologised to the customer for our colleagues departure and reflected that she shouldn't have done that. Lessons learnt: in customer situations take charge when things start to drift and customer shows uneasiness. Never leave a meeting (even if it starts late) unless it is finished and, finally, make use of your funny bone once in a while. It helps to lighten up things for the team.

Another interesting aspect of people leadership, which I think is the key, pertains to delegation and the art of tolerating and learning from our own and other's mistakes. One of the lessons I had learnt working with various chieftains is the art of knowing what to delegate and when. Timing is critical as there can be situations where one can end up messing things. There are instances where you will come across a boss who outwardly shows he or she is delegating, but is micromanaging the entire show through another set of team members. Trust and tolerating mistakes are the foundation of successful delegation and a great team becomes super when delegation happens across levels automatically and everyone performs their designated tasks.

One of the bosses I worked for managed this well. She gave the team complete freedom to run that part of the business, but had a monitoring and reporting system in place through weekly meetings. This was essential as customers would call up for various matters and she had to know the current status to respond to them appropriately. Again, she had this power of negotiating tough clauses with the customers and could present on any topic provided someone did a "Halo poly" with her on the slides. She trusted the team and if she had mentioned something which was factually incorrect, she had the guts to say she was wrong. Now this is a great trait which many bosses do not possess.

I had the ominous task of accompanying her in several Steering Committee meetings and presentations to the Board of an organisation on project status. These were not always pleasant meetings. Mostly, with the complex projects that we were working on, all things do not work as they are supposed to every time, and there were misses or problems not getting resolved, etc. To face the Board and answer tough questions is an art she introduced me to, and again when she stood up and spoke, she was doing it on behalf of the team knowing well the capabilities and the shortcomings. If I had told her that the timelines cannot be met because of X and Y reasons, she pushed back the customer when they tried to influence through the corridors of power. She had respect for the team and trusted the leaders and their judgment. We had committed a few glaring errors in a few projects and when I look back, I realise that without her support and willingness to tolerate these mistakes, we wouldn't have progressed.

I have tried to cover the various facets of management skills one should experience to become great leaders and bosses. The examples earlier signify a specific set of do's and don'ts which I think should be kept in mind when we as leaders start to manage large teams and try to be role models for the future generation. These, if kept in mind, would earn you respect of your team and this is what every boss must strive to achieve at the end of the day.

Uncompromising integrity is the starting point and there can't be anything higher on the list.

Listening Skills

1. Sit up.
2. Look interested.
3. Lean forward.
4. Listen.
5. Act interested.
6. Nod your head to show that you are tuned in.
7. Track the speaker with your eyes.

Listening skill is something we give up as we move higher in the hierarchy. This is something we have to pay attention to, as unless we give a patient hearing to the other side, we will not be able to comprehend the problem, forget about resolving them. This should be part of the Personal Leadership characteristic we build for us as we move on our journey of leadership. Bosses usually like to hear their own voice and in a powertrip do not find it necessary to listen to any one else.

Keep in touch with the technological aspect of the business as the ecosystem around us is changing drastically. If we are not in sync, we will be overpowered by our traditional thinking and problem resolution style which might not be the best fit for the occasion. A recent example will illustrate this better. When we talk of Software Development Life Cycles or SDLC, the most common method employed is the Waterfall Model. With the customer's timelines getting crunched, companies are looking at Agile Methods. If the team or the boss feels threatened by this new monster, I am sure there will be a huge reluctance to move in this area. Keeping abreast of what Agile is and how it helps boost the confidence of the team as well as the leader.

Implementation is the key. Think of Planning and Execution as two phases. A rule of thumb to remember is small p and big E, i.e., Execution should always be more than the planning in every aspect of the business.

You have to develop the art of thinking strategically as you grow in the organisation. Don't think of the immediate benefit to the team, but start thinking in terms of the benefits that will accrue to the company through the small action you take on a particular area or topic. As you are aware, the world around us is becoming smaller and smaller. With the global connectivity and interlinking of various aspects of businesses, a small innovation by any one individual can have a huge influence on the company or the industry at large. So keep the innovation engine running within the teams and encourage strategic thinking.

In times of a personal crisis, which could happen with any of your team members, you as a boss must provide personal support – it earns you respect and loyalty for a lifetime. This is one aspect which can never be underrated. Unfortunately, in our day-to-day stressful life, sometimes many of us do not understand the importance of this important humane aspect which a boss must do and display.

Finally, we have to lead people and everyone is different. The way we speak, interact and respond to each individual has much bearing on what type of leader we end up being. Building an atmosphere of trust, providing feedback without fear and showing empathy goes a long way in depositing emotional quotient in your account and, trust me, this always helps in tough times.

One of the greatest traits of a boss, I have learnt is to always think strategically and explore areas where no one dared to venture. I had a boss who could come up with an idea which makes you think differently.

6

A BOSS IS A PEOPLE MANAGER: AN HR PERSPECTIVE

Samir Kapoor
Co-Founder & Director
Corporate Affairs,
MILE (Management
Institute for
Leadership and
Excellence)

Managing people is not rocket science; it is even more
complicated, because you are dealing with people and
no two are alike.

In the year 2009, at the age of 31, Samir quit his corporate career and co founded MILE—Management Institute for Leadership and Excellence. For the world he is Dr. Samir Kapoor but for his students he is Papa or Big Boss. This name flashing on the mobile screens can get the entire campus running even at 3:00 am. His students particularly fear his innovation and creativity, ranging from running on streets to earn a day's living to making parathas for the entire campus for wasting food. With him around, everyday has something new to offer. There is never a dull moment. A man who likes to keep busy and keep everyone busy. He knows how to keep everyone's interest alive. A wonderful motivator he can even get a person who has hit rock bottom up and running again, and start believing and working towards perfection. A bit demanding sometimes his focus has always been in getting fruitful results in whatever he does.

His students say:

"His innovative ideas, zeal and energy are things to die for, he even beats us youngsters in these areas and this surely makes us envious."

"As a student the best thing about learning in his shadow is that you'll realise your hidden strengths and he will work along with you to further strengthen them. A true mentor, he knows his students in and out, and always strives to get his students the best there is, be it jobs, the profile, the faculty, the environment, etc."

"A person who is full of professionalism, discipline and the charisma to keep doing something different, never leave an opportunity, to learn whatever new comes across his way, and has always been a role model for all his students to imbibe qualities like him."

A few years back, when I was working in one of the leading MNC banks, we were struggling to retain our sales force, attrition being a triple digit number was killing us. The challenge we faced was two pronged. Firstly, no one wanted to take the responsibility, the idea was to find a fall guy. It had become more like a witch-hunt. Secondly, the business managers didn't know how to manage their attrition levels. The Sales Managers argument was that they were responsible for getting business and with these attrition levels they would never be able to meet their targets.

The unfortunate and evident flaw in this argument was that as a business manager, one of your prime responsibilities of managing people was not being acknowledged. Their argument, "If I don't push my people I would not be able to achieve my sales targets," did not hold any water, as there were managers who were running at far lower attrition numbers than others and were achieving their numbers consistently without increasing their blood pressure and screwing their teams. It took us sometime to get things in place, and the solution was simple. Something all managers have known "People don't leave organisations they leave managers".

While this is an overused quote, managers still don't know what it takes to be a good People Manager. The idea being that people should not only perform but outperform other teams and yet want to be with you. Here, I would talk about some simple yet effective ideas for business managers. Managing people is not rocket science, it's even more complicated because you are dealing with people and no two are alike.

Managers run organisations by managing talent and it's the talent of the employees that helps an organisation achieve its goal. As simple as this may sound, it involves much managerial acumen to achieve organisational goals.

With talent becoming the differentiator in today's economy, it is imperative that as a business manager you understand the importance of Talent Management and Talent Development. While this has become more evident in the last decade or so, visionaries understood the principle almost a hundred years back. "Take away my people, but leave my factories and soon grass will grow on the factory floors. Take away my factories, but leave my people and soon we will have a new and better factory," wrote Andrew Carnegie, the famous American industrialist and philanthropist in early 1900s. Nearly a century later, Carnegie's statement still holds true more than before.

Every manager is a Human Resource (HR) Manager; he hires, trains, sets goals, reviews performance, motivates and rewards his team. How you manage your team would have a direct impact on how they deliver your and, in turn, organisational goals. What differentiates an ordinary manager from an amazing manager? The transformation from an individual contributor to a people manager is nothing less than a caterpillar that metamorphoses into a butterfly.

Organisations conduct two day trainings, sometimes online training modules (which are worse) before they get a person in a managerial role; this is not enough. We need to understand that because someone is a good individual contributor it does not mean that he would be able to manage a team. The competencies required for a manager are different and are less industry specific than what most people would think. A good manager is a good manager in any industry or any kind of job. As long as it's about managing people, the principles are the same.

The good managers can seamlessly move across industry and do well wherever they go. So what is it that makes these managers succeed? The key is they are good people managers not softies, but people who know how to get work done. It's about managing talent, because that's what employees get on board – Talent.

Boss, or a Business Manager is first a people manager, and I would use these terms inter changeably. I would be analysing the role of a boss not only as viewed by a subordinate, but also as viewed by a HR Professional. I view a boss who not only spots talent, but also grooms and retains talent.

HR Professionals put in much effort to get good people on board and get demoralised when they see the Business Managers using talent as cannon fodder resulting in people leaving the organisations. I have tried to put my experiences with my bosses, my peers (who are bosses to some) and my experience as a boss in a format that would give out some effective strategies which can be used by peoples managers, across industries and all levels of leadership.

No one set of strategy will work for all managers and that is what makes managing people so interesting. You can learn from others experiences and use them as a backdrop for developing your individual strategy that fits your industry, personality and vision.

Insulation, the Art of Keeping Your Team Warm

I still remember the first time we were conducting 360-degree feedbacks at ICICIoneSource. For some managers it was an eye-opener. When team members have the luxury of giving feedback with anonymity, they make full use of the opportunity if they have faith in the system. Under the leadership of my then boss Aashu Calappa, the faith was rock solid, and the results were there for all to see. One of the feedbacks that many managers got was that their team did not feel the manager was motivating the team in case of a crisis. For such managers, when there is crisis there has to be a scapegoat.

Teams would never be able to work in an environment where an honest mistake can be fatal. I spoke to a few employees who were managing teams and their response was that they had come from an organisation which was culturally different. When probed, it turned out to be more of an individual style of functioning and not much could be attributed to the previous organisation's culture. Few employees went to the extent of calling their managers spineless, people who would not take a stand when needed and not protect their team. Then there were managers for whom their teams would do just about anything.

Let me tell you a small story.

I still remember it was a Wednesday, not because I have a fantastic memory, but because we had our Work Force

Management (WFM) calls on Wednesday's. The WFM call is more like a negotiating platform where Business Heads fight for new hires they need in their team. The talent acquisition team's capability being finite, one business head's gain is another business head's loss. On the call would be WFM team, talent acquisition leads, Business Heads and in-case there is a big fire, the HR head. The reason I say big fire is because in the ITES industry fire is Business as Usual (BAU), the number of times I have heard, "There is a big fire," made me wonder if I was working in the Fire Department!

This was a normal call with limited exposure to fire, but we had a new challenge this time. We were discussing the quality of hires, this is a nightmare for recruitment managers because as much as they would like to focus on quality the training team would never say the quality of hires is good. This is a professional hazard that every Talent Acquisition Manager would acknowledge. Luckily for me, Firstsource had one of the most dynamic training head one can work with. Maninder Kapoor Puri, no I am not related to her, in case the surname suggests as much.

Maninder was willing to take the challenge to train all the Garbage as trainers would say and Talent as I would like to put it. She appreciated the challenge the Talent Acquisition team faced and always had solutions for problems. But this time it was different, our team had gone out for a job fair and had messed up big time. The quality of hires was so poor that my recruiters didn't know where to hide. These are the mistakes for which people can lose their job. I spoke to defend the team but the gravity of the mess was astronomical. The question everyone asked was, "Who hired these people?" These were people who by no stretch of imagination were fit for an agent who had to take voice calls.

As much as I tried to duck the question, from the tone of the call I had understood that I was on a tight leash and had to respond. So I said, "It's me who has signed off on all these profiles." We had complete silence for about 30 seconds and then Maninder (I think she had a smile on her face when she said this) said, "I think you should attend the Calibration Sessions", and people burst out laughing. Calibration sessions are where trainers and recruiters sit together and understand what a trainable hire is. Somehow, I was able to wriggle out of the situation in one piece. As the DGM Talent Acquisition I could get away with this but had I put forward the recruiter, he would have been crucified. I had gained my teams respect; they knew I would stand by them come what may.

With this background we started our investigation into the fiasco. To my surprise, everyone was more than willing to take ownership of the problem. But I was not interested in whose fault it was, I was more concerned about our assessment process. How could a person get through three rounds of interview with three different people and not be able to speak to save his or her life. I was not willing to believe that my recruiters could have hired such people.

We took out all documents and at first glance we found out that a few people who were incapable during the training had scored the highest in our preliminary assessments. This came as a shock. We sat as a team to understand how this could have happened after looking at the papers and meeting the trainee, there was only one-way this could have happened. We were dealing with an imposter. We called the trainees and probed them and bingo we were right.

We finally asked these people to leave the organisation. The team came up with a solution of adding a photograph in the interview form, which would be taken at the time of interview with a webcam so that it could not be tampered. This solution was quickly replicated across locations in India and became a part of the Talent Acquisition Process.

Let's try to see how these things could have turned out had I not taken the ownership and insulated my team from the storm. Some recruiters name would have come up on the call and leave alone what this recruiter would feel, the entire team morale would have gone down. My investigation could not have led me to the actual problem and I would be sitting with one recruiter short and a demoralised team, which would be less productive and would shy away from taking tough calls.

But again, there are managers who would like to save their skin even if it costs their teams heart.

While this is not only a reflection of how I did as a manager, it also is a reflection of how the leader of the training, Maninder made me feel. Below is what my Linkedin reccomendation for Maninder read:

Yes I can. Three words that not many people can say with conviction. I had stereotyped training heads as individuals who did not have the courage or the spine to face the dwindling talent pool reality and always wanted readymade talent so that the trainer's effort would be minimal and chances of failure least, but this was before I had worked with Maninder. I had not met a training head who would understand and appreciate the ground reality and work with the Talent Acquisition team. The key here is working with and this cannot be lip service, it requires high levels of positive and continuous intervention. A lot of credit for my success as a talent acquisition lead has to be attributed to Maninder. She worked with me and my team personally and made the necessary changes in both Talent Acquisition and Training Processes and this was not a one time change. She had laid the foundation for continuous change by creating a dynamic self evolving system. Most people would believe that the two roles talent acquisition lead and entry level training lead are designed for a role conflict, but with the right leadership and people management skills, this role conflict can be transformed into a partnership, one that benefits the organisation. This I am sure could not be simple for anyone, but Maninder had the Domain Knowledge, People skills, Leadership skills, and could say the three magic words, Yes I can.

You can't Improve Something You Can't Measure

I was standing in the lobby of Standard Chartered Towers (SCT) at our newly built office at Goregaon, Mumbai, waiting for the elevator;

 this could sometimes be painful as three out of four elevators were turned off during non-peak hours. This was the bank's strategy of Green Planet by saving power, no pun intended. At two in the afternoon, in office where people find it difficult to keep their eyes open, after a heavy lunch, I was to meet Krishnan, my boss. He was the National Sales Director for SCB consumer bank. This position for most would lead them to have high blood pressure, but Krishnan was a different breed. He used to thrive under pressure.

The elevator stopped on the fifth floor, the Lion's den, as most sales people call it. About 10 meters from Krishnan's workstation I could hear him scream at someone, for the sake of confidentiality, let's say he was speaking with Rajesh, National Sales Manager for one of the Consumer Banking products. (Hopefully there was no Rajesh in his team). This is what the conversation was like:

Krishnan: Rajesh what are your numbers for the last month?

Rajesh: The market has been bad … the team has been trying … Blah blah.

Krishnan: Rajesh you give me the numbers.

Rajesh: The entire market is in a bad shape … we have had many leads trying to convert them.

Krishnan: Can you please give me the numbers Rajesh?

Rajesh: Zero.

Krishnan: For the last one month you have had no focus on your numbers. Zero is what you have done. This is not acceptable, if you can't manage your shop sitting in another location then please shift base.

Rajesh: Krishnan if you want, I can put in my papers.

Krishnan got wild at this and said, "Don't give me this emotional stuff. If you want to put in your papers go ahead, you are in the system to do a job. See how best it can be done. You cannot be doing zero sales for the month and not have an action plan around it."

In this entire conversation not once did Krishnan abuse Rajesh or got personal. In fact, I have never heard him use the four letter word. This is one thing I admired about Krishnan, he was an objective boss. Krishnan knew that Rajesh had zero sales, thanks to his Analytics stud Gagan. Krishnan would never go for a meeting without taking data from Gagan. You could never see Krishnan talking in the air, and he would always be on top of his numbers.

The best part about his management style was that he would never make motherhood statements. He would be specific and would try to focus on the problem and its solution, and not on the person in contention. He would keep driving people up the wall, but with data. His belief was, "If you can't measure it, you can't improve it." The rigor he got in sales was unbelievable. The National Sales Director was a difficult position to handle, thanks to the complicated matrix structure that most multinationals have.

The National Sales Managers were to report to their respective Value Stream General Manager (VSGM) and to Krishnan, but it was the VSGM's who had the budget. No National Sales Director had been successful before, but Krishnan was different. He took ownership of the entire sales machinery and created metrics that even feet on street (FOS) would understand. He created a performance monitoring system that could put most HR guys to shame. His idea was clear. The only way we would improve is by measuring the right things. By driving teams continuously he had done what no one had done earlier, made the National Sales Director role one of the strongest roles in the consumer bank.

What he did was simple; he saw where the team was, what were they achieving, where they could improve and showed them the mirror. The most amazing piece is yet to come. Krishnan did not replace any of the existing team members with people he knew. He worked with the same team and achieved just by measuring and improving. Nine out of ten things in the corporate world are not rocket science. But unfortunately, people like to show how complicated their work is, so they are viewed in a different light.

Back to the fifth floor, I went to finish my meeting with Krishnan. But during the entire meeting, I kept wondering how does Krishnan shift gears so fast, from sales to recruitment and back. You would never find him preoccupied. The moment you talk numbers you could see his interest levels increasing like the required run rate increases in the last few over's of a T-20 match.

There was this story about Krishnan. His wife Lalita had delivered a baby about a year back and people used to wonder if Krishnan would give Lalita a target that the baby should increase 1mm in height every week.

Your Team also Has a Brain Let Them Use It

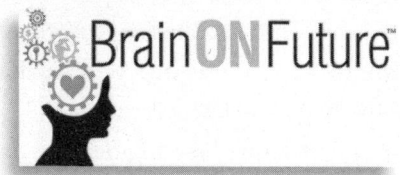

For almost a decade I have been combating with business managers, persuading them to take people who I feel have the requisite skill sets for the role he is being lined for. Hiring for some managers is like a nightmare and I would cover this later. Most managers are choosy about the kind of people they want to hire as a part of their team.

Hundred profiles, fifty shortlisted resumes, thirty interviews, four offers, and one joinee is how hiring usually turns out. One would think this hire must be awesome, and our business manager would have faith in him or her and his or her skill sets. But no, our manager would still not let this person think independently. He would want to do all the thinking and the new hire is left with the job of execution. This is like hiring a canon to kill a crow. I have come across many managers who would not be willing to listen to their team members. It's like them getting an inferiority complex if their team member comes up with an idea which is better than theirs.

It was 5 September 2004 and I had recently taken over the role of Manager Talent Acquisition at ICICIoneSource. The biggest challenge in this industry was to continuously meet the hiring numbers. Attrition rates then were double digit numbers, moving closer to triple digit. The industry was plagued with the problem of attrition and the direct impact was pressure on my team. This was like trying to fill a bottomless pit. Some organisations were hiring so aggressively, they were just short of putting up a board "Trespassers will be recruited".

Within a few days in the system I understood one thing clearly; meeting numbers was a hygiene factor, though there were other recruitment challenges that needed to be addressed. Somewhere in the struggle to meet the numbers we had understated other recruitment metrics. I was not comfortable with this and went to my then boss Shaily Gupta and discussed what I wanted to do.

I was planning to set up a Recruitment Call Center (RCC). It is simpler than it sounds. Shaily was initially reluctant about the concept and educated me on the consequences of not meeting numbers. She was one boss anybody would love to work for, objective and clear with what she wanted. She did not reject my idea, but wanted me to go to the drawing board and think about it again. I went back to make a concrete business plan, and then it happened.

One of our processes was moving out and we had people on the bench who had to be internally absorbed in different processes. The pressure was to relocate them quickly to different processes with in the organisation and not lose any people. This was my opportunity. We did not have enough positions to place these people, and I quickly went to Shaily and requested her to take five people from the bench and start up the RCC. This was the best time to go to your boss and ask for people from the bench as it was mandated by the Senior Management to absorb as many people as possible.

I used to sit at the Millers Road office in Bangalore. It was Monday, 5 September 2005 and I was to meet candidates for RCC–Team Lead Position, the most critical position in the RCC setup. Lydia Paul, my first candidate, walked in, very unassuming but with a pleasant personality. I was impressed with her confidence. Most people would have been petrified with the targets I spoke about, but Lydia was willing to bite into the challenge. After a thirty-minute discussion, I decided to take her onboard. As she walked out of my cabin, she was already running towards her first task, recruiting her team from the bench and she had to start the RCC operations on the 6 September.

The sense of urgency that she showed reaffirmed that I had made the right hiring decision. On 6 September 2005, Lydia came back with the shortlist of our team members. After meeting them briefly, I gave a nod and we were in business. So, as planned, we went live on 6th and our first call was made from a shared cubicle at Millers Road. In the days to come, RCC became one of the most reliable and cost-effective source of hire. Within three months, everybody in Senior Management was talking about cost per hire, a metric that was never given enough weight. This was a reflection of RCC's success and it has to be credited to Lydia who ran the operations better than I had expected.

The key to Lydia's success was her ability to accept new ideas purely on merit, irrespective of who comes up with the idea. If it was good, it had to be exploited. I remember one brilliant idea that improved the efficiency of RCC manifold.

After about four months of operations our team was burning data faster than job portals could replenish. And we were facing this challenge of getting data for calling. We had multiple meetings to address this challenge. Ideas varied from buying databases from telecom providers to Credit Card, all were shot down as these were a no-no from a compliance perspective. The best people to come up with ideas are people who are working on the ground, in this case our callers. One of the RCC callers went to Lydia and said: "We have a walk-in of about 80 to 100 people every day, what if we take 10 references from each of these candidate, we would have enough data. Let's call this refer a friend scheme." We thought not only would this data be fresh and exclusive, it would also be more relevant than what other sources can offer. Bingo! Had we hit a jackpot? I thought only time would tell, but on the face of it, the idea that was simple turned out to be a success. On this day I got to know one quality of Lydia as a manager that would take her a long way.

She came to me and said, "One of her team members has suggested an idea." Never did she claim it to be her idea, but she was proud of her team who had the ability to think. While she was dealing with simple callers, she knew her team members had a mind of their own and she had given them the liberty to use it.

Another interesting story that made me question my move out of firstsource tells you how even in a very short time a manager can make you feel engaged and in control.

Shaily Gupta my boss had quit firstsource and moved on so Aashu being Shaily's boss had to manage me and my counterpart Amar Salvi. While we missed Shaily, the idea of getting to report to Aashu was something that excited both me an Amar, we were hoping that Aashu would continue to be our boss. Aashu was the backbone of the Firstsource culture and working with him was like a dream come true. The reporting to Aashu lasted for a couple of months and we started hearing rumours that we are getting a new boss. I am sure most people who have worked know the power of the grapevine. Amar and I had multiple calls on this and were very unhappy that Aashu was planning to hire our boss inspite of our delivering on every single KRA. Finally the day came, I was in Manila setting up the Philippine office for Firstsource and my team called me, "Samir we have a new boss, he is from Accenture…how will we guys manage." I knew this was coming, but when it finally happened I was very uncomfortable and a lot of thoughts were going through my mind. Will I get my space to work, will this boss let me work the way I like to work, will he let me experiment, were some of the difficult questions to which no one had any answers. Amitava Saha, was going to be our new boss. I quickly went through his profile on linkedin and realised that he is an IIM Kolkata alumnus and my first reaction was, "He must be an arrogant guy." Next day I got a call from Amitava. "Hi Samir, this is Amitava Saha I am sure you know that I have joined as a part of the Talent Acquisition team… thought I would call and check with you if you need any support in the Philippines." There was something about his voice that was very comforting. What he spoke and how he spoke calmed my nerves and my first impression was exactly opposite of what I had thought of him. I was back in India and finally got to meet Amitava. While Shaily my earlier boss used to operate out of Mumbai, Amitava was going to be sitting in Bangalore, and this I thought was not good news. I was someone extremely independent and did not like people interfering in my work. I was like the seniormost guy in recruitment in Bangalore and now I had a boss who will operate out of Bangalore. Firstsource had multiple centres in Bangalore and I was operating out of the recruitment center. My first thought was that Amitava will start sitting at the recruitment center, which was in my mind My Territory. Amitava chose to sit at the RV Road center and I was ecstatic to know this. Little did I know that in the coming months my relation with Amitava reach a point where I would actually look forward to being with him and the team. I think Amitava had understood me well in the first few meetings and he recognised my strengths and weaknesses. He knew I was someone who had multiple ideas on the fly and liked to experiment. He gave me all the support and made sure that nothing changed for me. One incident that made all my apprehensions go away was when we had a meeting with our COO Raju Venkatrama, we were setting up four domestic centres and were supposed to hire 6000 people over 60 days. This was one of the steepest targets we as a company had seen. We were at Chennai, and had all the top bosses of Firstsource and Raju asked Amitava, "So how are we going to ensure that we meet these numbers?" Amitava said, "We have a more than capable recruitment team managed by Samir which would be able to deliver these numbers." He looked at me and continued, "Samir can you share your plan that you had shared with me earlier." For someone who was just a couple of months old in the system doing something like this is very difficult, he could have seen this as an opportunity to show how good he is in leading the team and how the old team was incapable of delivering. But with his leadership skills he would be able to get them to deliver. Little do people realise that leading is not always about being in front. As Nelson Mandela says, "It is better to lead from behind and to put others in front, especially when you celebrate victory when nice things occur. You take the front line when there is danger. Then people will appreciate your leadership."

I had to move on from Firstsource for some dreams I had, while Amitava wanted me to stay back. He knew that I was leaving for something that I wanted to do in life, so he let me go. On the last day at work, he and his better half invited me and my wife for dinner and by the end of the dinner I was wondering, "How in 6 months Amitava had created a space in my world as a mentor, a friend and a guide."

Spotting Talent

"I want a person who has done this job before." Like most business managers who I have hired for hiring a team member. The Job description rarely talks about the person a business manager is looking for. The focus is predominantly on relevant experience.

Specs read like this:

Need an HR Manager for the ITES industry who has worked in an ITES setup.

Or

Need a Sales Manager – Credit Cards for an MNC Bank which has been in Credit Card Sales for over 6 years.

There is no emphasis on the skills, attributes, and personality. Unfortunately, questions related to competencies are rarely asked. Business Managers need people who have done a similar job and are willing to pay more for it. I have always believed that we should give jobs to people who come with the right competencies. Prior work experience can be an added advantage, the moment it becomes a prerequisite, I know the manager I am dealing with is not worth his or her salt.

One of my summer interns, Salonie from Symbiosis Institute of Management Studies (SIMS), at Standard Chartered Bank had worked on a project for the launch of Post Graduate Diploma in Retail Banking and Sales (PGDRBS). While I was managing the recruitment function, she was a marketing intern and working on selling this course. I had observed her for two months and was impressed with her work. During the final placements, we were not planning to visit SIMS as we did not have any openings for fresh MBA. We were trying to negotiate with Business Managers to visit SIMS for marketing profiles, but all businesses wanted people with relevant experience.

Finally, the National Sales Manager, Liabilities, agreed to meet people for his sales team provided they came with some experience.

We had a few applicants who fit the Job Description (JD). As Salonie had worked with me for about two months, I wanted her to take the interview because I was confident that she would do well in the role. After a lot of persuasion, the Business Managers were willing to meet her. After the interview the Business Manager was impressed with her, but was sceptical as she did not come with experience. Finally, he agreed to take her on board.

We had made four offers, one to Salonie and three more to those who came with work experience. Eight months in the system and three out of the four people had quit due to high pressure. The only one who survived was Salonie. Had Business Managers understood the importance of competence vis-á-vis experience they would have had a wider talent pool to choose from and could have hired more Salonies from the fresh MBA talent pool.

Spotting talent is a skill every manager needs to have to survive, let alone grow in the organisation. Few managers have the competency of being able to identify or define talent. In fact I can count these managers on my fingertips.

Punit Modghil is one such Business Manager. I remember the first time I met him. I had joined Talisma, an IT product company, in India. My colleagues in HR had told me that Punit could be intimidating. I walked into his cabin, I think it was second from the left and I saw this young dynamic guy. I wondered if I had entered the wrong cabin. A ten minute discussion with him and I knew why people were intimidated, he knew his stuff and was clear with what he wanted; someone who would not mince his words. My meeting with Punit was to discuss his manpower requirements. He was looking for people for his presales team. I asked him if he would be ok to hire freshers and to my surprise he was delighted with the idea. Most Business Managers would give me a look of, "Are you out of your mind." After spending about thirty minutes with Punit, I had understood what he wanted.

Most people want a 100 percent fitment, the point is if someone is leaving his or her current organisation in a similar role, there can only be two reasons for it. First he is not happy with his current organisation or vice-versa, or second, he is leaving his job for better pay. The right reason to leave a job would be to get a better and challenging role. Punit said something that I still quote, "A 50 percent match is better than 100 percent as you are giving the employee an opportunity to grow in the system," after nine years it's still fresh in my mind.

Punit hired three people from diverse backgrounds, but all with the right attitude and competencies. A girl who had worked in the US in an advertising agency, a fresh graduate from Sri Ram College of Commerce and an engineer from Vellore Institute of Technology. They had nothing in common on paper, but as people they all had the required competencies that Punit was looking for. All three stayed with the organisation for a substantial period and did well and grew in the system.

Punit moved to another organisation in the UK and till recently was working with Microsoft. It's been nine years and it is not surprising that all these three people are still in touch with Punit because he spotted them.

A Rolex Worth a Fortune is Worth Nothing if You are Not on Time

Punctuality, or lack of it, is no longer an individual deficiency, it is a national epidemic. Not only does this hamper an individual manager's growth, it makes him less competitive compared to his global counterparts. While our salaries are moving westwards and getting closer to our western counterparts, there are some issues that need to be addressed to ensure we remain globally competitive.

In 2002, I was working with Huawei Technologies, a Chinese Multinational, managing training for the organisation. One of my biggest tasks was to conduct a training called "Welcome to India" for all Chinese employees coming to India. In the two years I spent at Huawei, I learnt about the Chinese culture and I do not shy away from saying that we can learn from them.

One thing I saw in them was their seriousness about punctuality and commitment to timelines. This was beyond compromise. I remember, in 2002 the Indian IT market was booming, but getting good talent was not easy. By the time a student was in the sixth semester of engineering he or she already had four or five job offers and every engineer used to think he was God's gift to mankind. We were facing major discipline issues. The office timing was 9:00 am but our engineers would mostly arrive late at the office.

The problem was not that they were coming late, the challenge was their attitude and that they did not think it was wrong. They would argue and make statements like, we need flexi timings, this is like a jail, and the organisations culture is all screwed up. The management took a call. We were shifting to SAP at the enterprise level and payroll was also a part of the implementation. What this meant was when you swipe in, it would show time in and when you swipe out it would note the time out. The organisation communicated that if you are late to office half day salary would be deducted.

Inspite of the uproar in the organisation we implemented this policy and not a single Chinese employee lost half a day of their salary, but half of their Indian counterparts had lost substantial amounts of their salaries. The Indian employees were livid, they could not believe it. According to them, it was ok to be late to work. Some employees even left their jobs because they could not come to work on time and believed that the company was being unfair.

This is one area where most Indians are guilty as charged in the fight for being globally competitive. Unless we get disciplined, we will get work only on account of cost arbitrage and not competence!

The Fear of Failure Should Not be a Deterrent in Challenging the Conventional Thinking!

During college days you have many friends but a few of them become friends for life. Nitish Bhushan is one such person.

Nitish, I thought, was a born leader; he had charisma which few have. As expected, Nitish was one of the first few to get a campus placement not because he was academically brilliant, but because no recruiter in his right mind could reject a person with such a positive attitude. Nitish joined an IT giant and he has been with them ever since.

Having specialised in HR, Nitish joined the corporate HR team. He started by managing the campus relationship with MBA campuses. This was the only year where he did not have a reportee. After the first year he was transferred to Kolkata as Regional HR Manager of East. He took a big leap by moving from a supervised role to a supervisor and from a dependent role to an independent role as a Functional Head for a region reporting to the HR and Business Head of the Eastern region.

Nitish had now got a flavour of team management and he was enjoying it. He had gotten into a role which complemented his personality. His team was in love with him as he changed the way people looked at HR and also his team. Though he was a young manager, people soon realised why he was given a role which people three times his experience could not handle.

He moved to Bangalore as Divisional HR Manager for a different line of business. This was a national role where he was responsible for policy making as well as execution. He initiated Graduate Trainee Programmes, and programs which led the organisation to expand manyfold.

I spoke to his team members and one thing that emerged strongly was that the energy that Nitish carries around him is immense. The never say die attitude is contagious and the team believes there is no problem to which Nitish does not have a solution. On deeper introspection, I realised it's his ability to pick something without the fear of failure which made him an effective manager.

I have tried to analyse his career. There were two points of shift. The first shift came in the second year of his career when he was asked to pick the role of Regional HR Manager for East. He was excited at the beginning about moving into an independent role.

He was also moving away from a role where he enjoyed being close to the corporate office, to a role where he would be handling people issues in a region that was struggling with people trouble. Just a day before he was to fly to Kolkata, he felt scared and felt like running to his extant supervisor and telling him that he wouldn't be able to do it. He was scared that he might fail. But Nitish decided to take the challenge head on and later excelled. In his hearts, he knew he had the capability.

The second and bigger shift came in 2006 when he decided to move from the role of Division HR Manager to a Product Manager's role in Wipro's Laptop business. It was a paradigm shift. He was changing his career with this role change. From a HR Manager he would metamorph into Product Manager wherein he would interact with the industry, global vendors, and global technology providers like Intel and Microsoft, put together product-marketing campaigns, learn technology and guide the sales team with it. I feel for a team manager adaptability is very important.

Let me tell you one thing, no other person from my class has had the courage of shifting into a business role. If someone would have told me ten years back that Nitish would do it, I would not have been surprised.

Perseverance, it is Contagious, if you can Demonstrate Your Team will Follow

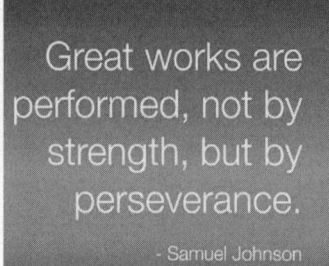

Great works are performed, not by strength, but by perseverance.

- Samuel Johnson

Nitish had taken the role of a Business Head at Wipro and was trying to learn the ropes. Shifting from HR to business was not easy. I believe we don't deal with rocket science in the corporate world. If one has the right competencies, skills can be acquired. This is the greatness of an organisation like Wipro which allows people to shift functions. Ensuring compartmentalisation does not come in the way of talent management. Within 6 months, Nitish knew what he had missed in life, he knew that he was made for this role.

I have spoken to many of his reportees and they tell me no matter how many hours he puts at work daily, he always looks energetic from morning till the closing hour and that keeps them on their toes. You can always see him striving for more. "He is persistent, he won't let go of an opportunity, and would always keep communication channels open with a prospect."

He never lets his team exit an account or an opportunity till he is convinced they cannot pick it up. Now the situation is that his team never exits an account or opportunity till they pick up the order. There was one such account where his team member Anish Gupta picked up an order after five quarters of relentless engagement and another where Adhir Jain did it after four. This is a reflection of the culture the boss has created.

Some deals can be long drawn and sales people tend to lose track of such deals as the pressure of a quarter is always there. If you lose focus, you lose the deal.

It was a day when Nitish was dressed in traditional clothes ready for his cousin sister's marriage. As luck would have it, a client Nitish was pursuing for months happened to call his team member Sahiba Singh saying, "I think we will take a call today on the vendor we are going to finalise." Sahiba was in two minds, she didn't know if she could close this herself and wanted Nitish to be on call, but she also knew that Nitish was out on a family function. Nitish had made it clear, "If its business I am available 24 × 7," but this was pushing the envelope. She picked up the phone and called Nitish. "Boss we have a call with that old client and he says he would close with the vendor today." Nitish without taking a second replied, "I will be on the call."

So there was Nitish all dressed up in a Sherwani taking a call for four hours straight. Result: The customer was so moved with their perseverance, persuasion, the relevance of what they were offering and the fact that he was on call for 4 hours despite his sister's wedding, he released the order to them. Most young managers and bosses lack this quality which makes them mediocre. They forget that the organisation's name and the designation on their visiting card is a privilege the company has given them and they are expected to behave as managers, they are the management, it's their company!

Nitish created a sense of belonging for his team members, showing them this is their organisation. It's been 8 years as a supervisor, he is yet to lose a single resource. I have known people like this, but 8 years is way too long.

Keep it Simple

In the corporate world you meet many people who use all sorts of jargon, the thought is, if you can't convince them confuse them. When you use complex ways to describe simple things, the essence of the idea is lost. People shooting in the dark and not knowing what they are supposed to deliver is a common phenomenon which is a result of poor communication. Managers who can explain what they expect from their team and an individual contributor who can explain to their bosses his idea, in my experience, tend to do better in their career.

I had just got married and moved to Bangalore and joined a Chinese telecom product company. Chandu, as friend's call him, was the Recruitment Manager and got me interviewed for this job. Since he had given me a good break, I wanted to meet him and thank him for the opportunity he had given.

As luck would have it, the next day Chandu called and decided to come and meet me in my hotel to see if I was comfortable. Within 15 minutes we had struck a chord and I thought that this place was going to be fun to work on. In a couple of months Chandu and I had built a good bond. He was a guide for me, giving me directions when I was lost. He would simplify the most complicated things and make them look easily achievable.

After almost 7 years, Chandu still has this knack of putting things in the most simplified manner. Chandu now manages HR at Qualcomm, which hires engineering graduates from premier campuses every year and this forms a chunk of their hiring. Being a Telecom product company, they invest in these bright minds and up-skill them technically. Chandu felt they could make them more effective by embedding corporate culture classes in their training. This was strongly rejected by the senior management as it would extend the nonproductive period for these hires. Chandu was up against a wall, it was a faceoff between one man going against the top guns of the organisation but he handled it well.

Chandu walks into a boardroom with the management team whom he had to convince. He has always been someone who walks into a room well prepared and knows how to adapt to situations. He has a knack of making things sound simple and relevant. According to him, it was not the management who was against the idea, they were unable to see what he visualised. It took him about fifteen minutes to soften their stand and then it was connecting with people individually, addressing their issues and proceedings. The last sentence though simple was powerful. Chandu said, "When an IT trainee walks late into a meeting, you say we are not hiring good people and while these kids are educated they need to be educated on corporate etiquettes. It's no rocket science, but it's important and I think, in the long run, worth it."

Had Chandu tried the HR and Organisational Development (OD) jargon, most people would have lost interest and the adventurous ones would have slept off. But by making this meeting meaningful and simple, he had it his way. The management gave him a go ahead on this. Over the next fifteen days, he designed the program, ran it past the management and launched it in India. The program was called College to Corporate. Today, this simple idea has proven to be so effective that it has been replicated across the world with a few modifications. In the US it is called Backpack to Briefcase.

Remember, if people understand it, they would be willing to take a chance. So try keeping it simple, you would be surprised with the results, even as a boss.

Create a Culture that Embraces Employees

This was the year 2004 and I was interviewing with ICICIoneSource. It was my final round of interview with the HR Head Aashu Calapa. I had to meet him at 2:00 pm. I came in a little early and was waiting in the lobby of ICICIoneSource at Millers road Bangalore. At 2:00 pm sharp, I was called into a cabin which, mind you, was not Aashu's cabin as he used to operate out of Mumbai. I walked into this small cabin which could hardly fit three people, we started our discussion and after about 40 minutes Aashu was done with the interview. During my meeting I could feel that Aashu as a person was someone who would always make people comfortable. During the interview, Aashu never mentioned his designation or talked about how big his role was. Trust me, today after spending a decade in the industry, nine out of ten interviewers talk about themselves during the interview. This was my first interaction with

Aashu. Little did I know that in the next four years he would play a vital role in shaping me as a professional.

Being the HR Head of an organisation provides an opportunity to create a healthy and a progressive working environment for the workforce. In the corporate world it is termed as Culture. The word culture can be related to the process of creating curd, you put one spoon of curd in one litre of milk and the next day in the morning you get a litre of curd. For an organisation this process takes far longer and is not as simple as creating curd is, but the end results are identical. When Aashu was leaving WIPRO and joining Customer Asset many people advised him otherwise. Most said, "*Arrey* why are you leaving an IT giant like WIPRO and joining a startup BPO?"

I don't know if this was by design or was it sheer luck, but I think the answer lies in what I see today. Aashu was joining Customer Asset to create a culture, a culture that made me stay with the organisation for four years which, coincidently, is the longest tenure that I have spent in any organisation. And leaving ICICI OneSource was the most painful decisions of my professional life. Till date, I refer to ICICI OneSource as My Organisation.

Over the next 6 months, I had become an integral part of the system. Our first offsite happened within my first year of joining and it was an amazing experience. I had slowly started realising what made this organisation tick. Firstsource was not the highest paying organisation, retention at a managerial level in a competitive market is not easy by any means. But as an organisation we were not loosing people at these levels, this was not by chance but by design. Not many people would look out for a change if they are happy in an organisation.

During my doctoral studies I had interviewed many people to understand attrition and retention patterns across dozens of organisations, and this is something that surprised me. Even at the entry level, people were not leaving jobs for compensation. People who left the organisation did get a hike in their salary, but their first step to move out of the organisation was not triggered by compensation. It was how they perceived their organisations. The decision that they were to move out of the organisation was always triggered by a reason other than compensation. Most of us who have worked understand one thing clearly that an organisation is a chain of I & Manager relationships, where I is an employee and Manager is his boss. The culture always flows top-down and this miracle of an organisation was created by Aashu, who created a culture that accepted people with their flaws and amplified their strengths, ensuring that every employee feels important and contributes.

Let's return to the offsite. I had attended a few offsites in my short career so far. Many such offsites can be intimidating for new employees, but during this offsite the atmosphere was relaxed and within a couple of hours I had realised that this won't be a witch-hunt. Over the next two days many new employees in the HR team got an opportunity to interact with employees from different locations. While teams were making presentations, other members of the HR team were encouraging them by giving new ideas and suggesting improvements or areas where the team could have done better. The tones of the discussion and the remarks were objective. Aashu is someone who would never be judgmental, he would always try to find a solution to a problem rather than finding someone who can be blamed for it.

After over 12 hours of presentation, it was party time; the mantra: "Work hard party harder" was something we lived by. We were having a great time and suddenly we saw the restaurant manager coming towards us requesting us to finish at the earliest as it was getting late. One hour and three requests later, we were almost pushed out of the restaurant. This was least expected from a five star in Goa. One look at the watch and we knew what the problem was, it was almost breakfast time 5:00 am. But we were not done yet and we decided to continue the party at one of our rooms. Some people were tired and hit the bed. People like me and the younger guys had not had enough and the party went on till 7:00 am. Then we decided to have an early breakfast and take a power nap before our first presentation at 9:00 am.

9:00 am board room environment and I find myself standing in front of the HR team making a presentation on our recruitment numbers. In the first six months of my employment with Firstsource, I had created a new channel of hiring RCC. This was a radical idea and it took me some time to convince the management about it and this was the first time I was presenting it to the larger HR fraternity of the company. It was a big day for my team.

Aashu being the HR head had been supportive of this new idea and had given us his full assistance. The presentation went off well with people saying great things about the new idea. My team and I were very happy with the response. I think the success of this idea was not only a result of how innovative it was, but was also a result of the organisation's culture that let me experiment with a new idea. That mind you, not too many companies can accept. Many times brilliant ideas are dumped because of lack of Senior Management buy in. The same could have been true for this idea and so I say RCC was not a big success because of how great the idea was, it was successful because I was in Firstsource. The RCC idea got me the "Innovative HR professional of the Year" award at the Deccan Herald Awards for HR excellence. I owe it to Firstsource which gave me an environment that made it possible.

There were other innovative practices that people in HR had come up with which have been successful. One such idea was Satish's idea called Footprints. Satish was the HR Manager for the Millers Road centre. He had a wonderful sense of humour and comic timing. While he had this amazing sense of humour, he could quickly change gears and become extremely demanding and negotiate really hard when needed, taking a lot of people by surprise. As the HR lead for the centre, he was always clued up about how the workforce is doing. He was always on top of data and not too many people in the system could challenge him, not because he was a senior guy but because he knew what he was saying. Even very senior operations

folk would go well prepared for a meeting with him. I used to look up to him as someone who was a senior resource but still had his feet planted on the ground. I think it was his understanding of the agent psyche and the environment of Firstsource that made him come up with this idea.

"Footprints" was like an invitation to all former employees to come for coffee with the Millers Road Management team to catch up on old times. Satish knew that not too many employee's feel comfortable returning to an organisation, it's like an ego thing. Satish rightly knew that no employee would approach the company to come back, but also knew if the organisation took the first step a lot of good former employees would want to return to the Firstsource Culture. The idea was a big hit. In the first few months we got over 70 people who wanted to join us back. Satish was taking substantial amount of load off my back by getting these numbers, as in the Contact Center industry the recruitment team is always chasing unrealistic numbers and rarely does the employee relations team contribute. But Firstsource was different. What is also important is that Satish never viewed Recruitment and Employee Engagement functions as silo's. I have seen many organisations where people try to showcase others failures and believe in one-up-man-ship. Satish had always made my team feel that we are a part of one team, and was there to support us and motivate us when needed. I still remember saying to myself, "Satish would make a great HR head." Today, seeing Satish as the HR head of Firstsource, I feel like an astrologer, but then I think its something a lot of people would have seen coming.

After four years with the organisation, I had decided to move on and, as I said earlier, it was one of the most painful decisions of my professional life and I don't say it as hindsight, I knew what I was doing. My farewell speech was given by Satish. He started by saying, "Samir has spent about 4 years with us but I think his contribution to the organisation make this seem a lot longer … his innovation and creativity…." I cut in and said, "Satish if the tenure seems to be longer than 5 years can I get my gratuity." To which the entire forum burst into laughter and Satish said, "See that's what I am talking about … in fact there are a lot of things I have picked up from him and not only has he contributed to the organisation, he has also in some way contributed to my professional life and I would like to thank him for that." What made Satish a likeable person was his ablility to acknowledge peoples contributions. He went on for about ten minutes but the first few minutes was so impactful that it had made me feel even more guilty of leaving such a wonderful place and people.

I wrote my last mail on 15 June 2007 at 1:09 pm.

Hi All,

I never thought I would be writing this mail. Leaving Firstsource was a thought that never crossed my mind and why would it - this is a fantastic place to work, learn, and make friends for life. This organisation (difficult [to] say "This organisation" when you are used to saying "Our") is poised to be the finest BPO in the world. I have seen this organisation create opportunities for people to ensure continuous growth by providing a learning curve that never ceases to exist. You all have given me the most satisfying 3.5 years of my professional life. I would like to thank you all for your support. I leave this wonderful place for reasons which are beyond my control.

I would continue to be an Ambassador of this organisation wherever I go. I would cherish these fond memories. I would like to stay in touch with you and will consider it to be my good fortune if I can be of any help to anyone in the future.

You can always reach me at samirkapoor@rediffmail.com

Regards

Samir

Being a recruitment person I got many mails. But there was this mail by Aashu. Rarely do people take out time to write mails to an employee who is leaving, forget the HR Head. They don't write mails, they just write them off. The mail below was sent to me by Aashu and it would give you an idea what is this fuss about culture, and why it's important.

Hi Samir,

Wish you the very best in your future career.

You have truly served the company exceedingly well by being the bedrock of the recruitment team in B'lore. The focus that you showed on recruiting at low cost was an eye opener for everyone. An innovation such as RCC and recruiting through advisors was truly outstanding.

Thank you for all that you have done for Firstsource.

I am sure you will rise to greater heights. Do keep in touch.

Aashu

What a comforting environment. Did I have friends at my workplace?

Handling Peers and Earning their Respect is an Important Aspect of Leadership

I still remember meeting Amar the first time. Shaily, my boss, introduced me to him at her office in Mumbai. I was managing the Bangalore hiring and Amar had just joined to manage the Mumbai hiring. My first thoughts were, I  have competition that was because after a long-time I had met someone who was as passionate about recruitment as me. Amar had a great sense of humour. In fact, a couple of minutes with him and one would realise he had a fantastic comic timing.

Amar dropped me till the lobby of 4D and I jumped into my cab to leave for the airport. I was worried I would miss my flight, as Mumbai traffic can be annoying. Malad and Mindspace may be built over reclaimed land on dumping grounds, but the Malad of today was nothing of what we knew, with tall glass buildings, and swanky residential apartments and huge malls. Traffic was nothing but natural. On my way back I started to ponder over the day's events. I started thinking that I was old in the system and Amar would take time to build his credibility.

Firstsource was still ICICIOnesource. We were about 8,000 people strong, with two Business Heads as our internal customers, but the system could be still complex to deal with. We had people who had been with the organisation for over three years and in a BPO environment that was long. I knew with Amar coming in, I would have to take my work to the next level for it to be appreciated. Being the younger of the two, I was less mature and more aggressive. I knew that Amar will make his presence felt. I had learnt that in the corporate world one should never underestimate competition.

I had started a recruitment call centre; a unit which would focus on direct hiring and this was a big win for me. We had been consistently doing numbers through this channel. I was nominated by the company for an HR award at the Deccan Herald Award for HR excellence; I won the award for Innovative HR Professional of the Year, I was on a high. For me it was like winning the Oscars.

We had started another initiative where we as an organisation would hire people through independent advisors; AP is what we called this channel. AP and RCC put together were giving us great numbers. Somehow RCC and AP numbers were not happening in Mumbai. I would think to myself why is this not happening? Is it because it is my idea that Amar is not pushing, because I was sure that this was not an issue of incompetence. I had always thought of Amar as one of the best recruitment persons I had met. I had seen the speed of his execution and his ability to drive numbers effortlessly.

Shaily, our, boss would ask this question all the time. "Why is it not working in Mumbai....our systems can't be people centric they have to be process centric, if it works in Bangalore it should work in Mumbai." Amar would always say that we are trying, but the numbers are not happening. He being the more mature one would ask me to share best practices. I started sharing how and why this works in Bangalore. Finally, numbers at Mumbai started to go up and I cursed myself for sharing the best practices.

I wanted to kick myself for sending Lydia my RCC champ to

Mumbai to train the Mumbai team. While I and Amar were in the same team ICICI OneSource and it was not that we were against each other, but we were still competition. We, like two fast bowlers in the same team, had a healthy competition. I loved my organisation and had helped it achieve a lower cost of hire by supporting Amar to get these numbers up.

I was wondering, "Why am I upset, if he is doing well I should be happy." I was only 27 and was unable to understand why this was happening to me. I kept thinking about this, but I couldn't find an answer.

A couple of months later Shaily called me and said, "We are nominating ICICIoneSource under the Innovative Practice category for the year at the Recruitment and Staffing Best in Class Award (RASBIC) for RCC and AP. I have asked Amar to develop the white paper and send it to them. I want you to prepare a two pager with your inputs and send it to Amar." I didn't understand why was I not developing this paper and why was Amar sending this to RASBIC. I was upset. RCC and AP were my ideas; these were my babies… why was Shaily getting Amar to develop this. Anyway, I finished my two pager and attached the document to my mail and pressed the send button, the last part was the toughest.

A couple of days later I get a call from Amar. "Samir we have won the Award, Shaily wants you to come down to Mumbai for the Awards." I said, "That's great news *Yaar*…can you tell me the dates when I should be there." Amar said, "Will keep you posted on mail, *chal* I need to get onto a call, will chat up later, congratulations once again."

It was D-day 19th January 2006, I was all decked up for the occasion, black suit with a nice blue shirt and a blue tie. The results were being announced. We knew we were among the winners, but under what category and what position was still a guess. I had butterflies in my stomach.

Finally our name was announced. R.L. Bhatia was hosting the awards and he said, "The Award for the ... goes to ICICIoneSource. I would now like to invite upon stage Mr. Amar Salvi from ICICIoneSource to come and speak to us about the same."

As Amar walked the Aisle to go onto the stage, I felt cheated. Those 10 seconds were like an hour and I thought this was not fair.

Amar spoke and what he said was something that made him taller. He said, "A very good afternoon ladies and gentleman, (then there was a pause...)you know the best part of sending the nomination is that the one who sends the nomination gets called onto the stage to speak about it ... actually the person who deserves to be here to talk about this award is my colleague Samir Kapoor.... I would like to invite him on stage to tell you more about this." I get up and started to walk towards the stage. During this walk to the stage I got the answer to the question of why I was upset with RCC and AP doing well at Mumbai. It was because I thought someone else would get the credit for the same. I felt I was so immature not to understand Amar.

I had realised that not only had I won the Award, I had won a friend and he had me as his friend and a professional admirer for life.

With talent becoming the differentiator in today's economy it is imperative that as a business manager or a boss, you understand the importance of Talent Management and Talent Development.

7

My Bosses and My Mentors

Huzaifa Khorakiwala
Trustee & CEO
Wockhardt Foundation

> *"If there is one word that would best describe my present boss that would be JUST. His justice is unique. He looks deeply and objectively at performance. His assessments of performance are also fair."*

I was born with a silver spoon in my mouth. My father, Dr. Habil Khorakiwala, Chairman – Wockhardt Group, tasted success very early in his career, as soon as he returned from Purdue University in 1966. Over the next 45 years, he built brick by brick and step-by-step a successful franchise in both pharmaceuticals and healthcare.

Under the pharmaceuticals was the flagship company, Wockhardt Ltd., with more than 8,000 employees and a market capitalisation of Rs. 8,400 crores as on 25 May 2012. Under the healthcare franchise, a chain of 9 hospitals were set up in Maharashtra and Gujarat over the last 20 years under the name of Wockhardt Hospitals.

I never had any economic struggle. Our standard of living was comfortable. With such a background, the fighting spirit needed in me to succeed was missing. I did not have much interest in inheriting a large business empire. It did not inspire me. My motivation to be a successful industrialist was absent. This was the case when I was 18 years old. I went into a depression for 6 months. I could not find a higher purpose of living. Money making did not interest me nor excited me.

My depression was the worst phase of my life. I lay in bed like a non-living entity. I was lifeless and spiritless. I had suicidal thoughts. If life did not have a higher meaning then everything seemed unreasonable.

I was deseperately looking for an inspiration. I was looking for something which could be my support, my pillar of strength. I was fortunate that during this time I came across a book titled *Nahjul Balagha* which contained the sermons and sayings of Maulana Ali (AS). It was the power of that book along with the inspiration and wisdom in it that I came out of my depression. Those sermons and sayings till date shine brightly in my heart and soul, and are the guiding light of my life. Beside this, the grace and *walaayat* (love) of the 52nd Dai, Syedna Mohammed Burhanuddin (tus), his *Mansoos* and his *Mazoon* have also guided me.

What started as the inspiration derived from Fatemi philosophy later on diversified to inspiration from other spiritual and religious books and philosophies. I read voraciously. The summation of my inspiration was penned down in a book co-authored by me titled *7 Human Values*. In this book we emphasise on the importance of understanding and practicing of the 7 human values of gratitude, forgiveness, love, humility, giving, patience, and truth. We say that these 7 human values are the path to inner peace and happiness.

We have digressed a bit from my background. After I came out of my depression at the age of 18, I completed my B.Com from HR College of Commerce and Economics. Thereafter, I worked for 2 years at the Wockhardt Hospital in Bangalore. Thereafter, in 1994 I proceeded to USA to do my MBA at Yale University.

On my return from Yale University in mid 1996, I handled different business verticals at Wockhardt ranging from international formulations, domestic business marketing, and animal health division. While doing this, I was heading the CSR department in

2005. I thoroughly enjoyed my work with Wockhardt CSR in the service to the underprivileged.

It was in September 2008 that I exited from business responsibilities at Wockhardt Ltd. and formed Wockhardt Foundation which would expand the work of Wockhardt CSR. My father supported me in this decision. I thank him for this.

My first boss was Mr. Rajan Sanklecha.

After I graduated from H R College of Commerce and Economics in 1992, I went to the Wockhardt Hospital in Bangalore as  part of garnering work experience before I would go on for my MBA in 1994 at the Yale University. Being a successful industrialist, my father chose my first stint in my work life carefully. The Wockhardt Hospital in Bangalore was away from my home in Mumbai. My father wanted me to live independently and gain some confidence. I was an out-and-out introvert at that age. I was 22-years old then. But still I had severe social phobia. I avoided social gatherings and meetings.

Mr. Rajan Sanklecha besides heading the Wockhardt Hospital in Bangalore was also a close friend of my father. Thus, my relationship with Rajan Uncle (as I fondly called him) was both professional as well as personal. But Rajan Uncle always put the personal relationship ahead of the professional relationship. He treated me with great love and affection, something which I missed from others.

Rajan Uncle was a gem of a person. He had an amazing sense of humour. His presence and his words brought an immediate smile on my face. He had a great emotional connect with nearly everyone. He was a man with a great heart. He was a people's man. His leadership was people driven.

He treated me like his son. Under him I did not learn great lessons in business from him. But he taught me great lessons in humaneness. I opened up as a human being under him.

At the Wockhardt Hospital, Bangalore, he gave me the responsibility to bring out a newsletter. I did so diligently. It was named *Heart Beat*. Beside this I was asked by my father to observe and learn in my 2-year stint.

I would rate Rajan Uncle as a boss with a large heart. His warmth, love, affection, and care for me as a human being is still shining brightly in my heart today. Today, in my leadership lessons I rate humaneness as the most essential quality of leadership. This I learned from my first boss, Rajan Uncle.

My present boss is my father, Dr. Habil Khorakiwala. As a leading industrialist and Chairman of Wockhardt Group, he is well known in the industry circles as well as among the public. Yes, my present boss is wealthy, powerful, and famous. He is indeed a powerful boss.

This part of the article has been the most difficult to write. It is not easy to write about an existing and critical work relation in a public forum without upsetting the apple cart. So the question arises, should I be safe in what I write or should I be frank? If I am safe and write only pleasant things, then the continuation in my present role may receive a permanent boost. If I am frank, then I may be crossing a thin line and upset my father. But the fact my dear friends is that even if I am frank, I will be safe. Because that is just the way my father is as a boss, fair and just.

If there is one word that would best describe my present boss that would be just. His justice is unique. He looks deeply and objectively at performance. His assessments of performance are also fair. He is a man with a practical bent of mind. His logic and reasoning stand behind his objectivity and fairness. So if you are a performer you will thrive under him. He will empower you and give you ample scope to perform.

However, sometimes behind the single-minded focus on fairness and performance, my father sometimes misses the Emotional

Performance (EQ) of his top management. There have been cases where some lovely, warm, and compassionate human beings have missed being rewarded due to their underperformance on  business parameters. It is rightly said that you cannot fool Dr. Habil Khorakiwala with your sweet talk. You will have to perform. There is no other way.

The other thing which creates a Communication Gap between my present boss and me is the dual and unique nature of our relationship. He is my boss as well as my father. As a son, it is my duty to be respectful and courteous to him at all times. As an employee, it is also the same. Thus, my respect and courtesy has to be two fold. This double folded respect, more often than not, makes me unable to strike an intellectually deep conversation with him. It is often a monologue where I take instructions. I find this a little unfulfilling as my intellectual depth is left unearthed.

One of the beautiful graces of my father is his wonderful charm. You will not necessarily find this charm in a normal social setting. But this charm comes into effect when he engages to explain a project or an idea. I have been left in awe of him when this happens. After he finishes with his lengthy narration, I become his greatest fan.

To sum it up, my present boss is a unique individual. In spite of being from a middle class family, he created a large business empire spanning pharmaceuticals and healthcare which currently employs more than 12,000 people. He has inspired the trust of thousands. He is a gifted and talented individual. As he nears the age of 70, the spark and glow which helped him create his success story is intact. The beautiful pink glow on his beaming face is a testament to this. He is my present boss, Dr. Habil Khorakiwala. I love him.

Bosses are of all types. Some are bossy. Some are sober. Others are hot-headed. Some are visionaries. Some are strategists. Few are tough taskmasters. Sometimes they have a rare human touch. Some inspire and others make the rest perspire.

Let's understand the word Bossy. When we say someone is bossy, it is construed in a negative sense. It implies the person is at least a little arrogant and throws his weight around. Oof! Shouldn't all bosses be bossy? Shouldn't they act a little tough and difficult to deal with? Many say if bosses are not bossy then they will be run over by subordinates. The subordinates will take them for granted. Though that may be true for non-inspirational bosses, but it may not be true always. Bosses who inspire can do away with bossiness. In fact, bossiness destroys inspiration. Thus, if you have the capability to inspire, then you will need to sacrifice your bossy attitude.

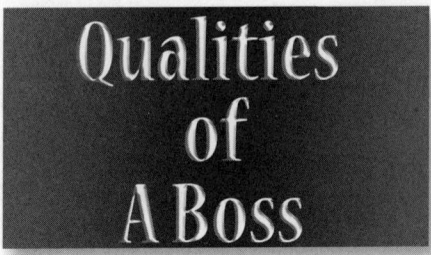

Let us now look at the 7 qualities of a top boss as I see them:

Trust

A boss must inspire trust. In return he or she needs to repose trust. It is rightly said trust begets trust. Trust manifests itself in sincerity, accuracy of facts, punctuality, and keeping your commitments.

Compassion

People do not work for companies, organisations or ideas. They mostly work for bosses. And what attracts them to their bosses? It is compassion. The ability of a boss to work with compassion inspires people down-the-line. Where there is love, care, and affection at the top, there is loyalty at the bottom.

Justice

Justice is the most important quality for a boss. A boss must be seen as one who deals with issues without prejudice and bias. He or she should not have any personal favourites. He or she must deal with every person and situation on merit.

Positivity

A boss needs to inspire hope through positivity. He or she has to have qualities of a fighter. When the chips are down, he or she leads through his or her optimism, hope, and positivity. A positive attitude and a cheerful disposition rubs off on others and it has the power to transform a dull and sleepy organisation into a vibrant, dynamic performer.

Wisdom

A boss needs to be a master thinker, strategist, analyst, and visionary all rolled into one. Through his or her knowledge and wisdom, he or she puts his or her stamp of correctness on his or her decision making. His or her ability to know what others do not, will radiate the glow in every action.

Help

The best bosses are not those who are difficult to deal with. Instead, they should be helpful and cooperative and play a proactive role in problem solving. When one needs help, the boss should always be there. The support from a boss, financially, intellectually, emotionally, and morally, means the world to the employees.

Joy

"My boss is so much fun to be with." How often have you heard this? May be not often. But in reality, a boss who brings joy and energy in his or her work with his or her sense of humour gives a new ambience to the work place. Yes, a top boss must bring joy to you and not sorrow.

These are my 7 qualities for a top boss. They are simple to understand, but in reality difficult to practice. Real work situations will put you at a loss when faced with dilemma and conflicts. Nonetheless, these need to be ingrained in your conscience and not just glossed over. In the success in practicing these 7 qualities lies the echo, East or West, my Boss is the Best.

Wockhardt Foundation has become a responsive breeding ground for implementing my management philosophies. As its CEO, I have been given ample scope and authority to lead the Foundation according to my vision and direction. To get an insight of the boss that I am, it would be necessary to share some of my management principles at Wockhardt Foundation. All people employed at Wockhardt Foundation are called Warriors.

Here they are:

• Action @ Speed of Thought

I believe speed is the essence of everything that we do. Without speed, we will be left behind. Our implementation will fail. Action @ Speed of Thought enumerates 10 points which every Warrior tries to inculcate in his or her being. These points help to guide him or her to be Speedy and Quick.

• Passion + Compassion

This is the motto for the recruitment policy. We hire people who have passion to achieve and deliver, and do so with compassion. Passion tests the energy and zeal. Compassion tests the love and warmth.

• Kar Seva

Kar Seva means to serve. This attitude is much needed in a social service organisation like ours. We often come across immense pain and suffering. In all these experiences, we must always keep in the forefront of our thinking the primary purpose of our work is *Seva* or service. *Kar Seva* is done monthly by all Office Warriors whose postings are not in the field.

• Response

Response is one of the keys to communication. All Warriors are taught to be quick as well as accurate in their responses. If there is communication, response has to be there. Communication cannot be ignored.

• Monitoring

Performance is monitored and feedback is given. Monitoring happens through systemised and regular internal processes.

• Transparency

Wockhardt Foundation offers a high level of transparency, both at policy as well as operational levels. Vision, mission, and goals are clearly defined. Also, there is daily reporting of activities among Inner Circle Warriors (office). Besides this, monthly performance ratings are arrived at through group presentations and 360 degree feedback.

• Human Values

Human values is the crux of what we do. The 7 human values, gratitude, forgiveness, love, humility, giving, patience, and truth lie at the root of our governing principles. Human values have been imbibed in the Warriors through a structured way of experiential learning.

Let me state a few do's and don'ts for being a wonderful boss to simplify our understanding.

DO's

- Be clear and predictable.
- Be just and fair.
- Be loving and compassionate.
- Be fun and playful.
- Be knowledgeable, impart the knowledge and add value.
- Be trusting and repose trust.
- Be positive and helpful.

DON'Ts

- Do not pounce on mistakes like a fierce animal.
- Do not rule by fear.

- Do not be difficult to deal with.
- Do not be inaccessible.
- Do not set unrealistic targets.
- Do not expect people to work like machines, or robots.
- Do not have narrowness of vision.

Many aspire to be a boss,
A position where you can't afford to make a loss,
And profits must multiply, always gross.

To me being a boss is a responsibility,
And a duty with accountability,
Where performance must be of the top quality.

A boss needs a heart full of love,
And handle his or her people with gentle glove,
Guiding his or her mission with peace and calm, like a dove.

If you are a boss, make sure your work is fun,
And the employees need recognition to bask in the sun,
As your company acts with speed and is on the move and run.

A boss needs to be fair and just,
And deal with all with trust,
And dependability and reliability must be the core of his or her character's crust.
A boss is human and prone to emotions,
So too he or she must caress others' emotions,
For these are the finer dressings of his or her job's motions.

Lastly, a boss is a boss, Someone whom you cannot easily toss,
And be warned of him or her if your achievements gather a moss.

One of the beautiful graces of my father, who is also my boss is his charm. His charm comes into effect when he engages to explain a project or an idea. I have been left in awe of him when this happens.

SUPER BOSS: TO BE OR NOT TO BE

Amit Malik
Director–Human Resources
Aviva Life Insurance
Company India Ltd

*As a matter of principle, leaders, however busy they are should never
cancel top-scheduled meetings. If there is a right intent to meet,
a meeting will never be cancelled.*

This June, I complete 14 years in the corporate world. Does
my tenure qualify me to write about how bosses should be or
not be? This was the question I had in mind when I was asked to
share my experiences. Even before I had the answer to the earlier
question, I had a series of more such questions like what will I say
that has never been said before? Who will want to read about my
experience when there are so many more illustrious seniors? Should I
be even accepting to do this? After 2–3 days of turning and twisting
these questions in my mind I went to a young friend. A person
who is all of 26 years and yet has a different perspective and way of
looking at things than what I have at 38 years. He heard me and
the first thing he said was, "Of course, you should." He then said
something that cleared my mind and hit the point home. He said
that in his 4 years of work experience he had seen people manage
bosses or become bosses, but met few who knew what being a boss
was all about and that too a good one. This made me think and I
found my path to follow.

I asked myself that in the last 14 years I have had 14 bosses and was it a coincidence or providence. These 14 include 3 women bosses which reflects the fact that there are still not enough women in leadership roles. Well, whatever it may be, of these 14 bosses I have a mix of good, bad and even ugly. Yes Ugly. When a boss threatens to destroy your career because you have been offered an assignment he does not want you to undertake, how else do you classify him? Before I embark on sharing my experiences, I want to acknowledge and thank all my bosses. I have learnt many things that have shaped me as a boss and as a professional that I am today. All my bosses have been an integral part of my professional life and some in my personal life. I respect all of them and if in the paragraphs below I mention examples that offend them, I offer my heartfelt apologies and hope in all my humility that they would accept it.

Everyone talks about what makes good bosses; whereas I want to share what not to do as a boss. In the next few pages I invite you to become a part of the journey wherein I will share my perspective on what I think being a bad or an ugly boss is all about.

Being a boss means you have a divine right to treat your team members as your personal property. They are there to serve the boss and look after the bosses needs. I still remember earlier I had a boss who clearly believed that ensuring the office boy got him his tea and clicking his slides in the presentation were part of my job. I needed to be one step ahead in understanding his needs and ensuring that they were fulfilled. If we were travelling together then it was expected of me to manage the car and his luggage, and even while he had an executive assistant to do all that. The beauty of the whole thing was that even the Executive Assistant (EA) too lost no opportunity to order me or my types around. It was an interesting phase and I started to ask myself if this is what doing an MBA from a premier business school got you. Today, when I look back I thank him because I exactly know how it feels and therefore ensure no young professional in my team experiences such a humiliating treatment.

I must share something interesting about another boss of mine who would always come up with what I had done wrong rather than what I was doing right and you know why? Because everything I did right, I was supposed to and that is why I was hired for, and for everything I did wrong I was expected to be apologetic and it was my good fortune that my boss was correcting me. I was alright with that approach but what was challenging was that there was a clear gap in providing me with insights or feedback on how I could bridge the gap between where I was and where I should be.

For him being a boss meant that his job was almost always about faultfinding and never on improvement or guidance. Every time I tried asking the steps I should take, I was told, "You are doing this job and therefore you should know it, you have great aspirations and ambitions and you can't even manage such a simple task" or even worse a remark, "What's the point of having a premier MBA graduate if you cannot find a solution yourself." It was frustrating but it taught me about self-control. It taught me about how not to lose my patience and keep going without retaliation.

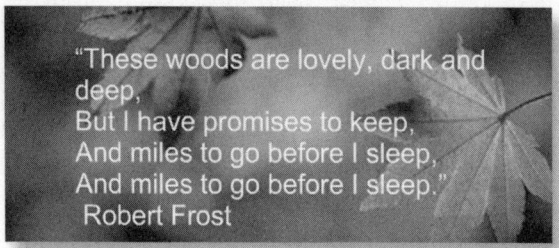

"These woods are lovely, dark and deep,
But I have promises to keep,
And miles to go before I sleep,
And miles to go before I sleep."
Robert Frost

I had on my desk a Robert Frost poem which said, "Woods are lovely, dark and deep and I have promises to keep and miles to go before I sleep." My respect for all my bosses who worked with me, taught me, took time to correct my mistakes and acted as mentors went up manifold during that time. I learnt that one thing is to have a boss who has the ability and the intent to guide you, but it is also important that one could reach out to other senior leaders who can anchor you and act as a coach or a mentor. Today I thank one such mentor who was my anchor and without ever being my boss, taught me many things and helped me bridge many gaps. Those nuggets of wisdom and small nudges in the right direction have been with me always. Thank you Sir: When you read this you will recognize yourself.

Bosses and appraisals go hand in hand. After all, it is a boss's prerogative to do a performance discussion and therefore one would say, "What's the big deal." I agree it is no big deal but it becomes a big deal when you have a boss who would always be unprepared for a performance discussion. I had a boss who believed that mere measuring the performance of a subordinate was too much of work for her. She also believed that giving *Gyan* and speaking good English is what mattered for a boss. Therefore, she never even read my appraisal document. As soon as the discussion began, she would ask me to summarise my performance and no matter how balanced I tried to make it appear, she would not even listen to me, and before I could even finish she would go off in another direction.

I would get to hear anecdotal feedback and when asked to substantiate her viewpoint, I was told to take it or leave it, as if the feedback was a gift from the boss or maybe a favour from the boss to a subordinate. Well I learnt my lesson and many a times I left the gift unopened. It made me realise the importance of performance discussion and how good bosses prepare for it and make it meaningful. Today as a leader or as a boss I make sure I set up parameters to measure and follow them up properly in a discussion. Not all bosses come unprepared for appraisal discussion.

I must confess one of my best appraisals or should I say a textbook appraisal happened when I had a non-HR boss early in my career. I then realised that maybe in HR we need to do a better job as we ourselves are custodians of the appraisal process. There are bosses who do a good evaluation but then some have a habit of surprising you in the appraisal discussion. It reminds me of a boss who would keep telling me that I was the man, how well I was aligned to the business, how he appreciated my ability to partner, but at some point during the appraisal, he would always surprise me by talking about things that were not mentioned in my Key Responsibility Areas (KRA's) or goals. It was clearly my fault that I had not included them post he had signed off my goal sheet but unfortunately I realised it during my discussion.

My business leader at the same time had given me a good feedback and because of the fact that he was fully aware of my capabilities and performance. This kind of understanding with business leaders was not liked by my boss and I was advised to keep my personal and professional equations apart. Most of the times I would ask myself why would my boss not balance out the feedback and understand or dive deep below the surface. The feedback left me wondering, as to what kind of a relation was my boss expecting from me, which would be neither too close nor too distant. These were clearly the most surprising appraisals of my career and I did learn that I hated surprises. Today, whenever I have a new team member, I clearly tell him not to surprise me as I have had enough to last me a lifetime. Remember, surprises can be sprung both by the boss as well as the subordinates.

We are born as individuals. God gave us different and distinct identities but unfortunately some bosses believe that all their teammates should be identical.

Bosses always compare employees with each other. Some statements that bosses make which might sound familiar are, "Look at him or her how confident he or she is" or "Look at him or her, how well he or she makes the presentation." You are also surprised by such bizarre statements as this. I had a person in my last organisation who was a genius in gathering shopfloor intelligence. "You both are from the same college then how come he is so smart whereas you are not." They clearly forget that sheep are cloned not human beings.

I must share how at one point I was compared to three of my colleagues because they had quietly and with lot of gratitude accepted their year-end reward and I had said that the numbers did not meet my expectations and were not in line with the conversation the leader had had with me a few months back when he had committed on certain numbers. When I persisted with my difference in opinion, I was told that I had less experience and was relatively new in the team. The boss forgot or rather never even once mentioned the fact that I did a far more complex role than my three peers. But I must mention that comparison need not always be negative or limiting. I clearly believe positive comparison helps bring out the best in team members, but we must respect the individuality of every team member. Comparisons are good to raise the bar, to motivate others, to achieve beyond the potential, and not to deflate the self-confidence or berate and belittle an individual.

The higher we move in the hierarchy, the busier we get. Yet it is important for bosses to find time for interacting with their subordinates or team members. As a matter of principle, leaders, however busy they are, should not cancel scheduled meetings. One of my managers told me that if there is right intent to meet, a meeting will never be cancelled, and this has stayed with me forever.

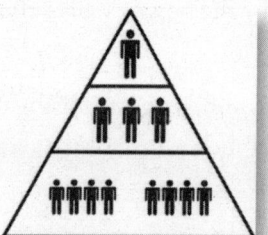 There is yet another type of boss who would always like you to be under stress or on your toes and that to with no specific objective in their mind.

One such experience is when I had just changed my job and was not aware of this particular trait of my new boss. Once he wanted to discuss something important, would say, "Amit we must discuss it today itself. Be around in your office and I'll give you a call." Just to keep a track I informed his EA there is an important meeting between me and the boss, and she should call me the moment he is free. After that I reminded her twice about this meeting and kept on waiting in my office. After waiting for several hours, when I called her again she told me that he had already left for the day!

I presume this was more by design than an accident because it happened twice more in succession. This was humiliating. Therefore, next time when he told me to be around and that he would call me, I summoned courage to ask him to give me some tentative time. He again said, "Just be around." I waited for several hours till it was late evening and I promptly left for home. Once I reached home, I got a call from his EA that the boss wanted me for the discussion. I spoke to him and told him that I had gone back home and he said, "But you know that I was still in the office."

During my appraisal he clearly told me that I needed to be in the office for longer than 9 hours that I was spending. He also had the habit of snooping over your calendars and would tick you off if you had no meetings scheduled after 6.00 pm. Such behaviour creates a bad working environment and people, instead of giving their best, are always projecting themselves as Busy while the actual productivity suffers. I really don't know why some people behave like this. It has nothing to do with efficiency, but I look at it as plain "I am the boss attitude issue" on part of a person in position of power.

How many of you have had bosses who clearly believed that as a boss I need to be tough to be respected? I have seen this in many forms in a few bosses and to varying degrees. It is important for a boss to be tough on occasions that require a tough stand. But how do you justify being tough by making your team members subservient all the time? Do we hire people who always say a yes to whatever we speak as bosses? Do we behave in a way that nobody ever dares to say no? I feel it is the most dangerous trend to have only yes men" in your organisation. If everybody agrees with you all the time then there will be occasions where you would create a disaster for yourself which could have been avoided had you listened to the different views of those team members who could have suggested a better solution.

Such bosses want their subordinates to be tough with the customers or their peers, but expect them to be subservient in front of them. You will never be able to motivate your team if you do not take their suggestions and encourage them to put forward their ideas. It is best to agree to disagree with the team members. It is good to encourage people to take up challenging assignments. I vividly remember an incidence when one of my bosses tried his best to dissuade me from taking an assignment which I was extremely keen on. Since I finally did take up the assignment, he held it against me and took it personally as a mark of disrespect. I have till date not understood that had I agreed to him and been cowed down in front of him, then how would this be a mark of respect towards him.

I firmly feel ego is one thing that makes or mars a good boss-subordinate relation. Bosses with big egos can never earn the real respect of their team-mates.

Another peculiar trait I observed is that bosses believe people should not work for money. I have had many cases where I have been told, "Don't bother about money." I have no disconnect with this line of thinking because I clearly believe that in a job money is one important factor but not the only factor. I have a huge disconnect with bosses who preach this and yet when it comes to themselves they do not practice the same philosophy. I have seen bosses at the highest level of organisational hierarchy who will fight for every single bonus and increment percentage for themselves and not rest till they know they have been taken care of at the end of the year.

I once was working on the year-end rewards file with one of my bosses who said, "Let's save some money and not be generous to all employees. If I save here, I have a better chance of getting an increment." I was dumbfounded and on seeing my expression he said, "Why are you surprised? After all, my boss also has a limited budget and I am only helping him allocate among his directs better." I felt sad that day. Another example I have seen many times is, when at senior management levels, people change policies to suit themselves. The strangest one is from one of my former organisations where senior leaders changed the company club membership policy to ensure they enjoyed these benefits post-retirement as well. One could argue that these are the perks of certain corporate positions. But I have seen people going beyond this and had the policy amended to ensure that after their demise the benefit should be passed on to their spouses. When such bosses preach austerity or not being prudent, it simply hurts. I feel such an attitude reflects poor integrity if you view it in the larger context.

I have elaborated enough on what bad bosses can do to your happiness and can create a stuffy atmosphere where people gasp for breath. I would now briefly explain about what I expect from a Good Boss – a Dream Boss.

- Speaks my language. Who understands me and knows what I am trying to communicate. Someone who hears what is said and possibly understands the unsaid part.
- Someone who believes in giving me constant and continuous feedback. Is someone who does not wait for two meetings in a year to share areas of improvement, but tells me there and then what went well and what could have been better.
- Someone who is transparent and has no hidden agenda. After all I am on my boss's team so what is the point of not being open and honest.
- Is well read and knowledgeable. I am here to learn and who better than my boss will be able to teach me, add value and help me become a better professional.
- Has high energy and can keep pace with me.
- Is sensitive and caring.
- Appreciates not only results but also the efforts and is a coach, counselor, consigliere and confidant.

Do you think it is impossible to get someone as described above? Let me tell you I have had a few who would have had most of these qualities if not all. I have been very lucky to have worked with some very good bosses who besides being good managers, have been great human beings.

In the end I think it's my duty to share what you must do to be a bad boss who is for example tough, hard, demanding, and insensitive. After all what is a boss who is not hated, feared or reviled, and to become one it is important to walk and talk like one. If you want to be hated by your subordinates, my not so easily digestible nuggets are:

1. Don't eat with the team. After all you are their boss and you cannot be seen in the cafeteria with the team sharing food. It's so boss like to eat at your desk or with the peers or equals. It is good to be friendly but not familiar with the team. Keep your distance and this is important.

2. Please ensure that you have a blocked calendar and everyone must take an appointment to meet you. It's your cabin and everyone enters at your pleasure. Your cabin is not a park that anyone can stroll in.

3. Make every minute count. Ensure people know that when you spend 30 minutes in a meeting how much that costs to the company. People need to be thankful for the same, after all you hold shareholders interest as paramount.

4. Be tough and merciless. If anyone makes a mistake it is important that not only does he/she realises it, but it is heard and known far and wide on the floor because people should learn from others mistakes.

5. Micromanage. You are the boss and you know it all, for you have been there, seen and done it all. Experience does count and matters and it's your duty and responsibility to ensure things are done as you want them to be done.

I have talked about the good, the bad and the ugly bosses. Some of the ideas/ nuisances that I have shared seem to be very elementary or basic. But I feel that these are the basic building blocks of building trust and mutual respect between bosses and their peers.

I will leave it to you to understand, assimilate and take your learning. If you decide to practice even one trait that I have shared as a boss, I would have done my job. Go ahead be a boss, and you have a choice what type you want to be.

There is yet another type of bosses who would always like you to be under stress or on your toes and that too with no specific objective in their mind.

9

Timeless Lessons

Rajat Mathur
Executive Director HR

*While watching him closely I observed that he always had a faster
and shorter way of doing things. That is why he never worked late.
He taught me that it is not about doing things for the present,
but doing things with the future in mind.*

Background

The best way to describe the way I have led my life is probably meandering through life. That does not mean I did not plan my career or consider some plans in my life. What that means is like everyone else, I have had my share of roadblocks and like a river meandering through its course, I have either struck hard at the roadblock, moved around, under, or over it. But once I have passed that roadblock I have continued to look forward in my life. This is partly because of my make up but also because of the different lessons that I have learned in my life.

I come from a defence background, where as children we led a carefree and somewhat protected life. That meant that we were accustomed to little in life

most of which was transient in nature. We changed houses often, cities every few years and learnt to adapt to change, and to make new friends quickly. But most importantly, we learnt the lesson of discipline. An attitude was developed that made us robust.

I had the opportunity to go to schools surrounded by children with similar backgrounds and took a keen interest in many extracurricular activities and sports. I still ended up doing well academically. Now I am aware that many people have a bipolar view on this and believe that extracurricular activities are at the cost of academics, but in hindsight I think the best form of encouragement I got was from my parents who insisted that I be an all rounder. The exposure I got shaped my life in more ways than one and as you read ahead, you will realise how debating or theatre or team sports helped me in interviews and in working better within teams at work.

I was not completely sure of what I wanted to do when I graduated. It was not the age of information and so I got a Science degree from St. Stephens College before applying for business schools, because everyone else was on the same bandwagon.

I did not choose my career line. It happened. When I chose to do an MBA, I had no idea of what civilian life was about, much less what an organisation does. In fact, I had never seen the insides of an organisation. A specialisation in Human Resources was by default. At that time it appeared to be the easiest exams to pass. I had no special love of working with people as so many new graduates tell me today as the reason for taking up Human Resource Management.

I have detailed a transition experience in the subsequent pages as I moved from the carefree college life to a decade of more disciplined corporate life.

My career moves were initially driven by my desire to earn more money and less from what I was being asked to do. I did little research to find my next job and was lucky to have secured better positions during most of my transitions. I changed a number of jobs, industries, locations, and roles including spending time as an entrepreneur for many years.

Unfortunately, in my lengthy journey I have not had a single boss that has been great. On the contrary, I have been fortunate enough to have many bosses who have been amazing and have taught me many things in my life.

I now work as an Executive Director, Human Resources, in a global firm. My remit is fairly large covering the Asia region and I believe I am learning every day of my life. The moments that I will share in the next few pages are a collection of instances that changed the way I looked at life. These have been defining moments for me, my moments of truth. No matter what you read and how you absorb these experiences, you will have your own share of your moments of truth. Don't hold on to them, but share them. I have shared these few war stories with many people and hoped that somewhere however small a manner, it has impacted their lives and their thoughts.

They may be small lessons, but these are what shape your lives.

1993—Time Flies

The year was 1993. It was my second day at work. Other than having done a summer internship at an organisation, I had never experienced the inside of an organisation before. I was a part of a fresh batch of trainees that had joined this technology company and we were all going through our induction programme. And I was late.

Now, for any of you who have worked in Mumbai would know that transportation has always been a challenge. It was no different in 1993. And for a non-Mumbaikar trying to travel on the local trains was doubly challenging. So after several attempts to push (or getting pushed) myself, I had managed to board the train, reached the station near my office, extracted myself from the masses, and taken a short detour to the washroom to make myself presentable again. I had made it to the office and till that moment I was proud of the fact I had only been 5 minutes late.

I did not know the gentleman standing in front of the class and addressing the group then and discovered much later that he was Senior Vice President in the company. I knocked on the door, asked for permission to enter the class as we have always been taught to do in all our education years and then mumbling an apology found me a seat at the back of the class after negotiating with the other interns in the room. The elderly gentleman had not said a word since I entered the class and waited patiently for me to settle down, took my note book out and got ready to take notes.

"If you are late, it shows that you don't care," he said. And I started to protest to that comment readying myself with what I believed were genuine reasons then for being just five minutes late. He held his hand up and said, "Son, I would like you to respond to me only next week at the same time." Then with a slight mischievous grin added, "Maybe same time next week but preferably five minutes earlier."

I do not recollect a single word from the rest of his session or for that matter the rest of the day. I was seething inside of me. How could someone accuse me of not caring but I had genuinely tried my best to get to work on time. No one had said this to me before and this sentence played itself again and again in my head. I could not wait for the week to pass so that I could respond to him and explain why I was late. I slept fitfully that night. It was definitely not the best start to my career.

I checked the induction schedule and noticed the gentleman had three more sessions with us over the next few days, two of which were the first sessions of the day and one session was immediately after the lunch break. I was so desperate to prove a point to him that on the two days that he had the first class, I left home 45 minutes before normal to be the first one in class. Luckily, one of the days he came to the class early to do some flip charts and saw me in the class but did not acknowledge me or comment on my early appearance. On the day he had his session post lunch, I raced through my meal and was back in the class fifteen minutes before the session was to start, thrilled that I could prove my commitment to him.

Exactly a week later, I was in class early. At nine in the morning the instructor entered and started to speak to us about performance management in the organisation. I was surprised he had not asked me about my response, but decided to wait (rather impatiently I must admit) for the session to complete. As soon as we ended the session, I walked up to him and reminded him that he had asked me for a response a week earlier.

"And your response is…" he said.

"I had a reason for coming late that day I said. I was new to Mumbai and I had trouble with the transport system."

"So what changed in the other two days that you were early for my class," he said. "From what I know, no changes have been made to the transport system."

"Because I wanted to let you know that I could come early if I wanted to," I said.

"Because you cared," he said, smiled and left the room before I could respond.

And then realisation struck me. I knew the difference in my thinking from the day I was late to the days I was well on time. It was because I really wanted to be on time to show I could do it. It was because I really cared and that is what he meant. Almost 20 years later, that lesson has been a game changer for me.

When we say, "Its ok, we are only going to be a few minutes late or we are going to be a few days late for a project." It's because we don't genuinely believe we have any skin in the game. There would be times when due to unforeseen circumstances, we would be delayed

but our responsibility is to make sure that we inform in advance whenever possible. It's frustrating to wait for people trooping into a training class or a meeting. As a matter of principle, I now start on time, even if I am the only one in the meeting. I don't allow anyone to come into my class late. That has made people unhappy, but often I find they are never late for my meetings or my training class again.

I always draw an analogy with catching a train. Is it possible, you consider being five minutes late to catch a train. I would think not. You would not want to walk to the railway platform to watch the last train compartment pull away from the station.

Sometimes we find solace in the fact we are not the last ones into the training session or the meeting. That we arrived late but then no one was there either and therefore our actions are acceptable. I go back to the train analogy. Would you feel better if you missed the train by five minutes while someone else missed it by ten minutes?

Remember, If you are late, it shows that you don't care. There are no other dos and don'ts associated with this lesson in life – this moment of truth teaches you that every moment I have matters. I would expect each of you to respect that.

1998—Smart Working

I was jealous of my boss. He never ever worked late. Maybe that is being unfair on him as there were times in the year when we were doing year end compensation exercises or preparing letters for promotions to be delivered the next day where he stayed with the team for as long as it took to get things done. But usually and by that I mean three sixty of three sixty five days, he would leave for home in time.

Contrary to the popular (but clearly erroneous) belief, he continued to rise in the organisation. I was intrigued by this contradiction of facts where the expectation was the more you work and the longer you work, the better is your visibility in the organisation and therefore the faster you would grow in the organisation.

But then, you try not to question your boss on his work habits despite the culture of open doors and first names coming into the country. I did envy his ability to manage his time and manage his career. I secretly started to observe what he did.

While watching him closely one of the first observations I had was, he always had a shorter and faster way of doing things for most of the to-dos he had on his plate. Despite all my efforts and trying to think on similar lines, I could not find the key to that secret.

Maybe it makes more sense to ask. I waited for an opportunity to come by and not long after that time, while working on a complex compensation sheet for all employees in the organisation, I realised that he had the ability to analyse and calculate faster than I could while sitting and facing each other working on two equally slow laptops.

Now to put this in perspective, I think I am good with my mathematical skills and Excel skills. I definitely believed I had the edge on him but he still got to the right number quickly.

After going on for an hour on this, I finally slammed my laptop in frustration and asked him how he managed to beat me every time on the draw.

He smiled (and I got more irritable) and asked me to come over and see his screen. At first I could not see the difference as he had the same data that I did although he had laid it out slightly differently. Then he gave me a one-line explanation that changed the way I did things.

"It's not about doing things for the present," he said. "It's about doing things with the future in mind."

"To put this very simply," he explained, "When I was putting all the information on the Excel sheet, I was thinking of what this data may be used for, what analysis may be asked on this data and how it could be formatted in a manner that it was easily usable yet gave all the information that your sheet has."

"Once I had thought about all the requirements of the data, the initial effort of putting the data together in the most practical manner was a one-time activity that may have taken a bit more time than when you put the data in your sheet for now and the future. I will continue to reap the benefits, while you will struggle to get what you want from the sheet."

It was simple, putting formulae in cells, linking sheets and simple things but the end result was fascinating and for everyone to see.

The point I am making here is not about being a wizard on the machine or on MS Excel, but having the foresight and thinking ahead for all the actions you take. You can do tasks but when you think of tasks in isolation, then you are only working in the present and the repeat benefits are lost.

A classic example that I see is when people prepare power point slides (and I know we do it many times in our lives) when they get frustrated, when their boss asks them to change the font or the colour, and they have to go to every slide and make the changes. There are tools and ways to standardise things that can help in making the changes with one brush.

But we don't think about the edits and the time it will take to make the edits when we are preparing a presentation. We want it to look the best and we over complicate it so it becomes difficult to unravel later.

This goes beyond preparing MS Excel sheets and power point presentations although both will save you a lifetime. It's also about how you organise your work life. How easily are you able to retrieve information and use it effectively? How do you store what you have done? How do you label your files?

I am sure you have had the frustration of not being able to remember file names when you need to find things. There is no right or wrong way of doing it, but one thing that works well for me in chronological filing.

So when I want to retrieve something my thought process is, "When did I last use it," then go by the year, month, week, and day to locate it. It works in most cases, but I have seen my manager being much disciplined about the naming convention he uses. It has time, topic, and subject on the file name for quick access. Again, it's about how far ahead are you thinking. Would you be able to find this file and remember this name after two years?

Remember, the area you work in does not change as rapidly as everyone believes it does. A lot of what you have done in the past is reusable. You don't have to be always focused on inventing a new thing. If you are asked to develop a Sales Strategy, a Business Plan, or a Performance Management System, chances are you have worked on something similar (and if you were smart about it, it exists as a template) in the past and can quickly find and replicate it. After all Performance Management Systems don't change every day.

Imagine the amount of time you can save by doing this. I have found immense value in this simple belief about thinking ahead and often get frustrated about how many junior colleagues who work for me are not thinking long and hard about the next day.

It's not rocket science. It's the science of the mind and everyone can do it.

2003—It's Your Life

I had now spent a decade working and I still believe that a lot of things have happened to me on which I either did not have control or had limited influence. Some of those things have been positive, but equally I have had my share of disappointments in various stages of my life.

As I was meandering through my working career in the first decade of my life, I worked hard. I did not plan as well as I should have, but at every opportunity that was presented to me, I worked hard to prove my worth. And, therefore I grew. The simple mantra was the harder and smarter you work, the more you will grow. And sure enough, there were times when I did not feel the compensation was commensurate with my experience or my contribution, but once that initial disappointment of seeing the bonus number was over, I put my head down and continued to plod along. I met my next boss who created an impression on me that was probably the single biggest transformational change in my life.

Well maybe I am exaggerating here, but this piece of advice I received from him changed my outlook to life.

I observed that my manager would rarely get stressed. He was as cheerful on a Friday afternoon as on a Monday morning and while we would all moan and groan about work and many other things, I never heard him complain. He would get exasperated sometimes, he wasn't perfect but in contrast to all the other managers I had worked for and all the other managers that worked in the organisation, he had the ability to remain calm and collected at every given instance.

This ability was discussed a lot amongst us and more with junior staff, but none of us felt it to be appropriate to ask him that question and time went by.

I was driving to work one day with him when we got stuck in a traffic jam. After being stuck in the jam for a few minutes, I started to get impatient and started to blow the horn. I did it for several minutes before my boss asked me what I was doing.

"Blowing the horn," I said.

"And the aim of doing that would be ...," he said.

"Oh, to get people to move ...," I said without thinking.

"You must have amazing powers in your honking to be able to do that," he said as he reclined his seat and closed his eyes.

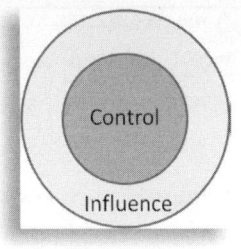

And that got me thinking. I found it a perfect moment to ask him one question I always wanted to ask.

"Why don't you ever get hassled," I asked.

"Well you would not either if you knew about locus of control."

"What is Locus of Control?" I asked.

And then began my biggest lesson in life.

"It was about knowing what you can control or influence and what you cannot. For example, this traffic jam. The blowing of the horn and others adding to the cacophony will only increase the noise levels but not get the traffic jam to go away. When you are able to grasp this simple truth, you will start to relax and think of more productive ways to use your energy and your mind. This is when you steal time back."

That was it. The single biggest lesson in my life was learnt that moment in a traffic jam. It was about learning how to steal time back from your life.

Sounds rather basic, but see what happens when you start to apply it in your real life. Over time and with a lot of practice, I was able to ask myself this question every time I came across a situation or an event.

Is it in my locus of control?

And so much of unnecessary worry has gone away from both my professional and personal life. But we are humans and we can't always control our behaviour and reactions. But even if you were able to do this for half the instances, that would cut down your stress levels by half.

Suddenly, there appeared to be more time to think constructively and it started to impact the way I dealt with people in life. A positive change for sure.

A few years later, another incident that was a life changer happened when in an informal conversation with him, he asked me what I would do if I had a million dollars (then a lot of money in my eyes) in my bank account that took care of all my expense factors in life.

I didn't have an answer to him then but did go back to him a few days later and told him I would run, hike, trek and do things that I was passionate about. He asked me why not do them now and I said it was because I did not have time.

He grinned at me and said, "I told you how to steal time back. Start stealing more of it."

That sounded like a perfect solution and looked easy, but it took me a while to get to the solution. It was as simple as it sounded. You can always make time if you are passionate about something.

So began my journey of pursuing my passions. Today, that has resulted in the birth of The Fight back Club where professionals like me try and rediscover their lives. There are no rules in this club. Just a bunch of people determined to follow their passions. This has over the past few years changed lifestyles, made people pursue

healthier options and rediscover happiness. Many of you may think this is idealistic and too far out there, but give it a try. I tell everyone I meet about locus of control and about regaining your lives.

You can steal time now before it gets stolen from you.

I observed that my boss would rarely get stressed up. He taught me to understand in every situation, what you can control or influence and what you cannot. When you understand this, you will start to relax and think of using your energy for more productive work. This is what he called as locus of control.

10

BOSSES: GOOD, BAD AND THE UGLY

Tanaya Mishra
Senior Vice President Group HR
Jindal Steel Works

> *Some bosses were classy, poised, had domain expertise and skill of the function they led.*

The Boss

Boss, this four letter word for an employee means his or her living world, especially for a full-time employee. The joys and sorrows, happiness and sadness, the thrill of recognition of a project completion, job satisfaction, fun at the workplace, and the overall joy of being an employee

to an extent is dependent on the boss. Bosses have a significant role to play in shaping a subordinate's working style, thinking pattern, overall attitude, as well as career growth.

I am currently a Senior Vice President in human resources for JSW, India's largest steel manufacturing company and with other verticals like energy, cement, infrastructure and ports, software and mining. I have also headed organisations ranging from insurance to retail to ITES to manufacturing. But to reach where I am, it took years of hard work, learning skills, adaptability, parent's blessings, and luck.

I am an Odiya and I belong to Cuttack. My schooling was in St. Joseph's Girl's High School. It is to this school that I owe a lot, as it built the foundation for me and helped me to relate to people across different spectrums and walks of life. As a student I was really attracted to western music and culture, and in those days the only teachers for this were my Anglo-Indian boarders. I was an extrovert and excelled in extracurricular activities, won numerous elocution and recitation competitions.

Odissi Dance

I learnt Odissi dance and did a post graduation in this field along with Hindustani classical music. I loved basketball and was in the state team when I was in 8th standard. My +2 was in Arts. I had to fight a royal battle at home to get into the Arts stream and not Science. I wanted to get into NCC which required me to go for camps including trekking, mountaineering, parasailing. In fact I was selected as the best cadet for my state and represented my State in the Republic Day parade and stood first to be on the elite list of 21 cadets who were selected for a youth exchange programme called Canada World Youth to go to Canada. The exchange was for 6 months and I was most of the time in Trios Rivieres in Quebec and had the opportunity to visit and perform at the Indian Embassy in Toronto. I did well in academics as well in the 12th and stood 3rd in the state. I did my graduation from the famous Ravenshaw college where the patriot Subhas Chandra Bose also studied. Post graduation was from Delhi School of Economics and personnel management from Vani Vihar, Bhubaneswar. This was followed with a bachelor's degree in Law and a Doctorate in Philosophy (PhD).

I have had the privilege of working across different sectors and had varied kinds of bosses, some terrific and some terrible. To some, I owe a lot in terms of learning the very basics of the function and some I would like to pretend they didn't exist but both taught me life skills. I became a better professional and understood the nuances of the corporate world.

Let me start with the initial days of my entry into the corporate world and how naïve I was. I remember an incident that left an indelible impression. I was posted in Bhubaneswar and there was a mandate to visit branch locations and customers. I was sent on tour to a particular location. Unfortunately, I was not privy to office politics and differences between my peer in Sales and the overall Branch Manager. Technically, the Sales professional was supposed to help a colleague in a support role. However, when I visited the location I found the Sales Manager missing as he was on a holiday somewhere else and was unaware of my presence. When I reported back to the Head Quarters my Branch Manager, knowing well that the Sales Manager wasn't present, asked me about the visit and if this particular gentleman had helped me during my stay there. To which in my innocence I declined, knowing little of what was to follow.

A meeting of all sales professionals was convened at a colleague's place, as most of them did not like the Branch Manager and took this opportunity to get back at him. The Branch Manager had his own little secrets of taking the afternoon off. In fact, as I reflect back, Bhubaneswar was a quiet little city those days where most of the staff was of sales, there was work in the morning and afternoon was siesta followed by relaxed evenings and some activity. Coming back to my anecdote, I was told to state that the sales representative was there but hadn't had the time to meet me. I don't really recall what the reasons were, but I had walked into a hornet's nest without realising.

The next day I saw the who's who of that particular company and this was followed by a one on one enquiry which was a dawn till dusk operation. I learnt a couple of lessons from this assignment; you don't necessarily have to state the stark truth.

Along the way of my growing years as a professional, I learnt some home truths, some that people may even deny, such as the skills of networking and its benefits, marketing oneself, delegating, awareness of what's happening through the grapevine and another beautiful concept of monkey off my back, looking good. These are the realities of the corporate world, however harsh they may sound. I have been a victim of innocence a number of times. I have had bosses who thought who were god's gift to mankind and threw their weight around.

I also believe in the theory of What goes around – Comes around. Let me cite some experiences that I have had. I had a boss who thought as a CEO, his duty was to humiliate and show that he was there, and was rude and curt. These were the experiences that left scars and I associate them with pain and tears. After many years, as I progressed in my career, one fine day I was told that a Concierge service CEO who had been trying to get my attention and I didn't understand what I had to do with this particular service and delegated this to our administrative department. As I passed the reception I saw the man who had given me so much pain. I was surprised to find that his presence did not bring the kind of wrath I expected it to bring, instead there was a sense of sympathy towards his state and I also remember giving him the contract.

There have been bosses who were just there in terms of existence. They never really met you or spoke to you, but probably wrote generic emails addressed to the department. They were harmless souls whose aim in life was to lead a retired life, do minimal work and ensure that they appeared good in their bosses' eyes. This meant speaking initially in Town Halls to ensure they marked their attendance to the crowd. But some were absolutely spineless souls who just could not say no to their supervisors. So in reality the king in this case the MD, a CEO who considered the senior management as his Ministers and the overall population as his fiefdom. In fact, there was one particular MD who believed everyone of the 3,000 employee base should be transferred to Operations immaterial of whether the employees in discussion had the necessary skill or not. If there was a refusal, then they would be transferred to remote locations. The last that I heard of this gentleman was that he was in prison.

The lesson learnt is that if you treat your employees as your personal staff, you may not go very far in your career. And if you toe the line of your seniors and behave like a *chamcha*, you will never earn the respect of your subordinates. Last but not the least, bosses who take erratic decisions or autocratic decisions and are vindictive will always be hated for sure.

Some bosses were classy, poised, had domain expertise and skills for the function they led. I would like to name this particular boss that I had in DHL, way back in 2000. She laid the foundation for me in terms of overall exposure to the function. She had an anglicised accent, her four by two smile and a laugh that had four intonations, from the softest to the loudest, but she knew her domain and knew it well. She ensured that you learnt on the job, let you think, explore and gave you exposure to the foreign world of the multinationals. During those years, it was a matter of pride and prestige to be sent abroad, it meant you had arrived.

My first international exposure was when I was sent to Singapore to attend training in Change Management conducted by Nanyang Business School with other colleagues from South Asia. I remember being in an exhilarated state, a bit confused and in awe. I also remember meeting another Senior HR Leader who went out of her way to show me Singapore. I am told she is currently the global head of DHL and my ex-boss continues to work with DHL in the U.S. Her name is Hermie Neri. Thank you Hermie.

I remember some very unique experiences which shaped my attitude and outlook towards life. DHL in India was a franchisee operation and was run by AFL Ltd. In the year 2000, DHL wanted to take over the franchisee operations completely. To ensure that the takeover would be smooth there was an Australian gentleman who was coming to India to do a recce or a look and feel. I was asked to assist him. What an eye opener the experience was. I first had to find an agent who would help in the process of expatriation. Way back in 2000 this was like hunting for a needle in a haystack till I found Lata Patel, then began the entire process of … how do you quarantine dogs that were shipped in? How do you deal and educate expats on culture, and the dos and don'ts … fascinating.

I remember personally going with this gentleman to see the plush houses in Mumbai. Oh my God! Who said Mumbai was constrained for space. I saw huge 4,000 square feet plush houses in the centre of the city with Jacuzzi, state of the art amenities. This was the time Enron had exited India and with it most of the expat population. We also looked at luxury cars. I learnt an important lesson, there were no limits to expectations and desires and that these were all relative. One has to set one's own benchmarks without comparisons, or being carried away by wealth and glamour. If you want to reach for the stars, define what you mean by that, internalise and make an effort to work towards them. I enjoyed my stint at DHL but chickened out when I was given the charge of going ahead with separations and deciding on which employee would continue with the parent and the one who would be sent to the Indian parent company.

My next stint was an interesting one as the Head of HR for SBI Life. I remember attending a panel interview, something that was the first and the last of its kind that I attended. It had stalwarts and my to be boss who was the Deputy Managing Director of SBI, a big name in the banking world. Senior officials in public sector companies take time off to attend to interviews and adhere to all laid out norms. Unlike what one hears of public sector companies, bank probationary officers are sincere, dedicated, and hard working. They are a combination of diligence and intelligence. I had the privilege of setting up this company from scratch as the third employee on rolls.

This was a true start up in every sense of the term; we had an incubation office that we took on rent. Later shifted from there to a building that was given to us by SBI and then like a giant octopus we spread our tentacles all across the country to reach where it is today, one of India's largest insurance companies. Not just that, I am proud to say that two of my former colleagues are powerful DMDs of the Bank, a prediction that I had made way back in 2001. One of them is in Africa and the other is the Head of Marketing with SBI General Insurance that I had a chance meeting with where both our airport buses landed side by side. I was headed to Bangalore from my current company JSW and he for Delhi, and we both met as if all those years hadn't gone by.

However, this was a challenging assignment in various ways. It was a unique combination of public sector, private sector and a multinational. SBI Life had on its rolls several secondees that included expats from Cardiff, officials from BNP Paribas as well as bank POs and, of course, there were regular employees such as we. This lead to many confusions. Let me name a few which I think will be useful for any person who has to handle such an assignment.

The French expats from Cardiff had to have an Indian salary with a compensation paid to them in their home country. Just how much, one did not know and had to make several enquiries to find out. That was the only time I saw a lot of value in consultants who got this sorted out. There were other issues such as accommodation and vehicles which BNP Paribas was providing, but for some reason could not come into the picture for some tax laws. The next one was even more hilarious; out of the three expats two of them had live in partners but were not married. Indian regulation refused to accept such relationships, so arose the issue of dependent visas and how could we organise those?

At SBI Life all matters about overall policies, practices, and compensation had to be benchmarked with other sister companies such as SBI MF and SBI Capital Markets. Though all three were different companies, treatment according to the parent company's instruction was to be the same. That brings me to my next issue for regular employees like us. Believe it or not, we got salaries for

6 months without proper appointment letters. One reason was that our MD and my boss were never sure whether the contents of the appointment letter were what they should be. Thus began my frustration as an HR professional. I remember drafting out a simple appointment letter, under various versions for as many as 20 times. After which it was a table item to be approved by none other than the Chairman of SBI himself.

I take this opportunity to describe my boss here, a bright and talented man who had impeccable qualifications and credentials. But there was one thing which was frustrating, his sense of perfection … that we felt, having made his decision he would never be firm and say go ahead. I guess, with brilliance and the will to give shape to the best, we went through versions and yet more versions, which meant that we spent time in re-doing all that we did with the hope the current draft was better than the previous one. Since our MD took a long time to give a go ahead and make up his mind, and even if he did, he kept on changing it. The common joke was that one thing would remain unchanged for him was his name.

Learnings in start-ups are immense. It constantly throws challenges that one has never faced before. It teaches one to understand the direction and urgency of a certain HR process at a certain point in time that one needs to concentrate on. It teaches an HR professional to understand the nuances of the environment that are unspoken like the culture, what to say and when to say, cultivating and nurturing interpersonal relationships. It teaches one to be aware of politics, coteries, alignments and power games.

In hindsight, I believe I got a good team which meant I was good at recruiting and I had a great equation with most of them. This is the reason that I am in touch with most of them even today while they are at senior management positions. Two of our then General Managers of SBI Life, who were probationary officers of SBI and non deputed to Insurance, are currently Deputy Managing Directors with SBI and one is posted abroad. One of our former employee, who quit, has made his mark in the corporate world and sits on several boards. My other colleagues that I were instrumental in hiring, one is a CFO of a reputed joint venture insurance company and another is in Hong Kong as a reputed investment banker. But where I failed miserably was managing perceptions. My youth acted against me as my MD always thought of me as a young manager and someone that he should ignore when it came to taking important decisions. I also could not align well with people in power with the JV partner. Another drawback was not being thick skinned and taking things to heart and deciding more from the heart than the head.

I decided to change as I felt the environment to be suffocating and stifling, another wrong decision in hindsight. I took what I got instead of waiting for the right opportunity to come along. Let me explain this a bit, when one is troubled one has to have patience and weigh each opportunity by fitment into an organisation, its culture, who does the position report to, and position of the function in the overall scheme of things. One has to have a clinical approach every time one is thinking of a career change and instant decisions are a complete no-no. The other must do is talking to individuals and finding out more about the organisation, its culture, and its people. However, one must be discreet as people love juicy gossip and it is invariably a small world and word does get around.

The next organisation that I joined was Group M, called WPP in those days as Director Human Resources. This was a merger where the reputed advertising companies of WPP in India, JWT-J Walter Thompson, Ogilvy and Mather, and Contract were merging their media units for the first time. This meant the same people who were competing for the same clients now were part of the same group and under the same roof. In simple words, competitors were now on the same side with their pent up emotions. Added to this complication was the fact they had different cultures, reporting systems, and perspectives to handle media. There was a division of different verticals within. There was Mindshare Fulcrum which was the Unilever media wing, Mindshare, Maxis had shared services like Finance, HR and IT. If one follows the Vedas one could classify them as Brahmins, Kshatriya, Vaishyas and Shudras, exactly in that order.

I was told that, two media heads who were vying for the top slot had been sacrificed and an expat CEO was brought in. Media is a strange world where it's all about people but where the human resources function is least developed and respected. Flamboyance, conniving professionals, politics, backbiting, creative, intelligent, artistic, watered down values are my interpretations of the media industry.

As the HR Director my team was limited to two people. One who was an asset and payroll manager and another a lady, who was a part of the furniture and about to retire. There was no mandate or vision or deliverable that was charted out. This was an industry if you were not part of the coterie or clique, then you are not meant to be. I think they thought it was fashionable to hire an HR person who would be around.

When I look back I wonder how I survived 1 year and 6 months but I did. The initial task was to bring all the compensation components under a single platform. I must say these were my initial days and I remember that I owe my then payroll manager, Sandeep Suchak, a big thank you. My understanding was limited and to try to work out components that were friendly to all wasn't easy. Let me also mention the media industry of then wasn't a big fan of hiring experts like the Hewitts and Mercers of the world to do it. I remember doing a lot of hiring. But this hiring was all through networking and no consultant was involved. So when recruitment agencies specialising in Media approached me, I had to politely thank them and continue doing my work single handedly.

I tried to put the policies, processes, and performance management in place and I think I did a decent job. But in hindsight, there were a number of things that I did not do well. If I prioritise them, the first on the list would be perception management which I think I did not do very effectively at all. One day I remember being summoned to my CEO's office, a Malaysian Indian, with a British passport. The conversation was around the fact that my vision was not really aligned to his vision and perspective, I remember being enveloped in an array of emotions … nervous, angry, and belligerent. I also remember telling him that I would move on immediately as my ego was badly battered and bruised. This was a polite way of saying I was not wanted.

Therefore, it is not only important to understand the boss and project an appropriate stance to create the desired perception but it is equally important to learn to adapt to a culture which could be vertical centric, in this case the media industry. This was one of the low points of my life, but people say every dark cloud has a silver lining. This was my turning point and from here onwards there was no looking back. But even in these low moments God sends you an angel, in my case it was Sapna, the HR Head of JWT. She was a high point in my life in the media, someone who was a friend, philosopher, and guide. She told me to take my time, cool off, get a fresh perspective, and move on.

During such low moments, you also find people who will be friends forever. This was when I met Sanjay who was then a Director with Emmay HR. I remember meeting a nattily dressed man and fairly young to be a director, Mr. Sanjay Shetty at Barista now called Palladium, for a formal chat to discuss career opportunities. The discussion was fruitful and we discussed aspects that would be interesting for me. I recall both of us trudging back to our respective work places and I remember Sanjay getting into a plush sedan and I thought, "Maybe I should become a consultant". Good lifestyle and I was certain a good pay considering what I had seen.

I kept pestering him up almost every other day asking him for opportunities and instead of being snooty, he was patient; he was a big pillar of support. I think every experience of ours with a brand is determined by the representatives of theirs whom we meet. Their treatment to us and our brand recall will be the person who is the single point of contact. I did meet both Monisha and Madhu, who were the founders of Emmay, both bright, fashionable, and young motivated entrepreneurs who probably changed the face of recruitment in Mumbai. I watched as Emmay was bought by Randstad and then being merged with Mafoi and the management changed. Things changed but what didn't change is my friendship with Sanjay who became a confident and continues to be so even today.

I got many offers after my stint with Group M, one of them was Syngenta, then there was Godrej and there were some others, but somehow they did not fascinate me. It was through Sanjay that I got interviewed at ICICI OneSource, a company that interestingly was in the same building. My first interaction was with Aashu Calapa, my boss to be. He was so different, mature, a philosopher at heart, warm and so easy going that I felt comfortable. I was also interviewed by Sameer and my word, he had an exhaustive list. In my heart I knew that I liked the place but would they have a position for me? Aashu had stated there were two positions, one in Bangalore and one in Mumbai, and he had met someone for Mumbai and there was no way that I was moving to Bangalore. So I had to play the waiting game, waiting for an answer and hoping against hope that some miracle would happen, and it did.

I got a call from Aashu's office asking me to collect my offer letter. Aashu narrated to me how a former Captain of the Indian army that he had liked and recruited for Mumbai volunteered to go to Bangalore to accommodate me, a stranger. This is my second forever friend Capt Anil Dhanker. Even before I joined I had much respect for this faceless human being who had sacrificed his comfort. I met Anil after a long time. Anil was a tall, reserved, well mannered, and a knowledgeable professional who had joined ICICI after his stint at IDBI.

I have very fond memories of this company, now called Firstsource. I had great colleagues who I still share a strong bond with. There were Laxmi and Parag, two wonderful people. I remember us getting into Parag's Santro and going out to have lunch, of chattering incessantly about processes, systems, and people. Parag is now with Accenture as a Partner and Laxmi as Vice President Customer Services in

Vodafone (don't know if they have had any more promotions). I remember Pooja at Centre for Cultural Resources and Training (CCRT) and Neil and his boys in Marks and Spencer. Sunita, voice training and how she used to be stressed all the time. Of how to ensure that agents on the floor had neutralised English and no Mother Tongue Accent (MTA), of the *pha,tha,kaas*, of how to say *thffank* you, with the tongue touching the teeth and not *tank* you. There was Tina Dhawan, a real darling. She was a thorough professional, extremely upright. Tina in those days used to be the centre head for the back office of Lloyds TSB in India. She played a crucial role in my life and had a tremendous influence in shaping my life. She is the one who taught me the basics of money matters, the joys of travel and seeing foreign lands, of good food and to enjoy life. Currently she is one of the head honchos at American Express

Being a third party BPO was stressful as one had to bid for business constantly and win them, as the bread and butter of the company depended on the client. But it was fun as well. I remember all the Business Development personnel walking around pompously in their suits, whenever we were pitching to a client and dressing up to meet clients, turn by turn armed with presentations and FAQs. This would be followed by suspense where all of us had to play the waiting game. Once the business was won then would begin the migration process. This was an event that agents and team leaders on the floor looked forward to as this meant a foreign trip and an event of shopping, gossip and stories of who was going steady with whom. Handling foreigners, their tastes, and their whims was another art that most of us learned. But this was a great learning considering globalisation.

A great learning in the ITES for HR Managers is dealing with a plethora of issues. These issues could range from ones like sexual harassment to ones like theft, sex change issues, sexual issues, and homicide. The reasons for these I realised was primarily the background of the associates who took up jobs at call centrs. Many such incidents some complicated ones with sometimes no help from either of my bosses and no acknowledgement from my HR colleagues in most cases. However, this is where my operations colleagues gave me support. These were learning life skill lessons, facing challenges that life threw at you like a full toss that you had to bat and hoped that it was a six because one had no experience or training or support from any quarters.

This is where I think orientation to a culture is important. Let me cite one example for the readers. I remember waking up to the loud noise of a text message in the stillness of the night at around 2 am. The message said one of the agents had committed suicide at the Chummery that they were staying in. The case was complicated as he was not our regular employee but someone who had failed his voice and accent test with us and had had a string of failures with other organisations as well. However, as a benevolent organisation we had provided accommodation and he was staying with us.

I remember requesting my subordinate who used to handle MIS and the Human Resource Information System to retrieve data to get further details on this candidate. He was in office by 4 am. We discovered the person belonged to a remote area in the North East. The boy had planned his own death and his suicide note was in red, blue and green. He was dressed for the occasion with a bandana, sun glasses and smart clothes. Then followed the *Panchnama* with the police and getting someone to collect his body as his step mother, who was a house help in Mizoram, flatly refused to come. She denied having anything to do with her stepson. Through our bank contacts we were finally able to locate a friend of his. Flight tickets were sent to him so he could come for his friend's funeral.

Let me not divert too much from the topic of bosses. This was a matrix reporting structure and I fell in between and felt like an orphan who neither of my bosses wanted to own, and I was in a no man's land. I had two great people who were my bosses, and till date I adore and respect them and am still in touch with them.

However, as professionals there were many areas I think needed a lot. My HR boss was a great guy but I found a complete lack of ownership as he thought I belonged to operations. There would be no reviews, rare one on ones except for appraisals. The other thing which I learnt and don't do, was his encouraging subordinates to speak against their boss, in this case me, without actually getting to know the reasons as to what were the real issues. My other operations boss never had time for HR as he was bothered about Earnings Before Interest Taxes Deductions and Amortisation (EBITDA), headcount and attritions.

He was such a number's man that our conversations would be about numbers with no discussions on softer issues. This is something every boss must never forget. Softer issues are the hardest to handle and hit you the hardest when they boomerang. However, this was a great company and probably I would have continued had it not been for the fact that despite my hard work, dedication and passion, my efforts were not recognised as promotions were being meted out to people who managed perceptions well. My reaction to this was voting with my feet, a decision that was another turning point in my life.

I joined as Head of Human Resources of Shoppers Stop Limited, India's leading retail company and the pioneer for retail in India. Shoppers Stop as a company was extremely systems and process oriented. The quality of human resources was also fairly developed. The company was customer centric and believed in delivering excellent customer service. Every employee was first a customer care associate followed by the designation. The company was headed by then the Managing Director Mr B.S. Nagesh, who was considered a pioneer and father of retail in India. He was a visionary, the brain behind launching many brands like Crossword, Brio and Hypercity which is a leading name in hypermarkets as well as getting international brands like Mothercare and Mac into India.

I reported to the CEO, Mr Govind Shrikhande, who was an inspiration. His simplicity yet thoroughness in everything he did were something I remember and try to follow to this date. He was a great HR Leader himself. He always led from the front. I remember the enthusiasm and personal attention he gave many of the schemes that HR ran and he believed in the personal touch. He would address the ground staff himself.

He believed in training. Even people like me, who were not from retail, were trained by the best international faculty to understand retail terms like Gross Margin Return On Floor Space (GIMROF), Gross Margin Return On Labor (GIMROL) and Gross Margin Return On Inventory (GIMROI) and the overall science of retail. The HR practices like running in-house assessment or development centers for identifying talent across-the-board and the sanctity and adherence to the process. The process like the Baby Kangaroo program used for identifying and nurturing talent from the associates on the floor is still a success. This program has changed the future for many. They have risen to be store heads taking charge of stores worth crores of business.

I had a great team and a wonderful group of people reporting to me who I still am in touch with. There was Suketu who was my head of Learning and Development (L&D). He is now the head of L&D of Mahindra Finance. Then it was Vikram, who moved as Head HR Tata Battery, and Paul, GM HR with Gujrat Ambuja (Holcim). The team was young and vibrant. There was Kalyani, bright, enthusiastic, and ready to take on challenges, Bhuvana, Priyesh, Kaajal, Kapila and the list goes on…. We did some real good work and I think the best part was that we enjoyed ourselves and had a good time. We worked hard and partied as well. The only party pooper was the lady, who joined as Chief People Officer (CPO). She was supposed to be the group head for HR, someone who hardly worked and would go around people's desk saying how bored she was, always looking for opportunities to belittle people. Her role was to direct the respective businesses in HR to the HR leaders and define an overall strategy.

My next assignment was Holcim, the world's largest cement manufacturing company. I joined as CPO of ACC Concrete. My exposure to multinational culture was at its peak here. Functionally I reported to the CEO, Hans Fuchs. Hans was of Swiss origin with a British background. He was an exemplary leader; a leader who walked the talk, a taskmaster but extremely fair, who rarely got swayed by hearsay though he knew everything that there was to know. He has been the best boss that I have ever had. He had a vision, fire in the belly and the grit that distinguishes the leaders from the common mass. He was somebody who had great faith in his team and believed them to the core. A thorough gentleman, he inculcated some deep-rooted values both on professional as well as on the personal front which I live by even today.

My functional boss was also a Hans, Hans Mielants of Belgian origin who was based in Zurich. He was an extremely competent professional and was well versed with aspects of the business as well as human resources. He took pains in going through all the details and reviewed all the initiatives that we rolled out. The exposure he gave and the growth he provided was phenomenal. He recommended me to be part of the team that was global for Society of Human Resources Management (SHRM) US to write out their examination questions. He even recommended me for an assignment in Zurich. A fantastic boss. Thank you so very much Hans. I would always remember Hans M as he was the only one who came close to challenging my distinctive hearty laugh. ACC Concrete Limited (ACCCL) was a fantastic assignment for starting a project from scratch and taking it to great heights. It was a unique opportunity for me as I was challenged by people who had been in the manufacturing industry for over two decades (this was my first stint with a core manufacturing company) and every time I had to give my best. I had to use all the tricks of the trade which I had learnt over the years to overcome the challenges and every time the best in me came out. This was also a place where I played a role as the conscience keeper and would give honest and candid feedback to my CEO on people issues, which he would take and implement.

There were occasions where we had differences and would deliberate on and reach a consensus. For example, once when we wanted to roll out the Vision, Mission and Values of the company. Hans wanted to hire an external consultant and I advised him against it as he himself was a great trainer. I remember asking him to do it himself, which he did and the impact it had on people was amazing. I also remember the tough assignments that he wanted me to discharge, such as downsizing within my second week of joining. This was 2008, and I didn't know the company or the people. This in hindsight was good, as I didn't have the emotional connect that would hamper objectivity. This was my first tough task and I accomplished the same with flying colours without affecting psyche and moral.

The next tough task that Hans gave me was to shut all our plants in Bangalore and negotiate with the unions. I being from the service industry had never handled Industrial Relations (IR), so the thought was not an easy one, but as a boss he stood by me and my COO, Ravi Chander, who was my execution partner. The entire project was completed with precision and finesse. As a boss what I learnt from him was perfection, extensive planning with alternatives like having a plan A and a plan B, execution, and completion of projects and assignments. Hans was a boss that I admired and who was a role model.

My HR Director was someone that I really admired. Since we were part of his region, South East Asia region, he ensured that we got to meet, interact, and discuss with the HR Directors of Singapore, Vietnam, Thailand, Sri Lanka and India which was represented by us, ACC and Ambuja. Hans ensured our exposure to best HR practices from across the globe which was a great learning experience.

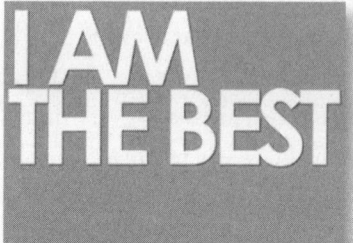 

The frog in the well mentality was something that one could relinquish as well as the pompous feeling of I am the best. We were given projects where we were encouraged to work with or in other countries. These were forums where we discussed our talent and secondments for them.

In ACCCL I had a wonderful team. There was Azhar who was a brilliant trainer, someone one could rely on for perfect execution and now a very dear friend. There was Dr. Bhoon, a retired Brigadier from the Indian Army and a PhD. from IIT who understood Operations well and the rest of the young teammates. There was Debra who is now heading HR in Doha and Sameer who was a dedicated professional who is doing well now. This was an assignment that I got a lot of job satisfaction from and in turn got a lot of recognition as well.

I then moved on to the JSW group....

He was an exemplary leader, who walked the talk, a taskmaster but extremely fair who rarely got swayed by hearsay, though he knew everything that there was to know.

11

A GOOD BOSS IS A GOOD LEADER

S.V. Nathan
Director–Talent Resource
Multinational Consulting
Company

> *He taught me the importance of simplicity in strategy;*
> *the soul of strategy is simplicity.*

An Introduction

What is leadership? The term gets thrown around a lot these days. What do leaders do that make them leaders? Are  leaders born or are they made? More books have been written about Leadership than any other subject. Can one learn to become a leader? I wish to address some of these questions and more through my personal narrative and offer some ideas on how one can develop leadership capabilities.

Leadership is a trait that is in high demand and short supply in today's world. As society fragments further and collective consciousness is dictated by television, people increasingly look to get what they can while they can. I believe the breeding of individuals who look beyond, look out for others and are looked on with respect, is central for the survival of the society and humanity itself.

In a long career, in various parts of the country and the world, has afforded me the pleasure, and sometimes the misfortune, of working with many bosses of various shapes, sizes, characters and dispositions. A summation of these experiences and the lessons I have consciously imbibed along the way remain a constant daily reference point.

For instance, the reason I shine my shoes every day: A young management trainee and fresh off the boat, I seldom took the time to polish my shoes or clean them each time after treading the narrow road I took to work. Well, I was not going to let clean shoes stand in the way of my ambition and success. Now, was I? My boss, a retired Captain of the Indian Army, was particular about well creased pants that slid down into spit-shined shoes. He, however, chose not to call me out for my tardiness. He waited for the day when, thanks to a summer shower, my shoes had shaken off their familiar layer of dirt.

"Well done, Nathan!" the Captain's voice boomed from across the corridor, "You shined your shoes today." A bit startled and embarrassed I mumbled my thanks and scurried back to my desk. He chose to catch me doing something right. Even though it meant I had not done it out of my own volition. I just got wet and my shoes got cleaned. He chose the one occasion to compliment me when I seemed to have got it right. I realised early in my career, positive affirmations are more powerful than negative comments and help change behaviour. And yes, my shoes have been squeaky-clean since. Priceless lesson learned.

Five Easy Pieces

Over time you get to be a good leader, a good manager and a good person. I have come a long way from being a management trainee I was 28 years ago and my bosses, good and bad, have been integral to that development.

Five Easy Pieces is a narrative of how I came by these five vital lessons that have held me in good stead and guided me in stormy weather in both my professional and personal life. Remember, I did not go out seeking them. They came by me through chance and kindness. What I can credit myself for is recognising the lesson and internalising it until it became integral to my thought process. Lessons only life can teach you.

The Five Easy Pieces:

1. The Ease of Ethics
2. The Courage of Conviction
3. The Innards of Inspiration
4. The Thing about Thinking
5. The Soul of Strategy

What follows is the story of how I came by these pieces....

The Ease of Ethics

I have been just lucky to have some outstanding bosses. How does one learn ethics? Classroom ethics are passé. Seldom in one's career is one privy to where the question of ethics is played out in plain sight. What matters is the insight. I had that privilege early in my career.

As a junior member of an Administration team I was tasked with doing a host of odd jobs. Not something that I loved doing. I just loved to get tasks cleared off my desk, knew how to navigate the system and how to get the stuff done. One such job was to fix the new CEO's back pain. So I rolled up my sleeves and got down to the root of the issue. His bed.

The company provided bungalow came with English Spring beds which the new CEO was not used to. A hardboard would be good for his bad back pain. I was ordered to replace the framework of springs with a flat plywood board. In those days you did not judge work. One quick trip to measure the bed and another to the local market to source the 10 mm plywood board and the job was signed, sealed and delivered. The case of the CEO's back pain was closed in my books. The next day, to my surprise, I was summoned to his office. I enquired if the modifications in his bed were alright and he replied that they were. He then asked me, "Young man, have you forgotten to do something?"

I searched my memory and my to-do list. There was the leak on the first floor bathroom, but that was not grave enough to warrant a reprimand from the CEO. He asked again, with more pronounced enunciation, "Have you forgotten to do something?" Now I was all jelly. A ball of fear took hold of my stomach and began to grow, it had to be the bed. I replied with feigned confidence, "No boss, I did all that was needed, I even checked last evening if the work was according to specifications and it was." "Think again," he asked and to reply to that I puffed my chest out and shook my head in vehemence. Looking disappointed, he reproached me with a question, "What about the bill?" I looked at him in surprise. What bill? All this was official expense, I thought.

He began to explain slowly, tapping the table with his index finger for emphasis, "This is a personal requirement, owed to my personal need and I would like to know how much it cost you to organise the board." He was serious about it. I rushed and got the bill to his office which he cleared and it was a small amount. Nothing I would have worried about. He did, though. Here was a person building the foundation of ethics in the grassroots of the organisation and doing it in the simplest way possible. The seed he helped sow took root and remains today as a lighthouse whose guiding light I use as a reference point in times of uncertainty.

One's integrity is sacred. It should remain uncompromised. Period!

The Courage and Conviction

Acts of courage stem from conviction. You stand up for an ideal, a value or a person you believe in. The strength of conviction is tested in difficult situations. The ability to stand up for me and brave the consequences of a bad situation is a leadership trait. And one can learn it.

courage and conviction

A hard land breeds hard men or women to handle hard ways. Bihar, before the carving out of Jharkhand, was just that, a hard land. With most of humanity working the mines, pockets of simmering communal unrest, roving bands of dons, and a nonexistent officialdom, reality was at times worse than a Bollywood potboiler.

It was then, four years into my career, that I found myself managing a transport fleet for a factory producing industrial grade explosives for use in mines and road building. The role involved keeping a fleet of some battered passenger vehicles, buses and 4×4s in running condition and on call 24/7. With a shoestring budget, ailing machines and road conditions that are fit for endurance tests, the role came with its share of challenges, to say the least. I was told that my predecessor had left the company complaining of deteriorating health and high blood pressure. What a happy situation indeed.

The fleet, in addition to a host of other duties, helped ensure the factory had an uninterrupted supply of ammonium nitrate, the base material used in the explosives. Large tankers of the material kept the factory supplied daily and were themselves subject to constant breakdowns. In a breakdown, a mechanic would be driven to the tanker to administer the necessary repairs and ensure the chain was unbroken. A break in the chain usually resulted in halting of production and that affected everybody's joy.

One day, the inevitable happened and we needed to chase ammonia, as we called it back then. We needed a car and none was available. The only car available was being repaired in the garage. Production came to a near halt as the grid collapsed. All hell broke loose. I was called to the CEO's office and was being unceremoniously yelled at by the exasperated CEO. It was a big office and daunting. I tried to explain but it did not help. How does any yelling help me? No idea perhaps it helped my CEO. It was a bad situation.

My boss (you will remember him from the shoe-shine story earlier) walked into the room and stood in front of me and gestured me to take a step back. He told the CEO that he and not I was responsible, and the CEO should speak to him. The CEO, not backing down, continued to level accusations of incompetence and lack of foresight at me. At this point, Captain turned to me, asked me to leave and wait in my office. I fled the place.

Later that day, the morning crisis had been addressed, production had resumed and things had been brought to an even keel. I was called again by the CEO and I feared the worst. He appeared calm and asked me to sit down and said, "I learned a thing or two from your boss today. Thank you." My boss's actions that day brought home to me that courage stems from conviction in his people. And have the courage of conviction to stand up, when needed.

The Innards of Inspiration

It is central to a leader's arsenal to be able to inspire people to reach above and beyond their perceived potential and create synergies within teams and groups that accomplish challenging tasks together.

It was late evening and the dust had settled on the town of Gomia. The Captain (my boss) had just ordered his first round of drinks in the Officers' Club even as the sun settled on a long day. The Captain was a man of substance and was in charge of administration, security, and facilities and was the go-to guy in any untoward situation. Our quiet chat was cut short by a frantic phone call for my boss. He came back, reached for his glass and tossed the amber liquid back in one fluid motion and gestured me to do the same, "You're going to need it", he said. With Captain, you did not ask questions, you just followed. So, I went.

He filled me in about the situation in one of the warehouses at the factory formula raced to the main gate. A band of armed thugs had taken over one of the warehouses in the factory by force and were demanding a supply of copper wire, a commodity of value in the local market. The guards at the factory were many but were afraid to make the first move. Their supervisor was hesitant and his fear played on the others.

On reaching the factory, the Captain quickly assessed the situation and made for the lone gun in the gun cabinet. It was an old dusty musket of dubious make and was more for effect, than for real use. The Captain grabbed the gun and found cover behind wooden packing crates at a location that gave him a view of the warehouse. After a whispered conversation with the factory foremen, we learned there were seven assailants, inexperienced and young, with five guns between them.

Captain looked around and then broke cover and began to run, yelling and sending off a few rounds into the air. The security chief and, a few other factory guards followed him with gusto. There were much yelling, flashes of gunfire and the sound of gravel crunch as the guards converged on the warehouse. I have no recollection of what ensued. All I remember is that one intruder lay sprawling on the ground, another two were apprehended, and one was caught trying to jump the fence; the other three escaped. As in the movies, the cops arrived when the battle was over.

In the celebration that ensued, I saw the Captain become one among the men and recalled to celebrate with each member of the team by the Captain. He never once spoke of himself. The cops rounded up the thugs and a photo was taken to mark the event. That day I learned what it meant to lead from the front and what it took to inspire belief and faith in people. It continues to be a constant endeavour to live up to the example the Captain set for me that day. Learning: Without fear look beyond oneself, for a cause in the thick of things, to lead in an inspiring way.

The Thing about Thinking

After a long stint in the adventurous lands of Bihar, I moved to a large multinational organisation and met the person who taught me to think and do, one who lived in a world of thinking through every small detail.

It began with my interview. It lasted close

to 5 hours where she understood more about me than most of my close friends and colleagues. I had the opportunity to work and interact with her regularly. One of the initial projects was to rollout the policies for the organisation. For a nascent organisation, they had to be built from the ground up. Of course, we had the blueprints from the parent organisation, but we had to reinterpret them in an Indian context.

They had to be worked on for cultural suitability and balance. The discussions and debates lasted over a month and each of them was a study on structural analysis and thinking. One discussion to remember was the one on Parental Leave for adoption. I held my ground that a special company would give paid leave for adoption and it was not redundant because other companies did not do it. Yet after a lively debate she prevailed on me, I came away understanding the difference between basing your thinking on experience as opposed to basing your thinking on what could happen tomorrow. A futuristic view was needed. She taught me to get to the heart of the matter by asking three vital questions:

1. Why do we do it?
2. Is this for the collective good? For today and tomorrow?
3. Is it something that people will truly appreciate and use?

It would have been easy to overlook the entire process, but I realised later that she taught me how to think progressively. She did it by guiding my thought process through dialogue and stirred me towards the right decision. She also left a trail for me to follow in case I lose my way. I have endeavoured to help create similar paths for people and organisations since.

Epilogue

Recently, I met a colleague who had adopted a child. She spoke volubly of the Parental Leave policy that helped her immensely. The policy was drafted eight years ago.

The Soul of Strategy

Working for a younger boss is a difficult proposition. The natural instinct is to reject them for their inexperience and lack of maturity. My instinct was proven wrong on this occasion.

Much of what we do is for today and in many ways we are a function of our learning. My young boss was fearless. He based his actions today on what the future would hold and relentlessly pushed us to do the same. He would often say, "As much as you're doing things right, are you doing the right thing?"

He had the uncanny ability to question the core of a project or a function with a sense of innocence. "Is this truly required?" one would often hear him say to the shocked disbelief of those around the table. The instance that comes to mind is when we rationalised the Talent Development function of the organisation. Based on a school of thought that each individual is unique and his or her needs are different, the function got to a level where it offered three hundred different courses. I was proud of the million hours of training that we were about to have. What high standards indeed.

The discussion began with him asking me about my vision of the future. Where did I see Learning and Development five years from now? I thought hard and painted a picture of a utopian future as best as I could. I had an elaborate plan and ready answers on what we would accomplish and by when we would do it. The first question he asked me, again with innocence, "How do you plan to do this, is there a framework of development?" I realised that all that I had said lacked conviction.

In our lives we have many variables that come to us. How do we simplify and put things in perspective. What matters and what does not matter? How do we separate what is not useful to us? Strategy is not what to do. He went to the drawing board and asked me to describe my plan. I felt defeated and low and yet saw the method in the madness. He was asking me to think.

I went to the drawing board and started to develop a basic framework, sans the embellishments of numerous courses and fancy programs. I began to realise that less was more. All learning and development was then turned on its head. Today, the function does a limited number of programs but does them well and there are customised learning maps for every individual. Yet, all of this falls under an overarching framework.

He taught me the importance of simplicity in strategy, foresight and the need to deploy underlying frameworks that would reach far into the future. The soul of strategy is simplicity.

The Closing

The journey has been long and fulfilling, and I am glad you have stayed with me this far. The narrative is only a small part of what I have learned and the people I have worked with over the years. I owe a debt of gratitude to my bosses. They have made me  the professional I am. They have made me the leader I am. I stand proud because of them.

They have helped me create these beacons so I may find my way home in bad weather. These sign posts tell me where I am and where I have come from. They guide my moral compass and navigate the murky waters of the corporate life.

But in truth, they are just Five Easy Pieces that I picked up along the way. Maybe, someone else has more than five pieces. Maybe, their pieces are different from mine. Maybe, they came upon/ across them in different ways. All I would urge you to do is this.

Be aware and pick them up when you find them or, in some cases, when they find you.

One's integrity is sacred.
It should remain uncompromised. Period.

12

MY EXPERIENTIAL LEARNING FROM MY BOSSES

Anu Vishwas Sarkar
Vice President
Regional Diversity Lead-Deustsche
Bank APAC
Global Diversity Lead-Service
Centre's Deutsche Bank AG,
Mumbai

Wonderful Bosses don't just manage performance effectively, but also turn into sponsors to help you with opportunities for a successful career.

I did not want to be a doctor like my parents and my sisters opted for a radical career path in the context of my family which largely had doctors and engineers. I went for a MBA education and specialised in Human Resources. I will be honest, opting for HR was not a scientific decision. I knew I wanted to pursue MBA but was unsure on the specialisation. I arrived at this decision after talking to several people and understanding what each of the specialisations really meant and the kind of work involved in the business world. The more research I did, the more I got inclined towards HR and found it resonating with my strengths and passion. And that led to the beginning of my professional journey.

"My manager is terrible. She hardly communicates, and least about the things which are positive or my achievements.

However she is brilliant in identifying 'serious' mistakes in punctuations and fonts. Her definition of wrong is doing things in any other way but her way."

"I am tired of listening to my manager's problems, her negative views on everyone at work and how nothing is right in the system. Every time I go to her for some direction or inputs, everything else comes in from somewhere. It gets really exasperating when she catches hold of me in the evening when I am about to leave for home to be with my family."

"My manager thinks himself to be smarter than what he is and only likes people who are like him. I lost another assignment as he is more close to another team member who goes out for golf sessions and drinks with him and, therefore, has a stronger relationship with him."

The list of complaints can go on and on. I have heard it from the floor of the trading room to the floor of call centres. I have heard this in informal chats over coffee in cafeterias to formal skip level meetings. I have heard it from my peers about their managers whom they role-modelled previously and wanted to work with. But this note is not a note to complain, this is a note to celebrate, refreshing all the moments I cherished during my more than a decade long career and give due credit to all my wonderful bosses.

So, did I ever have wonderful bosses to work with? Yes. Did I work with bosses who I could not relate to? Yes, that too. Did all the bosses, who I worked with, had faith in me or vice versa? The answer is mostly yes, but I had a mix of bosses too. Out of the several managers I worked for, some of them were extra-ordinary in some way or the other. And from my other bosses, I learnt a lot. Yes, I am lucky and I sincerely hope everyone becomes as lucky. I have fond memories of most of them. There were moments of incredible excitement, extraordinary achievements, indelible highs and unfathomable lows, but each of those moments made my present and my future too. I got an opportunity to work with managers across countries, genders, and functions. I never understood when I started to become a reflection of them, in some way or the other!

Let me dive deep and ask, "Who is a wonderful boss?" I have spoken to many about this not only while writing this portion but it is one puzzle which everyone attempts to solve at least once in their life time, irrespective of where one is  in the hierarchy? Is there a straight answer? The traditional wisdom might refrain me from providing an answer because I am not aware of any universally applicable and a globally accepted formula. Even if there have been attempts to write what a wonderful boss does or can do, I am fairly confident that putting those rules in to action is a long journey and sometimes people simply do not know how to act on them.

Having a wonderful boss, for me, is like a feeling which comes from cherishing experiences built over time. This experience is all about daily transactions which make a day, month after month, and year after year. This experience is what made me grow as a professional and experience what I attempt to provide to my team members.

I started my career with a large Indian engineering organisation as a Management Trainee in Mumbai. This organisation was and still is one of the most respected Indian Multinational Corporations (MNC). I was proud to be a part of it. When I joined, I was overwhelmed with the size of the business, scale of operations, number of people, and the precision with which shop floor was working. That was one of the greatest starts I could have ever had. Since then scale never scared me. As a part of the Management Training Scheme, I got exposed to late nights during performance cycles, part of the innumerable organising committees of multiple events and also supported New HR Initiatives programme. I still fondly remember those heavy Excel files, hurriedly reaching out to the vendors for our events to fix the last minute glitches and how some of my proposals on New Initiatives got shot down on account of being overly ambitious.

I worked on transactional activities to being part of some big projects. But what I most fondly remember is how my manager used to patiently translate each of my tasks into projects. He made me learn the skill of defining jobs and linking it to something big. When I look back at those experiences, they were fascinating because I never studied about those projects during my Management education, nor did I have enough understanding of how to accomplish those in an organisational landscape. But I started enjoying it the moment I experienced things are getting done. My manager ensured that I got early successes in my career. He knew that today's victories will be the foundation for tomorrow's success. What a wonderful quality to possess as a manager.

In my first job I got an opportunity to work on various projects across HR and enjoyed my learning and development experience the most. My manager gave me some of the most challenging assignments there and had very high expectations from me. My success in those assignments gave me a tremendous sense of achievement and confidence. I still remember how happy I felt when I designed a training workshop (my first one) to which my manager was invited to facilitate in a number of industry forums, campuses and then wanted me to facilitate it myself. I always felt I was not ready and could never do it. However, he pushed me into it which led to many sleepless nights, lot of anxiety and finally the day arrived. My manager worked closely with me but on the day it was my show.

It was the first workshop facilitated by me for a challenging group of mechanical engineers who were much senior in age, experience and designation to me. The programme went off well. I still recall how my manager seamlessly stepped in during challenging questions which gave me tremendous confidence. I enjoyed the experience so much that I wanted to do more such workshops and dive deep into the topic. This led to my long standing career in talent development. Good managers give you various options to help discover where your strengths and passion lie.

In terms of sectoral exposure, I have moved a long way. After joining an engineering organisation, I moved to a high pace driven, people centric, one of the largest banking and financial institution with offices around the world, and a strong retail presence in India. Here I joined the management and leadership arm of the training centre. My role was to design solutions and facilitate workshops. I could never have taken up this role or discovered that I enjoyed facilitation so much if it was not for my previous manager.

This organisation proved to be a real learning ground for me as a Learning & Development professional and I got to do some of my most challenging assignments here.

I then moved to one of the leading global universal banks with a strong investment banking focus. I have done multiple roles ever since I joined the bank seven years ago. In my current role, I head Diversity for the bank in Asia Pacific region and for the bank's service centres globally.

When I joined the corporate world in 2001, I saw different canteens for different employee groups, attendance registers at the entrance, different sized chairs for different corporate titles and a hierarchical environment largely focused on India operations. And today I work with an agenda which encompasses people across more than 17 countries and 3 different regions. I work with people from different genders, generations, sexual orientation, ethnic backgrounds, nationality, etc.

I work in an environment where one's role and agenda matters more than one's corporate title, and people respect one for the value add one provides. My  managers have provided me the flexibility to work from various offices in different locations. People are geographically spread across the globe and work efficiently only due to the trust in relationships, which are very often between people who have never met and come from different cultures.

People often ask me, as I moved across sectors and organisations, have I seen peoples profile changing across sectors? Yes. Have I noticed any change in the organisational cultures across time? The answer is yes too. But I feel that the concept of a wonderful boss did not change with sectors but the concept of successful manager kept changing. Well, let me elaborate on it. When it is only about two individuals, attempting to create a wonderful relationship with utmost honesty, it is easier. This is a place where context has little role to play. But when success becomes the lens of evaluating a relationship, context plays a critical role. Therefore, it is easier to find wonderful bosses if you do not focus on success but focus on a relation.

It is critical we recognise what we want out of this relationship – do we want proximity to successful leaders or do we want to be around authentic leaders. I always wanted a wonderful boss first and I got many. I took care that I do not ever evaluate them on the success parameter. Incidentally, today some of them are epitomes of success in their respective businesses, they are role models of hundreds, maybe thousands too, and people will eagerly wait to listen to what they have to say in town halls. Sometimes I feel happy I got an opportunity to get an insight into how humane they are, even when leading large teams. At the workplace, sometimes when things go wrong, I need to get a reassurance, I have help available and these leaders gave me that assurance subtly yet definitively.

I believe that great organisations always attempt to create a superlative leadership standard and managerial experience for everyone.

An important aspect of leadership is sponsorship and not every manager is a great sponsor. Some of the best managers have played the role effectively and without which the journey for me would have been different. Many researches show and my experience as a Diversity Head was that very often sponsorship is key to advancing careers, helping team members get the critical assignments, greater opportunities and, importantly, visibility at the right forums. This becomes even more important for women where they tend to focus more on performance and letting it speak for itself.

After a certain level, who you know becomes equally important as what you know and that is where sometimes women lose out on important high profile assignments. Sponsorship comes more naturally to men and shows the impact on representation of men at senior levels. Though I read about it and hear it all the time in my discussions, I also can relate to this issue being a woman myself. On reflecting, I feel that my managers have been playing the role of a sponsor and helping me build my presence in front of important stakeholders. There have been times when they were willing to take a chance on me more than what I thought I was capable of.

As a result, in my career, I got some big projects when I felt I was not ready, and today, being candid, I must confess that those discussions stressed me more than motivate me. However, I understood early that good managers who are sponsors have a lot of their credibility at stake. If they take a bet on you or ensure you get noticed, you better be good. I took up some of these assignments and worked hard not because I thought they will give me my next promotion, but because I did not want my managers to feel let down and my motivation was to make them feel proud of the decision they trusted me with.

I feel this is also important for a relation between a boss and a subordinate to flourish. It is a two way street and every working professional must understand this. In hindsight, they gave me a  few experiences which were career turning points for me and perhaps

I would have never raised my hands for some of the opportunities, if it was not for the confidence they gave me. Wonderful Bosses don't just manage performance effectively but also turn into sponsors or advocates to help you with opportunities for a successful career. Let me recall a few special incidents from my professional life which stand out.

I remember when I had joined my current organisation as Head Talent and Development (T&D) for South Asia and was primarily focused on India. This was much in line with my prior experience. In due course of time, I got an opportunity to work with my Regional HR Head for APAC as my direct manager had quit soon after I joined the team. It was a learning experience to work with her. I was young and fresh for the bank and had several opportunities to explore and prove my capability. However, the idea of being new and suddenly exposed to a senior member managing the team was sometimes intimidating. I learnt some of my best lessons that time. I enjoyed the role I was hired for, established the T&D function and could certainly see my experience being leveraged effectively.

I was also keen to experiment and explore areas that don't take me far from my core area of expertise (People Development) but yet add another dimension to my perspective. I was keen on areas like culture, team efficiency, organisation development, diversity, etc. And there came a one on one opportunity when I bounced off a few ideas with my manager on rolling out a few global initiatives in this region. That conversation led to the start of the diversity journey in APAC. What fascinated me was the way this was handled by her in a region where there was no stated appetite from our clients, no understanding on the business case for diversity, and no expertise or resources in the existing APAC HR team.

My manager decided to take a chance on me not only on the basis of my performance as I had no prior experience on diversity, but more for my passion in this area. I agree this could not have come my way if I was not performing well in my role and had been able to provide faith to my manager that I will not let her down. However, I am sure not all managers could have taken this risk. I was soon given this portfolio at a regional level in addition to my development role then. It was a huge step for me and an unknown territory, both in terms of job content and stakeholders. I was suddenly expected to create an agenda on something which I was passionate about and had no experience or background supporting me. I was now dealing with my global diversity team which had people who have been Diversity professionals for a lifetime.

I was expected to manage stakeholders at APAC leadership levels and clients who had limited understanding or appreciation of the concept. Diversity was at best understood as something related to harassment and discrimination at workplace. As I started on this journey, I had many fears, concerns and was not sure if I was ready. What I was always confident about is that when I needed some answers or a sounding board, I always had my manager. A manager who had faith in me and trusted me and, more importantly, clearly expressed that she was always available for me.

I remember sometimes when I felt I had made mistakes, felt very disappointed with myself and wanted to give up, I got a tough feedback which was not easy but not once did I feel the feedback meant criticism, and I knew it was meant to make me succeed. Through these lessons, I learnt not only about creating a meaningful agenda from scratch, but more about how my manager groomed me for a role which required a high level of interaction with senior stakeholders. She is one of the best HR professionals who I have worked with and is good at stakeholder management. She is a unique blend of strategy and execution. Often she would spend time in reading my emails, business proposals, and coach me through the process and, most importantly, was always available when I needed her time.

The biggest lesson I learnt here was that as Manager, giving a hot job is not enough. A wonderful boss has to guide through the process and set up the person for success and not failure. I never imagined that the additional portfolio of diversity started as a project work would lead to a full time agenda for the bank. Today also we are grappling to find out answers to questions but the questions with which we grapple today have changed. Today many more minds are at work not only from HR but also senior business leaders.

Sponsorship does not only mean giving stretch or visible assignments. I have seen it playing in daily conversations and is easiest for managers as they know their team the best. My current manager who is the Global Head of Diversity is perhaps the biggest advocate of sponsorship as a good leadership practice in the firm. I see her playing this effortlessly as a manager and making it simple though the concept sounds complex. She demonstrates this in various ways which have had a huge impact on my career. For instance, she never leaves a chance to talk about my successes wherever she can and wherever I deserve. She is constantly talking to my senior stakeholders and understanding their feedback which helps me grow further. She is constantly looking for ways to provide me with more visibility with key stakeholders and often more than what I would ask for. She is a senior leader who has come from the business. It has been an enriching experience to work with her and understand how business people think, communicate, and like to see information. She has given me tremendous flexibility and empowerment to do my job my way, but yet I feel a great sense of alignment with her strategy and her vision. I feel few leaders are able to get that balance of control and empowerment right.

I have learnt some interesting ways of leading from her. She is task focused yet concerned about the people aspect. She is constantly challenging and making the team think differently. She expects her team to develop commercial acumen and work as true strategic partners with the business. She not only expects, as any good manager would do, but demonstrates these expected behaviours in action and role models them for the team which is what makes her stand apart. She has coached me on many occasions where I have joined meetings with the seniormost stakeholders to see how she deals with a conversation and that has often helped me get a foot into the door.

Moving to Singapore was a part of this strategy to help me be closer to my clients and establish relationships, build credibility and take my agenda to the next level. Though that meant moving many pieces on my personal front and taking a risk after coming back from my maternity leave, soon I realised how much that added to me as a professional and how that made me more effective in my role and helped me build perspectives by living in a global environment. This was yet another example for me on how a wonderful boss is not thinking about the role but also exploring strategies to groom you and provide you experiences to help you shine in a role.

One of my biggest learning's from my experience with her is her ability to adopt new ideas, new technologies and use them to be more effective professionally. We often talk about Gen. Y's love and adaptability for new technology and often stereotype that baby boomers are close to experimentation or using new methods of doing work. With my manager, I believe she is the best example to challenge such stereotypes. In my opinion, in most organisations, we overdo with confidentiality of information. To a significant extent this is valuable, but I feel this is sometimes overused and perhaps we reach a point where we don't want to be vulnerable with too much of feedback coming our way.

For instance, at the bank, we recently moved to a very unique communication platform which in simplest terms is our version of facebook. I heard multiple concerns from various people on the utility of this platform and could see some resistance in the name of what we work with is sensitive. I am truly amazed to see how my manager adopted this platform and how we created one of the fastest growing communities of diversity on this platform. It led to a movement where suddenly thousands of people were engaged in our agenda, wanted to know more, contribute, give ideas, and be a part of our journey.

We provide most of our information on this platform and make it available to employees and soon realised the benefit of being transparent and how this has strategically added value to what we are trying to achieve. I recall how one of the senior leaders thought this platform will open a can of worms whereas what I learnt from my manager is to be effective and sustainable, "Let the can open and then clean up if required and use the power of multiple people or minds". She believes in establishing feedback channels and is constantly asking the question – "How do we get better?"

As a manager, she demonstrates by examples and expects us to constantly think, challenge and find out newer ways of working and be transparent as a team. I see her adopting the principle of openness and transparency in every transaction which has helped us create a team where we leverage each other's strengths, share knowledge and best practices and work efficiently with defined resources. This level of transparency and open discussions have helped build trust in a diverse team of individuals who have perhaps never met each other and come from five different regions, multiple nationalities and still work cohesively as a team. Wonderful bosses demonstrate behaviours they expect from their team and create an environment of fairness, transparency where everyone wants to constantly improve and give their best.

I would like to share another important incident which taught me a different aspect of managing people. In year 2009, I was in the family way. It was a time for immense change around me. I was in the early stages of giving shape to a regional diversity agenda. My spouse, who has been of tremendous support throughout, after a long stint moved jobs. One of my managers moved out and a new manager came in and most importantly post my maternity leave, we were to relocate to another country. We both were standing at the cross-roads, exploring what to solve and how to solve. By that time, I was senior enough to hear horror-stories from my female friends on how the initial excitement of conceiving a baby, the anticipation of hearing the first cry, and seeing the first smile dies down by the time a lady goes on maternity leave. One of my friends once narrated this to me:

For the last three months before going for my maternity leave, the only areas where me and my manager have been conversing is how I am going to handover my projects, and if I can delay my leave and join back early. How will I cheat the organisation if I don't join back and what are the different ways I can be reached. And on the last date there was an All the Best and Get Back Soon post-it on my desk.

I feel the serenity prayer by Reinhold Niebuhr will be in order here. "God, grant me the serenity to accept the things I cannot change. The courage to change the things I can. And the wisdom to know the difference."

Now, let me tell you my story. At the outset, I must say that my managers played an outstanding role to ensure this phase remains as a phase which I would always look back with fond memories of how managers can handle concerns of both the sides gracefully yet objectively. Yes, I had lengthy discussions of high impact projects, handover of key activities, phasing of activity calendar, my joining back plan and many more. But all these discussions were thought through and immaculately executed that I am proud of them. The special event of my life remained special and will always be. Not only because I made it special or my family wanted it that way but my managers and colleagues, everyone around me wanted it that way.

Caring

My son was born on 10 October. We received innumerable gifts, cards and texts from different parts of the world. Two messages stood out. One was from our close family member and the other one was from my manager. The card read, "The picture which you see on the card is of a ladybug. Here, we believe that the ladybug brings in good luck. This ladybug, will not only bring in good luck for your family but will always protect your son from everything evil throughout his life. With all my wishes…." This was so personal and reassuring that even today my eyes get moist when I read this note. My spouse and I still hold this message close to us because for a parent, nothing else really matters. (Emotional touch and care is of utmost importance and touches a chord close to your heart. This is something which bosses must keep in mind. These gestures appear to be small but have a high impact on people you lead).

Then started the grinding period for a mother where I almost forgot that I ever worked. There was guilt on one side of leaving Shreeyansh, my son, and going for work. On the other hand, I was so unsure of how will I be able to manage so many new things together, how will I catch up with so many projects which happened in my absence. I simply did not realise when my managers reached out to me gradually, warmly and softly, and integrated me with my work-life. There was no single announcement of change which happened in my responsibility area without adequate heads-up to me in my absence. I was also touched when my regional reporting manager came from Singapore on business to Mumbai and made sure to visit me and bless my new born son. He had two objectives to achieve – one to meet my son and wish us and secondly to slowly help me reintegrate into work, share all that has been going on while I was away from the workplace, and more importantly help me orient for my post maternity country relocation to Singapore.

He spent several hours with me and my spouse to answer our questions and clarify all our doubts and concerns. I recall how much we appreciated that evening with him as that made us much more comfortable with our decision in the middle of several changes we were going through. Strictly speaking this gesture was not required in professional terms, but the impact it had on me during one of the most sensitive stages of my career was significant and I give much credit to him for being so patient in easing out from my country and maternity transition at the same time. On the day of joining, it seemed the workplace was looking forward for me to join. And the moment I joined, all my apprehensions took a flight out of the window. One of my key learning's is, "wonderful bosses need to find out a way of how they can be a part of special events in their team member's life."

If it was not for him, I may not have had the courage to take this assignment right

after my maternity and still be productive from my first day of arrival in Singapore. He not only ensured I have a smooth transition, but very subtly took all the steps to bring me up to speed in a new country and help me build my brand and establish credibility. He did that by making me attend various senior forums where he could have covered my remit, but he always pushed me to come and present my agenda. At first, I did not get his point and felt he was delinking me from his team but over time, I realised what plan he was working towards. His mantra was to surprise the audience but never to surprise me. He always gave me heads-up to prepare well to present at forums where people expected him to present. He slowly started to take a back seat and gave me all the visibility which on one side created some anxiety for me but on other led to a great sense of confidence and responsibility. Wonderful bosses invest their time and take pride in grooming their team to the next level and do it without calling it out.

My journey from there would have looked very different if it was not for him who set this fantastic foundation for me. Over the years there have been many times when I was down, I did not know what is to be done, how certain projects were to be dealt with, but some of my wonderful bosses saw that as an opportunity to strengthen our relationship. They have given more than they should have; they stood next to me. However, they never did it for long, nor did they do it too many times. They knew exactly when to move on. Sometime they saw it through, sometimes they did not, sometimes they even pushed me into difficult situations, but every time I came out of such situations, I came out stronger as a professional and a stronger human being.

There was one incident which comes to my mind immediately. In my role, I was a part of a steering committee for the inaugural Asia Pacific wide regional conference on Promoting Diversity Agenda. This was a two and a half hour participation-by-invitation conference where the most senior employees across the region fly-in. The client list is illustrious as it can get and the speakers travel across the world. The success of the conference was important for the firm to set a new direction and make a significant contribution in this region on Diversity where the concept is still nascent. For me, being the Diversity Lead for the Region and a professional, this project was important. Therefore, it was a high stake situation, a lot of respect and brand that the firm created were at stake, the credibility of the steering committee, many of whom have been a role-models for so many, was at stake.

This project was more complex than it looked to be for a two and a half hour conference. The planning started almost nine months ahead to ensure the dates do not clash with the firm's global calendar of business events and the regional events of other corporations or organising bodies. It did not stop here; there were decisions which needed global and regional alignment, sometimes buy-in from all the key stakeholders and some of these decisions were complex enough to be deliberated for incredibly long periods. Then the already committed engagements of the speakers, creating a premium experience among all the attendees and, above all, creating an exciting format for engagement between the speaker and the audience are just a few out of many more. One of the most interesting insights of this format was every minute is critical. Every minute sub optimally delivered in the conference would have been an opportunity lost. There were no chances of making any mid course correction because there is no mid point practically in a two and a half hour conference.

Given the conference invites senior Leaders across the region, we also took an opportunity to plan additional strategic initiatives in the same week and make use of their physical presence in one location. This was my first time and with several key stakeholders engaged in the conversation across the globe, I just had to get it right. I remember how overwhelmed I was and was finding difficult to deal with multiple priorities in that week. I can never forget how my Manger flew in from Hong Kong and camped with the steering committee for a week to ensure the conference succeeds.

The steering committee consisted of the most senior leaders of the region. Therefore, neither was there a capability concern nor was there a lack of commitment from any of us. We had put in tremendous amounts of efforts to get everything going. Invites were specifically designed, promotion campaigns were all over the city, the stage and ambience created in the convention centre was exceptional, the line of speakers were one of the best available, but still he made it a point to go through it all over with me. Both of us briefed each of the speakers for sharpening the message, looked at almost all logistical details, asked anticipatory questions, checked for back-up plans, helped us take some conference decisions and, on the day before, created excitement, momentum and connected us to a legacy.

He knew the amount of pressure we had due to various stakeholders engaged at the last minute. He made sure to call me and be a sounding board where I could speak out my mind, express my frustration, and helped me refocus on my job. His decision of being physically present in Singapore for that week was a surprise to me. He only had to say, "Anu, you focus on the conference and I will take care of the rest," given there were several other important activities planned in that week. I did not ask for it but his presence made a difference to me and gave me much confidence. I felt I had some one standing beside me and I gathered a sense of strength.

On the day, he was a part of the success which we all created and at the end doled away every bit of credit to me and moved out. This was not the end. Wherever he went thereafter, he never missed out a single opportunity to talk about our conference and how the steering committee made it come alive. After the conference, there were a flood of congratulatory emails, special notes and warm hugs. And this is how a wonderful boss can support a girl from one of the small places of India going across countries. The learning for me was wonderful bosses help their team members succeed and stay at it.

There were a few other Learnings from this incident. My manager led gracefully despite pressure without making it evident for me. This is not easy, certainly not easy for anyone. Externally, the brand of the firm, created over decades, was at stake and internally, the credibility of the steering committee, many of whom are role models to many, was at stake. The scale and the complexity of this conference could have been immensely imposing. Good Managers show grace under pressure. As I grow older, I recognise how rare I get to experience this trait.

While working with him, I also realised that sometimes some bosses know more about what their team members want than the team members themselves! This was a tremendous insight for me.

What I am going to say now may not be equally acceptable to many. Never mind, let me still say it. At least it might remain as a thought with some. In my current firm, I have completed seven years. Some of you might laugh at me, some of you might say, "I am a fossil," and some of you might say, "There's no one in the market to provide me with a role." But I am happy I did it like this. One of my key take-away is, one needs to invest in a relationship, be it with a firm or a manager. Once you have invested in a firm, you create a support infrastructure around. This support infrastructure will help you succeed sometimes. Sometimes, this infrastructure would like you to succeed more than what you want out of yourself. Over time, there is a momentum which gets built around you where even individual managers sometimes keep aside their preferred styles of leadership and submit to the greater purpose. I have worked with several bosses here perhaps many more bosses than what I would have got if I had switched firms, but my observation has been: "wonderful bosses are always a part of your career even if you are not with them any more . . . and sometimes you don't even know how and when they contribute but they certainly do."

More often than not, as a team member we get caught in the whirlpool of, "should not the organisation provide me with what I want and then ask for contributions?" And sometimes managers think the reverse, "Contribute first and then ask." I have been a part of these never-ending debates enough and more. And suddenly, "Organisation becomes them and never us," for an employee. My first question has always been that who owns this relationship? I sincerely think this relationship is as much to the bosses' as much as it is to the team member. But the nature of the relationship sometimes makes us see this as an either or relationship rather than an and relationship.

This relationship is about powering together. I am yet to see a successful team which is driven only by the managers or by the team members. In some cultural contexts, keeping aside power distance sometimes gets difficult, but the more I see an unstoppable team, the more I am convinced about the way forward. The need to make this relationship work is equally split. The irony is, more often than not, one side expects the other side to initiate conversation of powerful together, and the wait continues, sometimes forever. My learning is, there are no two sides in this relationship, there is only one.

I have been fortunate enough to work in multiple countries, with people from multiple nationalities and multiple generations, however, I am yet to come across a team member who does not like her or his manager to be away, be it for business or personal. The answer mostly was the sense of letting be on one's own. Hearing this, I asked, so what happens if the manager lets her or his team member be on her or his own when physically present around you? I was told, "Then the manager is not a manager enough." Therefore, managers face a vicious crossroad.

The firm which I work with operates in an extremely matrixed environment. The number of managers I report to directly and indirectly are three and I have stopped counting the number of stakeholders who I need to align for the work which I do.

The most authentic thing about us is our capacity to create, to overcome, to endure, to transform, to love, and to be greater than our suffering.

And yes, before I forget, all these managers operate from three different time zones. Therefore, as a team member, the days of walking into boss's cabin, whenever there is a red flag, is over. Also the days of close supervision are over. Today's boss only wants reassurance from the team member that projects are under control. Today's manager wants escalations to be made at the right time. The fact is today's manager does not have an option but to trust his or her team members. And today's team member does not have an option but to own up. If these ways of engagement are established early, then the foundation for this relationship is set right.

One of the key Leadership traits which are non-negotiable for me is authenticity. A lot of wonderful bosses, because of their success, get a stronger feeling of their own infallibility. But I was fortunate here too. Most of my bosses admitted to themselves and to me that they are imperfect. And for me, it is absolutely acceptable to be imperfect as long as you recognise that others are also imperfect. With one of my wonderful bosses the journey we set out on was to grow together individually. One of my key takeaways from this relationship was that even when two imperfect human beings are together, the relationship still can be meaningful, forward looking and perfect. My wonderful managers, have almost always seamlessly blended their staidness with their sense of being human.

I always knew that my managers can deal with every matter with speed, precision and without getting perturbed, but since the time I got to know that my manager, sometimes, is as vulnerable as me, I have started connecting with their whole self. My manager is also like me. I have experienced this from managers from both the genders and different nationalities, which really goes beyond the traditional wisdom that typically female managers and Indian managers open up more than anyone else.

As I come to the last phase of my note, let me pause and summarise all my learning's. In summary, these are the behaviours that have made an impact on me and I would like to demonstrate to my team members as I grow in my role as a manager.

Final Tips

1. Wonderful bosses are great mentors and effective Sponsors.

   - Identify stretch roles, take a chance and support them through the process.
   - They don't take no for an answer, if they are convinced. Rather help answer, "What's it going to take to help you be successful at it."
   - They work hard to allow you to come out of their wings and shine.
   - Help build your personal brand and visibility.

2. Wonderful bosses show flexibility of styles.

- Balance of strategic and visionary, yet are into details when required.
- Balance of control, alignment and empowerment.
- Do not need to be an expert at everything but should know how to manage a bunch of experts.
- Balance of professionalism, humility and accessibility.
- Wonderful bosses demonstrate grace under pressure.
- Know when to step in and stand by you.
- Support you during times of pressure when it is easy to get into a blame game.
- Make things right when they are wrong and don't let their egos come in the way of doing the right things.

4. Wonderful bosses understand the power of diversity, authenticity and vulnerability.

- They understand that being authentic sometimes makes you vulnerable.
- Understand if you can't be authentic, you can't be productive.
- Value the diversity of people, styles and thought, and use it to the advantage.
- Get to know their team well beyond their Job Descriptions to allow space for authenticity.
- Do not follow a norm of success and consciously go out of their comfort to build diverse teams.
- Model the behaviours they seek.

5. Wonderful bosses talk straight.

- They give feedback as it is and don't shy away from the tough messages.
- They give it timely and are prompt in not only constructive feedback but also passing on the positive feedback.
- Genuinely use feedback as a tool for success and not to communicate failure.
- Make sure your success is their success and celebrate it.
- Are transparent and fair to all in the team.

This is not to say that I have not had a share of my bad experiences or not so wonderful bosses. We all live in a realistic world and come across all kinds of people and all kinds of managers. The old saying, "People leave bosses and not organisations" is true for me and the reverse is equally true for me, i.e. "People stay for bosses and not organisations."

I have not elaborated on the managers who did not tick a number of above behaviours or did not fit into my framework of a wonderful boss. The reason being as I earlier mentioned, this note is to celebrate and share my experiences of my wonderful bosses and, more importantly, I must admit I have had few managers who did not add perspectives to me or did not contribute to my career. I have certainly grown with managers with whom I did not have the best of my experiences and, in some respects, learnt many managerial lessons on what not to do as a manager, which is an equally important insight. But I wonder have I been lucky to have had so many wonderful bosses or experiences to cherish, who have taught me much more about Leadership than what I could have gathered from literature.

When I think deeply about it, many times, I get a sense that that the best boss or wonderful boss concept is backward looking for many. What I mean to say is we, almost always, tend to start with our last boss and not the current boss while looking at good qualities. We always look into the past. It seems to become our second nature that it is only hindsight which makes us realise what we had missed? I am no exception to this. Initially, I had worked with a boss, who was conventional in nature, yet used to hear me out till I would not have a single word to say. One of my managers gave me great visibility without my asking for any. My other manager always used to look at my work with hawk-eyes but got the best out of me. One of my managers helped me build a network across the most senior leaders in the firm. One of my managers took special care to ensure that the show-stoppers are always kept at a bay.

When I was going through it, more often than not, I did not appreciate how they had all contributed to my growth. Yes, it would have been great to have all these qualities from the same manager, but God takes time to walk into life, isn't it? To be candid, I never expected it too. Therefore, my only suggestion is let us not take the present for granted. We should identify good things in our present boss that will make life better and more productive, else the search for a wonderful boss can prove to be endless....

A manager giving a hot job is not enough. A wonderful boss has to guide through the process and set up the person for success and not failure.

13

Vandana Saxena Poria *OBE*
(Order of the British Empire)
CEO
Get through Guides

Navigating the Signposts of the Business World: How a Wonderful Boss Can Guide you Effectively

"I believe that bosses act as signposts and help you navigate the journey you undertake. They help you find the right path even if it seems hidden, difficult to find or simply impossible."

As we all know, life has many journeys in store for us. Our working life is one of our most important journeys. This journey shows us what we are and what we are capable of. Where we can excel and where we recognise there is room for improvement. I believe that bosses act as signposts and help you navigate the journey you undertake. The right boss will help you find the right path, even if it seems hidden, difficult to find, or simply impossible.

I decided to write this chapter to show how a good boss can have such a different and dramatic impact at various stages in one's life. So rather than write just about him and his brilliant attributes, I decided to show how he has and continues to influence me from the first day that we met until the present day. I am eternally grateful for the lessons that were taught consciously and subconsciously over the years.

I first came into contact with James Cooper in 1995 when I was 24. My first interaction with him was when I was in the role of a customer. I had been put through to him as I was looking to buy training services from a UK listed company, BPP Plc. He had picked up the request and called me back. At the time, I was based in Bucharest, Romania, working for Ernst & Young (E&Y). My staff needed training and I had experienced BPP Plc's training firsthand as I had studied with them for my Chartered Accountancy exams in the UK. James had called me, as the person who usually dealt with overseas training was on holiday, and I had asked for a swift call back. At the time I spoke to him, I had no idea who he was. He explained in detail how the training would work. He knew the products and services inside out and at every point he gave me alternatives as I was concerned about costs. He followed up and ensured that I was satisfied with the decision that was made. He also introduced me to the responsible person that I could book further orders with.

My next interaction with him was about seven months later. I had spent a lot of time training my staff at E&Y and realised that not only was there a huge need for training, but I also enjoyed teaching the staff. I had found my calling, but how was I to make teaching my profession? A friend and I had now decided we wanted to quit E&Y and move into training full time. The obvious journey was to contact BPP Plc and see whether they would let us train on their behalf in Romania. So I called up James. He was surprised but not dismissive of our idea. However, he was cautious. He said that BPP would be willing to discuss this but I would need to come to London to have a chat. I went to the UK and met James face to face in January 1997. At that time, I still had no idea exactly who he was within BPP.

It was 2nd January 10 am and I remember thinking it to be strange that he wanted to have a meeting on that date. Most people were still recovering from the new year festivities. James, however, seemed fresh and relaxed. James asked me several questions about our set up and what the market was like. He then explained BPP was quite ethnocentric and risk-averse so did not feel that they would be interested in expanding outside the UK. This was another interesting thought, how narrowly focused they were but also how successful they were in their niche.

At this point I asked him who he was within BPP. He apologised and gave me his card. It was only when I saw his card that I realised he was a full Board Director and responsible for the most successful divisions within the BPP Plc Group. So the first lesson on this journey was the lesson of humility. He had never overplayed his position, nothing was too low-level or highbrow for him and that, subconsciously, I deeply admired in his behaviour.

James, however, was interested in understanding the potential opportunity that a region he knew little about could be. His mind was always calculating the next step and trying to work out the best route to get to his goal. He, therefore, agreed to come to Romania and asked me to plan a short 3-day trip for him in March or April. James had a small pocket diary with him and within seconds, he had worked out which week he would be able to come out. So here was the next lesson. He was an organised guide. He helped me understand what his objectives were, if there was a sustainable, profitable market for BPP training?, work out what the important elements of setting up a BPP centre would be, and left me to work out if I could pull the trip together. And so began my journey in training.

During the intervening weeks, I built up an itinerary for James, with visits to potential clients, meetings with potential trainers and a visit to a prospective training centre. The trip to Romania was quite successful. Many blue-chip clients were ready to sign straight away for courses and James could clearly see that there was a market. But here was the next lesson I learnt from him. He had to balance the opportunity with the risks that the BPP Board would perceive. In the end, he created a win-win situation. He agreed to give my colleague and me a franchise to run BPP. BPP would invoice and collect the money and then it would advance us a percentage to run the operations. At the end of the year, we would do a final tally and share the remaining revenues.

At this stage, James could have just left us alone to get on with growing the business. He, however, chose to continue to guide me and help me create paths that would lead to successful journeys and guide me away from paths that would not. For example, a potential training opportunity came up in Greece. I called James for advice on what to do. He realised it was for an important BPP client and cleared his diary to come with me for the meeting. By coming to the meeting, he empowered me both in my eyes and in the eyes of the client. the client realised that they were important to BPP and that BPP trusted me to deal with this client going forward.

However, in the end the Greek company were not willing to pay the minimum rate set by us internally and James told me that despite investing time in this venture, we should not take on the assignment. I wanted to take the assignment on, but he talked through the transaction with me and made me realise that my time was more valuable than the revenue that would be brought in through this client. If I spent that same amount of time on trying to gain more profitable clients, the journey would be more profitable for us. He helped me reflect on the advantages and disadvantages. But the final decision was mine and I agreed with his logic and we dropped the client.

By this stage, James had seen that I had a subconscious ability to develop business, train people and develop a team. I was still young and oblivious to my own strengths and weaknesses, but he was able to extract the essence of my good points and bad points. Time and again, he would send me opportunities, each one testing a different aspect of me. He was trying to see how I would react with different assignments and see how well or badly I would do. The aim was not to see where I failed, but where I needed help and extra guidance. This included giving me the opportunity to write a textbook for BPP on International Accounting Standards. Asking me to represent BPP in contract negotiations for work in Slovakia and doing some training in the UK.

Each time he would set the guidelines and I would report back in. He would then see where I needed extra support. For example, in Slovakia the client required that we provide training for 14 different exams. My team in Romania, which was closely located to Slovakia, could provide training for eight of the papers. James introduced me to others based in the UK who would be able to teach the other papers. He realised that this was an expensive proposition.

But at the same time, he would never send me into the lion's den without support. He would always ensure that I was ready for the task. For example, early on, he judged me and realised that while I had the ability to teach, I had never been trained to teach. BPP's training for new trainers then was world-class, so he sent me on the course, to give me the tools that I could apply while teaching. I knew that I enjoyed teaching, but I had no idea about how to do it professionally. During the course, I took to teaching like a duck to water. I did not realise it at the time, but I had found out later that James had been extremely involved in developing the whole recruitment, testing and teacher training course that BPP had.

He believed that within 5–7 minutes of seeing someone try to teach a simple topic (with some previously explained guidance), you could tell immediately if they would be a good teacher. He and the team at BPP were rarely wrong on this. He understood the most important outcome for the customer, that is a good teacher who can teach the student how to get through a competitive exam. This meant ensuring the recruitment and training process of a BPP teacher was extremely robust and progress could be monitored. He had recruited high quality people to run each of these areas and they reported in based on key objectives. For new trainers, the objective was based on student feedback on the trainers.

About 12 months later, BPP Romania was successfully providing courses to most of the blue chip companies in the country and we had also branched out into teaching in neighbouring countries, including war-torn Serbia. James sensed that BPP Romania's success could be pivotal to BPP Plc's international growth. So he was interested in exploring whether the path we were on in Romania could be replicated in other countries. And he believed in the growth story enough to set up a new division at BPP, called BPP International, which would spearhead growth in Eastern Europe initially, with the intention of expanding outwards.

At that time, James empowered me again. He realised that he would need someone who had lived abroad and understood how different markets functioned to lead the new operation. Moving to a new country and setting up a business can be a daunting task, so he felt confident that someone who had experience at living abroad would probably fare better than someone directly from the UK. He thought of me. So far, my journey had been mainly in Romania, where I lived, worked, spoke the language and had a huge network. James wanted BPP plc to take a new journey and branch out into the international world. He had seen my courage by giving up a secure job to do something I was passionate about and also my tenacity in expanding the business in Romania.

I was now 27 years old. He threw me a lever, a real opportunity to take my journey to a different level by asking me to set up the international division, move to countries and replicate Romania's success. I felt honoured but also hesitant. Could I really do this? Without formal training? Could I really move countries and set up successful businesses? I had a huge advantage in Romania as I knew the market well. I was up for the challenge but not sure I could succeed. James had thought this through. He was ready to support me with the same unbiased guidance that he had given me setting up BPP Romania.

We were now at a crossroad, with many paths in front of us. We had so many countries we could potentially expand into; which should we choose? So that is when we both went away and did our independent research. James helped me come up with a way to rank the countries and decide which one we should target. This system of prioritising helped narrow down the number of paths in front of us. It also helped me see paths which were steep with high gains and paths which were more gentle but with lower gains. We both agreed that Russia, Czech, Poland and Hungary were possible options as next target markets. On further research with more relevant criteria, we narrowed onto one path, Russia.

I went on a look-see visit to Moscow in June 1998. Before I went, James and I wrote down a brief list of what we needed for the business to succeed. He always concentrated on the big picture of viewing the path, who were the clients that could take us to instant profitability or near profitability, and who could be easy wins. So we concentrated on taking our training offering to the Big four Accounting firms and the large UK Multinationals. I had to use contacts to get meetings with these, which I did with surprising ease. James, however, was not surprised. He expected this to be easy for me as networking and getting meetings was one of my core strength. I started to become aware of this strength when he was totally unimpressed at the number and quality of meetings I had fixed. This was now a given and I had to work on developing other parts of my character to continue to grow.

In June or July, I spent a week in Moscow. It was an amazing place but very different from Romania. I managed to have a few intensive Russian lessons and got the hang of the Cyrillic alphabet. James again was not surprised to hear this. He knew (whereas I still didn't) that I was a natural with languages. He had identified another one of my core strengths, and before my going to Moscow, had facilitated these language lessons with a group company. He knew it would give me a little more confidence in a new market.

While it was a little frightening, hearing the Mafia stories and seeing many men in black suits with dark glasses, I was pleased with how the meetings went in Moscow. Generally, the clients were receptive and there was interest from everyone. It appeared our competitors were not providing much customer service, nor were the pass rates high. I felt confident that I would be able to crack the market. James and I poured over my findings when I got back. We made a budget and together worked out it would probably take three years to break even. I was getting excited as we were starting to create the path that I was supposed to walk on over the next three years. I now had to arrange for the move, so I spoke to relocation agents about moving towards the end of the year. However, what we were not prepared for was the Russian Crisis of September 1998. Business literally dropped off a cliff overnight. So all our hard work and preparation had gone up in smoke.

Did James regret or resent this? No, this was business. One path was destroyed but if you looked carefully, several other paths were still there. We still had our initial research from other countries. We had of course looked at the Czech Republic, Poland and Hungary. On the morning that the crisis broke, James phoned me up and said, "OK, so plan B, I think Poland".

On reflection, James subconsciously knew that the change of direction from Russia would have a huge impact on me as I had been working towards that move relentlessly. So he realised that it would be better for him to choose the new path and to help me understand his choice. Although the Czech Republic was a suitable alternative path, it was a much smaller country and the gains potentially lower. So it was a gentler and easier alternative path. Hungary, in James' eyes, was a weak path as they had no direct need for our services. Poland, on the other hand, was a much bigger country of 40 million people and there were many of our potential clients out there. So the switch to the path of Poland was the best choice.

I remember thinking at the time about how unemotionally James had made the decision. Even though both of us had invested time and effort into building the path to Russia and that was now wasted, he did not spend any time on thinking about the destroyed path. It was like an act of nature had destroyed that path and there was nothing that could be done about it. Move on.

So, we now had a pivot leading to a lever which would build a new path. James' thought process was the pivot and he was moving me on track from the Russia path to the Poland path. I was the lever that would build the new steep path. James decided to come to Poland with me for the first look-see visit. We had some interesting meetings and through the British Embassy, understood the Polish economy and the extent of British Businesses in Poland. I was not prepared for how much the Poles then looked down on the Romanians. They kept saying that what would work in Romania would not work in Poland, as Poland was much more advanced than Romania. I quickly learnt that I would have to play down my Romanian experience and play up BPP's listed status and 25 years of experience. James was amused at my change in business development tactics. But again for him, this was a given core strength of mine.

He pointed out to me that he liked my ability to adjust according to the situation and this would be critical if BPP International was to be successful. I realised that I had learnt this from him, his ability to pick up a direction and just move events around to make something happen like BPP International.

During that trip, I also saw a different side of James. He was annoyed with me as I had not given him some reporting data that he had required. He was also annoyed that the hotel we had chosen was a pretty expensive one. But even when he was annoyed, it meant that the conversations were brief and to the point. He never got angry and I had never seen him lose his cool. From this incident, I learnt about two major weaknesses of any business: reporting deadlines and costs. These are fundamental to staying on a path, indeed in ensuring the path continues to be built and is a strong clear path. James was an expert at both.

He delegated efficiently and also monitored the key outcomes efficiently. He distilled the essence of all his divisions, so he knew how the year would pan out. For example, in the training business, students sign up for exams. In order to predict training revenue, James set up systems to get information fed to him on the number of student enrolments on a week-by-week basis. He would look for trends in when people signed up for courses, so he could then predict with a great degree of accuracy what the final revenue would be, just from observing trends in the early weeks of enrolments. If the figures were looking lower than expected, he would look into where the student enrolments were lower and take some form of corrective action.

Back to Poland: I stayed on in Warsaw for four days after James left. I was extremely disturbed and overwhelmed. This new country was expensive, we had an entrenched competitor that clients seemed happy with. I knew no one, I could not speak the language and I did not understand the business dynamics. I felt completely out of my depth. I remember sitting in my hotel room doubting myself and wondering whether I was worthy of running this new venture.

At a time like this, it would have been easier to turn to James and ask for more guidance. However, I realised that it was time for me to walk by myself along this new path, see what was around it and then start building the path in the direction I knew would help the business succeed. Great words, but how do I start? I am not embarrassed to say that I shed more than a few tears. At 27, I felt I had been given a gargantuan task to complete. Idly, I picked up a local English speaking business newspaper called the Warsaw Business Journal. I noticed in the corner on the front page, an advertisement for a business mixer that was being run by the newspaper, in conjunction with Pricewaterhouse Coopers. It was for that evening in fact, it was starting half an hour later. I remember clearly sitting there on my bed and thinking about going. I remember also thinking that actually I just wanted to turn over in bed and go to sleep. Things always looked better in the morning.

Just then, I remember walking over to the mirror and saying to myself, "James has so much faith in you. You owe it to yourself to go. At worst it will be a waste of an evening (which would be exactly the same as if you stayed in this hotel room for the night). At best, you may make some contacts and after all, networking is your forte." I floated back to several conversations with James, where I realised that he was more of a loner. He on his own would have found it difficult to go to a brand new country and force himself to network.

His forte was analysis, reflection, strategy and implementation. While he was very good at asking the right questions to the right people to get the information that he wanted, when he was one-on-one with someone, he found it tough to just get out there and meet new people. He and I were very different. I was not so good at the analysis, but comfortable with meeting new people. So we potentially had a winning combination if I could show him that I could really network to bring in business.

So I picked myself up, changed and forced myself to go out to the Marriott on that cold, dark winter's night in Warsaw. I got to the venue and felt incredibly intimidated. Luckily I found a group of women almost immediately and hit it off with them. "What do you do?" asked one of them. "I work for a company you have probably never heard of and I will be moving out here to set up their Polish subsidiary," I said. "Which company?" they asked. "Oh, it's a listed company called BPP and provides training in finance and accountancy," I answered. They looked at me and laughed. One of them said, "Oh, I did my Chartered Accountancy exams with them," and one of the others piped up, "Yes I did CIMA with them." The third said, "Oh, I was with FTC, their competitor in the UK."

As luck would have it, two were senior managers from KPMG, one was a publisher and the other worked in the CFO office of Unilever Poland. This was the proverbial manna from heaven for me. All the companies were clients in other countries but, more importantly, here were women I could relate to. I explained to them that I would be moving to Poland in a month's time to set up BPP. Within 5 minutes, I had the name of an estate agent who would help me find a property to live in, a reliable taxi company, restaurants that did vegetarian food and, of course, personal contacts for meeting potential clients.

They were keen on meeting and welcomed me into their group unconditionally. It was incredible. Again, when I told James about this on the phone, he listened and then laughed. He said, "Well you know I am not going to say well done, because that is what I expected of you. Now get on building the business." He immediately told me that besides the activities I had planned, he had spoken to the language division who could get me in to meetings with their corporate clients. While the person who was responsible for language training would not be the same for management training, they would have the contacts to put me in front of the right people.

The risk of going out and the people I met that night, coupled with the contacts from the language business became levers to accelerate the development of the road that I had started to build. While James had not taught me that directly, his other lessons helped me get to this conclusion.

In it also lies one of the most important lessons that I learnt for myself. The one that you have to experience and understand by yourself and the one that all the great business leaders understand implicitly. You only have 24 hours in a day and everyone has the same amount of time, but it is how you choose to use those 24 hours that determines how well you build your path, how quickly you build it and where it takes you.

Although James was in the background as I developed the business in Poland, he increasingly left me by myself to figure out what to do. I think in his mind he had given me the guidance he could and it was now time for me to walk independently. Was I ready for it? No. Is anyone ever ready for it? I don't think so. I made many mistakes in the following 18 months, which I blame myself for and not him.

At the same time as I had moved to Poland in the beginning of 1999, a UK member of staff moved to Czech Republic to build the BPP business there. I had also recruited people to run the Slovakia operation of BPP where we had been running courses for a couple of years. James and I used to catch up during this time, once every few months. He always looked at the businesses objectively, always based on the financials. I, on the other hand, always viewed the businesses based on the number of clients we had won and kept. He kept drawing me back to the financials and I kept on going after new clients. We were treading the same path, but looking at it differently. That was a fundamental difference between him and me. I was very much a people's person and he was in some ways more of a loner.

He stayed out of the limelight, in the shadows and watched performances in a constructively critical manner. He looked at how they were pieced together and whether they would stay pieced together in the future. He was always looking to see how well the road was being built and what avenues were being developed off the main road. He was against dramatic development, preferring slow and steady. I, on the other hand, was hot-headed and looked for quicker and bigger wins. I learnt that his way of viewing the path was a much more robust view, as it was built on analysis of facts and figures, leading to a better way of extrapolating where the road would go and therefore what resources would be needed to keep building the path.

Towards the end of that year 1999, the Polish and Czech centres of BPP were starting to flourish. We had managed to start winning business away from competitors and build our businesses, although as expected at this stage they were still loss making. The Slovakia centre was also doing well. It had in fact become the only training provider in Slovakia for international finance qualifications. It was difficult controlling and monitoring the growth as it was happening so fast. I was also still relatively young and found it tough to remain authoritative with the people who were reporting in to me, especially as many of them were older and more experienced than me.

I did not voice this concern to James and in a way this is one of my biggest regrets even to date. I now look back and remember this characteristic of James clearly. He would never offer advice unless specifically asked for. If I asked it, in an unclear way, the answer would be equally unclear. So as a boss, in a way he reflected me, as he wanted me to make the decisions.

At this point, at the end of 1999, our journey together came to an end. My part of the business merged with another part of the BPP group, the language training part. I was asked to manage this new division and I was to report directly to the CEO of the BPP plc

Group. On reflection, I was probably not ready for this increased responsibility but, as stated before, are you ever? James and I kept in touch on an adhoc basis for a while, before I really did lose touch with him.

But some people come into your lives for other reasons. And will stay with you throughout. James was one of them. I was lucky enough to work with him again when I approached him to help me work out how to set up a business in India producing quality textbooks at an affordable price for students. He invested in the business and became a non-executive Director of Get Through Guides. But that's another story and another set of memorable lessons.

Unfortunately, as can be imagined, there are not so many great bosses out there. I have also had my fair share of not so good bosses. In a way, they were not willing to signpost the path or help me walk on it. I think they were on their own journey and did not make time to help those under them create a path that would ultimately help them, the boss, get to their destination quicker.

When I first arrived in Eastern Europe and was working for an accountancy firm, I had a boss who was working so many hours for clients that he had little time left for me or other staff members. We were a young team then and crucially needed help with time management and prioritisation skills. However, as is commonly known, you learn by example and, unfortunately, the main example we saw was always that of being totally overworked and chasing your tail.

I remember my first week in the office where I was left to my own devices to review an audit file and decide on the strategy for the current year's audit. After three years of experience in the UK, I was not ready to take this on and had no real guidance. I took the thin audit strategy document to my boss. He did not have time to read it or give me any input, so I had no idea if what I had done was correct or not. I felt like I was in the dark and there was not even a torch, let alone a signpost to help guide me. I asked others around me but in some ways asking others to give you a torch can be a confusing move. You are often not sure which path they are showing you and whether it is appropriate for you. In the end, I used the basics of auditing standards to come up with an approach that worked for this client.

Overall, my instincts were good, but there was a lot of time that could have been saved had my boss reviewed the strategy document earlier. So the path had become unnecessarily longer and more complicated, simply because he did not put in time at the beginning. I could not have known which direction to go in for the audit with my very few years of experience. If he had shown me a glimpse of the path, with perhaps a few signposts, I would have got there much quicker. However, I always believe that the glass is half-full rather than half-empty.

By going through this more difficult path, I learned how to become more self-reliant and how often there are tools around that can make the job easier. You just need to have the courage to make decisions for yourself. I guess it is not different to a baby learning to walk: if you keep moving all the obstacles out of the way, she will never learn how to navigate and will always see any large obstacles as blockages that cannot be passed through and so the baby gives up. However, if you leave a few obstacles lying about, after a few falls, the baby learns to navigate around these obstacles and can start to think for herself about what is and is not possible.

Another boss I had was the exact opposite of James. Let's call him bad boss, or BB. BB had no people skills whatsoever and believed the best way to deal with anyone was to bulldoze them into agreeing and continuing on a path. It was either his way or no way. I think the months that I spent working with him were the worst of my life. While BB had set up some successful offices in the UK, he had no idea how to share that knowledge with people who were working away from him, or adapt his knowledge to foreign markets. He was the true meaning of the word ethnocentric. He simply did not believe that any centre could be successful unless it was using the UK method of developing and running business.

So, over a period of time, he started to impose his ideas onto me and my team. This had disastrous outcomes. First, senior staff started to leave as they could not handle working for someone who had no idea of the local market conditions. Second, student numbers started to go down as he made us try techniques that were negative for our students.

I remember being in a meeting with him where he unilaterally tried to change my bonus agreement. Even if he had orders to do this from above, he made no effort to help me understand why the changes should be made and why in the longer term it would benefit me and other staff. His attitude was simply vicious, accept it or else. For a professional services firm, this was unacceptable. He had no idea of balance and how I needed to understand so I could convince the rest of the team to also accept the terms and conditions. If anything, he pushed me into a corner where I felt like I had to fight back. He never thought of how to make it a win-win situation. He wanted me to be an identical mirror to his views. He did not want any reflection and adjusting of his view.

Like James, he believed in following the numbers and was continuously monitoring results. This was usually a positive. However, that is where the similarities stopped. He never looked at where I needed to improve or provide guidance. He just expected me to get on and do things for myself, unless it suited him to do otherwise and often did not consider the consequences of his actions on the rest of us. He also had no regard for some of the most important of corporate rules. For example, he had often told me how none of us should ever speak about confidential matters to do with other Managing Directors (MDs). About a month later, I happened to phone him and he immediately started ranting down the phone about an MD that he had just sacked and proceeded to tell me in great detail about a fraud the MD had been involved in, then all the problems the MD had been having with other staff, thereby exposing the names of other staff who were still working for our organisation and disclosing confidential information of what they had been through. While it was very useful to me to be aware of these activities, I feel that he had breached the trust of staff who was still working for the organisation.

In terms of being a pivot, I honestly think the genuine lesson that he taught me was how certain people are so self-obsessed, that they cannot be pivots for others as they are too caught up in their own lives. Bad boss was also having an affair with someone relatively senior in the finance department which further undermined credibility in all of his subordinate's eyes. So he almost refused to make time to be pivotal to us in our lives, which was a great missed opportunity as we had an excellent team which was starting to deliver well.

Enough about my personal bad bosses. Having now been based in India for seven years, I have noticed characteristics of good and bad bosses even more. I feel that in India, many younger bosses are not given sufficient training in becoming a wonderful boss. If you think about it, even education teaches about leadership and management. It is always from the bosses' point of view. Actually, what is needed here, and elsewhere across the globe, is a different emphasis on the course, how to be considered a wonderful boss. The topics may be the same, but in the wonderful boss course, the emphasis is on how the people below you will be supported by your changing behaviour and how they can help you make those changes. Too many employees in India are completely terrified of their bosses so cannot even converse properly with them. We have to move away from this behaviour if we want to empower staff and help them build paths which will help move us all closer to our chosen goals.

I will end with the biggest reflection that my best and favourite boss, James indirectly taught me. We have a saying in English, "Give a man fish, he eats for a day. Teach a man to fish and he eats for a lifetime." James taught me to question this statement which has always been considered to be wise. It needs to be adjusted. In my view: if you have the wrong teacher, he may teach you to fish in an area where you don't have fish, or fish for fish that are harmful for you.

A wrong teacher can teach you to fish in an area where it will be unsustainable or fish for fish through methods that are ineffective. So perhaps we should change the saying to: "Give a man fish, he eats for a day. Teach a man to fish well and he eats for a lifetime."

The addition of the extra adjective changes the whole connotation of the sentence. I believe that is what James taught me. His unending patience, his analytical mind and his ability to foresee problems and solve them before becoming problems was mind blowing. The fact that he would then take the time to show me how he came to the conclusions and teach me how to do something right is the biggest blessing any boss can give his junior. Thank you James for the support you have given me and continue to give me. I am very grateful. And I hope that in some small way, I have been a wonderful and good employee that has also helped you see worlds that you may not have seen, had our paths not collided many years ago.

Too many employees in India are completely terrified of their bosses, so cannot even converse properly with them. We have to move away from this behaviour which will help us all to move closer to our chosen goals.

14

My Wonderful Boss

Sunil Sinha
Chief–Group Quality
Management Services
Tata Quality Management
Services, Tata Sons

A terrible boss can devastate not just your career but even your life. A comprehensive study in Sweden revealed that those with bad bosses suffered 20 to 40 percent more heart attacks than with good ones.

People join companies and leave their managers. This was the clear and firm conclusion reached by the Gallup Organisation when it conducted a widely quoted study, interviewing about two million employees at 700 companies, more than a decade ago. The study found that employees rate having a caring boss higher than they value money or other fringe benefits and perks.

Bosses are important to all of us. Having a wonderful boss enables the subordinate to contribute his or her best to the organisation. Studies have revealed that for more than three-quarters of employees, dealing with their bosses is the most stressful aspect of their job. A terrible boss can devastate not just your career but even your life. A comprehensive study in Sweden, a few years ago, tracking more than 3,000 executives for a decade, revealed that those with bad bosses suffered 20 to 40 percent more heart attacks than those with good bosses.

I have stayed in the Tata group for 30 years which bears testimony to the fact that I have been lucky to have good bosses. Hence, it was difficult for me to pick my Most Wonderful Boss. My journey with the group began in Tata Steel, which besides being a leading global steelmaker, is known as an institution for leadership building.

I served Tata Steel for 18 years in different capacities and functions including project management, total quality, international marketing, shipping, chartering, and human resources. My exciting journey with the group then took me, for two years, to Tata International and then, for the past decade I have been with Tata Quality Management Services (TQMS).

My personal journey was enriching in Tata Steel because I got a chance to work with several great and wonderful bosses. My first boss, who selected and hired me after I graduated in mechanical engineering from the Bihar College of Engineering, was Dr. Jamshed J. Irani.

Dr. Irani was also the one who later gave me a break to do something different from what I had learnt during my engineering career. During my career with Tata Steel, Dr. Irani invited me to be one of the members of the task force for implementing Total Quality in the company.

At Tata Steel, I also had the opportunity to work with Mr. Bushen Raina, who was the Head of International Trading, and I learnt my lessons in operational excellence from him. I also had the chance to work with Mr. Firdose A. Vandrevala, who was then the Vice-President, Marketing and Sales, at the company. I learnt a great deal from him about how to leverage people power in transforming an organisation from good to great.

Common Thread–My Wonderful Boss Over Many Years...

After I moved to TQMS, once again I got a chance to work with Dr. Irani. In fact, if there is a common thread running through my career with the Tata group, it has been the opportunity to work with Dr. Irani, who I would unhesitatingly select as My Wonderful Boss.

My career progression in more than a century old Tata group, India's most respected and admired business house, which comprises of over a hundred companies operating in seven business sectors, has a presence in more than 80 countries, employs more than 4,50,000 people and has revenues of $100 billion, has been closely associated with Dr. Irani.

From the time I met him first in 1982, at my job interview conducted by Tata Steel to recruit fresh graduates as apprentices, till 23 years later when I became the Chief, Group Quality Management Services of Tata Sons, Dr. Irani has been a mentor, guide, philosopher, and a guru for me.

What a remarkable and a wonderful boss he has been over these decades. Born on 2 June 1936, Dr. Jamshed Irani did his masters in Geology from Nagpur University before acquiring a Doctorate in Metallurgy from the University of Sheffield, England. He worked with the British Steel Corporation from 1963 to 1968, when he joined Tata Steel at the urging of JRD Tata, the late Chairman of the group.

"Quality Kingpin…"

Dr. Irani, who received the Padma Bhushan, and an honorary Knighthood (Knight Commander of the Most Excellent Order of the British Empire – KBE) may be best remembered today as the leader whose visionary stewardship turned a tired and ageing Tata Steel into one of the world's most efficient steel enterprises and set it on the path to becoming a global force. But an equally important, if less visible, contribution of his has been in making quality and business excellence central to the function of Tata enterprises. Known as the Quality Kingpin, he helped take business excellence to every corner of the vast Tata Empire.

His passion for quality took root during his time with Tata Steel from where he retired as managing director in 2001 after a remarkable career spanning 33 years. As Chairman, Tata Quality Management Services (TQMS), Dr. Irani played the role of a guide and mentor to mature the organisation that has become the crucible in which a raft of ideas and initiatives about business excellence, climate change, affirmative action, and more have been incubated, nurtured, and laid out for implementation across the Tata family of enterprises.

As mentioned earlier, my first interaction with my Wonderful Boss happened in 1982 just after I had been selected by Tata Steel following a campus interview. Dr. Irani, who was then the Deputy Managing Director of Tata Steel, was the Chairman of the interview panel. I subsequently joined the Engineering division of Tata Steel in Jamshedpur and started my career with the group.

My next interaction with Dr. Irani happened some time later, after I was put in charge of a project to set up a DG set based power plant. The company was looking for someone new to study the issue as it was felt that older people tended to discard new concepts. The challenge was to break all existing norms and install the plant within 6 months.

Since I did not know many norms, it was easy for me to set up new ones. I met the challenge and the diesel plant, comprising of 16 generating sets of 1 MW each, which was crucial for the success of the steel project was inaugurated by Dr. Irani ahead of the time schedule. The importance of the project can be reckoned from the fact the return on investment on this project was a phenomenal 900 percent. Dr. Irani appreciated my work.

This was a time in my life when I liked doing new things. In 1989, I had applied for a Rotary Club group study exchange programme which would fund the successful candidate's trip to another country for a brief study. There was just one opening for Jamshedpur and I was selected and got a chance to go to Sweden.

I went to Dr. Irani and told him I would be travelling abroad for the first time and would like to see some more things. Despite having met me briefly in the past, he immediately recognised me and acknowledged and recalled that I had worked on the power plant. He said he would like me to visit some of the steel plants in Europe. When I told him I did not have anything to do with steel making, he said it did not matter. He emphasised I would gain a lot from seeing the processes. He arranged for me to visit some of the newer plants in Europe. It was a great opportunity for me and a good break to learn at an early age. He always emphasised on capability building by visiting modern plants.

The Total Quality Concept...

This was a time when major changes were occurring in India. Tata Steel was looking for something different to do. It was the time when the Indian economy had started opening up. We had begun to hear of new concepts like the Total Quality programme that was being implemented in Japan.

In 1992, when Dr. Irani took on the mantle of the Managing Director of Tata Steel, he faced a major challenge of ensuring the steel company remained competitive and profitable. This was against the backdrop of the recommendation made by McKinsey and Co. in the late 1980s that the Tata Group should exit the steel business as it was value eroding for the shareholders. In 1991, the opening up of the Indian economy threw up a plethora of challenges, the major one being of the need for the steel company to stand on its own feet and become competitive rather than make money on a cost plus basis and break its past which had rendered the steel major ineffective in the achievement of operational efficiencies.

Therefore, Dr. Irani was confronted with the situation of having to make the elephant dance. The plant was undergoing modernisation in stages and he believed that this phase in the history of Tata Steel was dedicated to the modernisation of minds'. He believed that it did not involve expenditure of huge sums of money to create physical assets. Instead, it would take on the far more difficult task of orienting our greatest asset, our people, towards meeting the challenges and opportunities of the future.

One of the foremost achievements of Tata Steel under the stewardship of Dr. Irani was the phased reduction of its employees from over 78,000 in 1993 to around 48,000 in 2001, a move often referred as achieving downsizing without tears. 78,000 plus employees in 1993 collectively produced just 2 million tonnes of steel, when the market was becoming extremely competitive. An attractive golden handshake scheme was devised which offered a separating employee the same level of salary till the time of his scheduled retirement and a host of facilities. Indeed, it was so attractive that once at an external meeting, Dr. Irani was asked how he had introduced such a scheme. He was told that either Tata Steel had a lot of money, or that he did not have any brains. An unfazed Dr. Irani stuck to his guns and explained the rationale behind the unparalleled scheme.

Another challenge Dr. Irani faced was that of having to deal with requests for favours when the time came for a renewal of lease of the Chromite mines in Sukinda in Odisha. While the favours requested involved a far insignificant amount as compared to the investment of Tata Steel, under his leadership the company chose to opt for a partial renewal of its lease of mining rights rather than to succumb to unethical practices so characteristic of the Tata group. In order to implement the Total Quality Programme for enhancing operational excellence in Tata Steel and making the organisation competitive, Dr. Irani wanted to set up a small team of youngsters to work on the Total Quality Concept and promote and implement it in the Tata Steel group. On 30 August 1989, he called five of us and said he wanted to set up this Total Quality group. I told him that none of us knew even the "T" in total quality, and a little impudently questioned as to why was he selecting us. Dr. Irani admitted that even he did not know the concept and that he was going to Japan to learn about it.

He said, "If I am convinced, I will set up the team, which will report to me and change the culture and way of working at Tata Steel." "All of you have to learn the concept and implement the Total Quality programme in Tata Steel at the earliest."

The great thing about Dr. Irani was that he believed in walking the talk. He went to Japan, underwent the training programme and learnt about Total Quality. He absorbed everything he saw and heard, and took down copious notes, handwritten and in painstaking detail.

Till today, I have preserved a photocopy of those notes with notations and words underlined for emphasis. The notes revealed the meticulousness and single-minded focus Dr. Irani had about what he saw as his mission of building quality into the DNA of Tata Steel. Those notes were the first documents on quality that we had at Tata Steel.

Once he accepts to lead a project, he puts his entire force behind it. He would not lead from behind. Dr. Irani would do exactly what he said he would do. There would never be any dissonance between his words and his actions. This was a fantastic characteristic of his.

An Important Break…

After his return from Japan, Dr. Irani set up the Total Quality team as promised. It was a very important break for those of us who had been handpicked by him. It was an honour to be noticed by him and I now got a chance to come very close to him.

Once he visited one of our training programmes to interact with our batch of engineers. At the end of the visit, we assembled for a group photograph. We had a chair for him to sit and the entire batch stood behind him. He pulled me from the group and made me sit on the chair and he stood behind with the group. It was a symbolic assurance of trust and support that has remained etched in my mind since then.

After my stint in Total Quality, he asked me to implement the concept in a department. He initially sent me to the International Trading division, then to Shipping, Chartering, HR, and later to Tata International. When he took over the chairmanship of Tata

Quality Management Services (TQMS) in 2001, he offered me the chance of working with him yet again, an opportunity I eagerly accepted and grabbed.

Dr. Irani brought the same rigour to this initiative that he had shown while making quality central to the way Tata Steel operated. TQMS was transformed from an organisation that merely conducted assessments to an in-house consulting arm for companies in the Tata Group, paving the path for it to look beyond quality and business excellence to subjects such as innovation, climate change, and affirmative action.

My transition to TQMS was a great change in my professional life. This was the first time I was operating as an executive from the corporate centre and I did not belong to a single company. This transitioning from a mindset of being associated with a company to not being specifically associated with any one company within the group, was a huge change.

I had worked in Tata Steel for a long time. We had this saying in the company: "You can take a man out of Tata Steel, but you cannot take Tata Steel out of a man." People have difficulty in unlearning what they have learnt and shedding their baggage from the past. For me that was the big challenge: to unlearn and shed my past baggage and become objective and neutral about what I do as I serve the cause of facilitating business excellence in numerous companies of this vast group. It was an arduous and long journey and stretched nearly eight years to come to that level, but every minute I reminded myself that I did not belong to a company but to the group.

Asking the Right Questions...

Again, much of the learning for this came from the TQMS Chairman, Dr. Irani, and from the Board. He constantly kept asking me whether a decision or action to be taken was good for the group. Good and wonderful bosses have the ability to ask the right questions. Often, they don't give you the right answers; you need to search for them. But, good bosses know the right questions.

Once the right questions are asked, you begin your journey in the right direction.

Dr. Irani trusted his subordinates and his style was to give freedom to the CEO. However, this freedom to operate was given only till the time he felt the CEO deserved this freedom. If you had earned the freedom  and worked well, he would continue to give you a free hand. I was fortunate to get this kind of freedom. But this kind of freedom also came with great responsibility.

It was a key leadership lesson I learnt from Dr. Irani: about when you need to control and when you need to let go. Good bosses know this, when to become a Commander and when  to become a General. They switch between the two roles well. Dr. Irani did this very well.

This freedom that he gave his CEO kept my team motivated. When they saw their boss had trust and freedom, they were inspired to perform beyond targets and expectations.

I also learnt the importance of communication from Dr. Irani. There is no end to how much you can communicate. Communicate, communicate and communicate: these are the three most important things for a leader. Dr. Irani had this ability to communicate effectively and in a simple manner. He knew how to get his message across.

When the Total Quality programme was introduced in Tata Steel, Dr. Irani used to often deliver lectures. We used to celebrate November as Quality Month. He would go to ten different locations and deliver the same speech. Once we asked him did he not get bored making the same speeches? "No, that is my role," said Dr. Irani.

"People are not bored, as every time there is a different audience. I have to continue telling them what is important. And since it is important, I will repeat it a hundred times."

Dr. Irani had a simple definition for Total Quality. Q stands for quality, he said. While the small "q" stands for product quality, the capital (or big, as he used to say) Q stands for quality in everything, your response, writing, process, and customer-orientation. He emphasised on the need to move from the small "q" to the big one.

Dogged Persuasion...

For an entire year he kept talking about the small q and the big Q. At the end of the year, he wanted to take a stock of the situation, whether he had made the employees understand the concept of the big Q. An agency was commissioned to do a study, and the survey revealed that the communication had not been effective and the concept had not been understood. The general awareness of quality was not very high.

One of Dr. Irani's senior and cynical colleagues told him that he was on the wrong path. Tata Steel was an old company and these things would not work. He told Dr. Irani that a donkey could become a better donkey, not a horse.

Dr. Irani, however, was not disheartened. He said we are not donkeys. "We will take one more year, but we will make this company gallop," he added. He continued focusing on the small q and the big Q. The message finally touched a chord and Tata Steel began embracing Total Quality. Interestingly, it was the first group company to win the prestigious JRD QV award, instituted in memory of the former group chairman Mr. JRD Tata, which is given to a Group Company that surpasses high levels of excellence across its operations and serves as a role model in the industry.

"Quality is not an add-on for companies," Dr. Irani said in an interview many years ago. "Quality must be in the DNA of an organisation; it must be inherent in all activities of a company and its employees. Without quality an organisation cannot survive and there cannot be any advancement for employees or surpluses for the organisation."

At Tata Steel, Dr. Irani initiated a slew of measures that in a few years enabled the company to not just turn the corner, but become one of the world's most efficient steel producers. The People Factor, so vital in everything Dr. Irani has been involved in, became the cornerstone of the company's revival.

"An employee must have more to offer the organisation than mere loyalty," Dr. Irani remarked once. "There has to be knowledge, initiative, leadership; you have to contribute, you have to add value. You cannot sit and expect the company to keep you just because three generations of your family have been employed. That's what used to happen in Jamshedpur before we changed things."

Transparency and Fairness...

Another important learning from Dr. Irani was the concept of fairness. When you are leading, you should not only be fair but should be perceived to be fair. I see Dr. Irani to be a benchmark in this regard.

Once a letter comes to him, he does not read it the second time. In his view, whatever be the decision, saying yes or no or forwarding it to someone else, has to happen in one go. I confess I have a long way to go before I come up to that level. Dr. Irani was fantastic in taking quick decisions.

Let me cite some examples. There was a time when I was working in Total Quality in Tata Steel and some designation changes took place in the company. I believed that I did not get the right designation. I spoke to my bosses including those in Human Resources, but nobody was able to help me. I was not happy with the situation.

About a year later, I went to Dr. Irani and told him I was unhappy that my designation was not commensurate with my background and responsibilities. He listened to me very intently and said he agreed with me. He wanted to know why I did not approach him earlier. I told him I did not want a favour from him. He said it was a wrong decision and I should have done it earlier.

He then called up his assistant and asked him to take out a circular promoting me with immediate effect. He asked me whether there was someone else in my department in the same predicament. I informed him that there were two others who were my juniors; Dr. Irani said it would not be fair not to promote them. So even without meeting them, he asked his assistant to promote them as well.

Another instance I recall was when I told him that I was unhappy that I had a small flat to live in. But this time he refused to allot a bigger one for me. He heard me out and said he appreciated my feelings, but he could not give me a bigger flat as I did not have the necessary points for such an entitlement. "If you had come from some other department I would have considered it," said Dr. Irani, "But you are from my department and I cannot do a favour for you." I was satisfied because the manner in which he turned down my request was transparent and fair. He had the ability to say no in a nice manner.

Learning from Leadership During a Crisis….

 Outside the usual business environment, my most significant learning from Dr. Irani was during an unfortunate event, a crisis that occurred at Jamshedpur on 3 March 1989.

In 1989, I was selected for a Group Exchange programme and was due to leave for Sweden. The candidates for the exchange programme comprised of delegates from various parts of the state of Bihar and I was one of the candidates from the Tatas. Mr H.P. Bodhanwala, who was then the leader of our programme, invited us to Jamshedpur for a meeting on 2 March 1989, so that we could attend the Founders' Day celebrations the next day. (3 March is the Birth Anniversary of

Mr. Jamshedji Tata, the Founder of the House of Tata's). And indeed this was good because Founder's Day celebrations at Jamshedpur are held in a grand manner, possibly akin to that of our Indian Republic Day celebrations.

At the end of our meeting on 2 March, Mr. Bodhanwala put his hands in both his pockets and told us he had his pockets filled with VIP Passes for the Founder's Day celebrations the next day. One of the pockets was filled with Golden passes which would entitle us to the enclosure at the forefront of the celebrations and the other was containing silver passes that entitled one to a seat at the rear. He asked us to select one pocket and as luck would have it, I was asked to choose on behalf of our delegation. The pocket I tapped on contained the silver passes!

The next day, as we partook of the celebrations, a ghastly fire broke out at the enclosure where the Golden pass holders were seated. As we were seated in the silver pass area, our delegation escaped the impact of this terrible accident. Perhaps it was our luck to have won the silver passes and the others around were destined to this dastardly blow of fate. The fire spread across the entire seating area, ravaged the celebrations and took its toll on young and old, the officers of Tata Steel and their precious family members.

The aftermath of this tragedy was more than overwhelming. Hundreds were hospitalised for wounds caused by severe degrees of burns and there were many casualties. Dr. Irani was then the Deputy Managing Director of Tata Steel. He and his wife Daisy were seen daily at various hospitals in Jamshedpur where the affected were sheltered, comforting and consoling the bereaved. The management of Tata Steel spared no efforts to rehabilitate all who were impacted. Dr. Irani spearheaded this direction….

Quick Decision-Making…

Quick decision-making and fairness of his decisions were characteristic of the style of Dr. Irani. I have over the years tried hard to emulate him, but found it challenging.

I remember when I was directly reporting to him, he told me I had the choice of either taking a decision on my own or referring the matter to him. If I wanted to be a good leader I had to take the decision myself; there could be the likelihood of his reversing my decision occasionally. He also used to threaten me if I did not take a decision quickly, he would do it on my behalf.

Apart from Dr. Irani, there were important lessons I learned from other bosses as well. When I moved to the International Trading division in Kolkata, I was looking after the Southeast and South Asian markets. The head of the department was Mr. Bushen Raina, who later became the Managing Director of The Tinplate Company of India Ltd.

It was a major change for me as I moved from the role of an internal consultant to a hardcore selling operation. Initially, I was uncomfortable in the job as I felt my bosses were becoming unreasonable about the price I was getting, the quantity I was selling, the speed at which I handled the documentation and tackled customer complaints.

I felt stressed in the beginning, as apparently unreasonable demands were made to stretch my potential. If I had set a target to sell 1,00,000 tonnes of steel in a year, I was asked why it could not be 1,50,000 tonnes? Of course, when we ended up selling 1,25,000 tonnes, I realised the human potential is unlimited. It can be stretched by raising the bar. There are leaders who raise the bar on expectations; if you raise the bar, the entire organisation starts moving up.

I worked with Mr. Raina from 1994 to 1997. I would say that Mr. Raina was an unreasonable boss ... more unreasonable towards himself than on others as he had very high standards of performance expectations, both from himself and from us, whether on expectations of sales quantity, or Nett realisation, turnaround time or documentation time. But we realised it was because of these traits of Mr. Raina that our team used to over perform. He also gave us full freedom on decisions. I remember that we used to complete the documentation for pre-shipment in 15–20 days. He gave us a non-negotiable apparently unachievable target of 3 days for completion of pre-shipment documentation from now on. The team thought through and worked out all possible innovations and finally achieved this over a cycle of 4 days, an inconceivable task.

Though Mr. Raina was most often seen as unreasonable, he trusted youngsters and continuously encouraged them with his go for the kill management style. Indeed he groomed many youngsters who later on became the CEOs of other Tata Steel Group companies. His leadership style was developmental and indeed hospitable as well.

After my stint at Tata Steel Ltd., I moved to the Shipping and Chartering Division of Tata Steel (which is now formed into a separate company called TMILL). I served there for 3 years; I found it an exciting organisation, formed by the consolidation of two businesses. Then one used to hear of the emerging thought process in Tata Steel that HR function should have Line Managers in order to be more effective. In fact, the Management of Tata Steel was on the lookout for inviting high performing Line Executives into the HR function. Quite naturally, most Line Managers were not too keen on this as they considered this a sidelined posting.

One fine Sunday evening at 7 pm, I got a phone call from Mr. Firdose Vandrevala, commonly referred to as FAV, who was then the Vice President, Marketing and Sales of Tata Steel. He told me that I had been selected for the position of handling HR in the Marketing and Sales function. My first reaction was one of obvious reticence, I did not want to get sidelined and did not hesitate to inform FAV about this. He summoned me to a meeting with him the next morning, informed me clearly that this was not a sidelined role and gave me the offer of handling Shipping and Chartering and HR in Marketing and Sales. After understanding the importance of the role, I opted for the HR role and that is when a new chapter in my professional life began. Later, I discovered that FAV had consulted many members of the Senior Management of Tata Steel before selecting me and they had expressed confidence in me, on which his decision was based on.

I worked under the guidance of FAV for two years from 1998 to 2000. He brought in my role as a listening post, handling HR in Marketing and Sales. He gave utmost importance to the HR of business and as was explained to me, the reason I was chosen for this role.

However, I must mention this was not my first meeting with FAV. In fact, the most memorable time when I had interacted with him earlier was when I was on an overseas trip in 1989 and that is when I had discovered his People Orientation. I was committed some amount of forex allowance before proceeding for the trip, and as a part of my tour I reached a destination from where I had to proceed to

Europe. The promised forex was getting indefinitely delayed, and I found myself in a quandary and was unable to proceed on my journey. I dialled my boss Mr. N.P. Sinha at his residence to ask him to bail me out. Due to some recent reshuffles and transfers, his residence number had been interchanged with that of FAV. FAV took my call, asked me about my situation, and asked me to hold on for 24 hours. Without reference to any other of my superiors, FAV spoke to the office of the then MD, my other wonderful boss Dr. Irani, and to my surprise I found the amount due was remitted to my account within 12 hours. Such was the people orientation displayed by FAV, even for a colleague who was not from within his department, but was in trouble in a foreign land.

I found FAV demanding about performance expectations. He gave me an interesting guideline on my role as a Listening Post. He explained to me that when I had to meet him, I would represent other colleagues and carry with me the message of the people down-the-line to FAV, but when I had to meet these colleagues, I had to carry with me the message of FAV to the others. Either way, I had to carry each time someone else's message.

While FAV was demanding, I found him to be reasonable. In an earlier stint, when I was in Chartering, he was heading Trading in Tata Steel. Invariably, there would be a tussle between these two functions on the availability of material at the port versus the availability of ships. In fact, often ships were requisitioned while the steel material was still being rolled in the mill. This was a well known fact and at Chartering we would requisition ships with this knowledge, there was a huge cost involved in keeping ships idle. One fine day, FAV called me and fired me stating bluntly that shipments of material to be traded are being held up due to lack of ships and should we deduct the loss from my salary. I sought a meeting with him and the next morning I challenged him stating that if he could ask his people to show that 12,000 Tons of steel was available, I would arrange a ship; otherwise no one had the right to ask me for ships. FAV did his own investigations, and ended firing the materials team and unhesitatingly conceded that my contentions were right.

Among the bosses I have worked with, FAV was the one who was the most data and logic driven. He was a benchmark in creating a data system driven organisation. He also had a wry sense of humour, which would enable him to get away with cheeky statements with his seniors.

At TQMS, the Chairman and the Board always asked questions like why can't we take this whole exercise to a world-class level? Or, what does it take to make the entire programme world-class? All this sets you thinking in a different manner. Good bosses have the ability to push the envelope and take you to the next orbit of performance.

This is the same quality that I notice in my present boss Mr. Prasad Menon, the present chairman of TQMS. While Mr. Raina used to raise the bar in a commanding and forceful manner and FAV in an equally commanding but more aggressive fashion, Mr. Menon does it a lot more simply and nicely. If you set a target, he will raise the bar by asking why it is not 10 times more. You finally realise it is possible to raise the bar by at least five times.

These are the bosses with whom I realised it was possible to get an organisation to work at its optimum level. I am told often at TQMS that I am unreasonable. I tell them it is by choice: I am unreasonable even with myself. I am able to stretch myself, not stress out to do much more.

My learning's from my bosses and my own views, based on a career of over 30 years in the industry, can best be summarised as follows:

I believe that it is our tradition to let our work speak for itself. The profession is bigger than the professional. Professional success in my definition is not an uni-dimensional quality. It has many facets. A successful individual is not just someone at the zenith of his or her professional career but also someone who is ethical and lives by a sound value system. An unethical person may also appear successful, but is not something we want to emulate nor is it success in its true sense of the word.

I believe there are five key aspects that define a successful individual:

1. Passion: There is no substitute for this. In fact it does not matter where you have studied or your background for as long as you have the passion for your work, everything else falls into place. Passion infuses everyone around you to give their best too. The only thing to remember is passion must be tempered by an ethical temperament. One should never give up one's values in one's climb to the top.

2. An ability to keep learning: It is said education is a lifelong occupation and it has never been more true than today. We live in a world that is defined by change. Things I learn today will be obsolete five years hence and I have to recognise this and keep myself open to unlearning and relearning constantly.

3. Humility: This is the hallmark of a great person. Success is temporary but the life that you build for your family, friends and colleagues is your true legacy which will be remembered for a long time thereafter. This is possible only if you are humble and do not let your success get to your head. Arrogance too breeds its own variety of success but that is not what we are talking about here.

4. Communication: A leader has to communicate clearly, logically and from the heart. In a way this flows if the earlier four qualities are present. It also depends on the ability to keep absorbing new thoughts and new ideas from books, the people we meet, and the places we visit. All of this adds to our power to communicate.

5. Adaptability: This in a way follows from the second aspect. I have seen that successful people learn from the best practices of others. They adopt all that is admirable in other people without changing the core of their being. This is possible only when we are open to learning new things all the time.

Finally, all of these earlier aspects would be rendered ineffective if we do not have a positive outlook. It is vital. In my personal life, there are several instances of being able to tackle the worst crisis with a cheerful disposition when I have allowed myself to believe that I can do it. Your body language has to be positive as that will allow the rest of your team to absorb and deliver to the best of their abilities. This just proves an adage, Success is not an individual sport, it is a team game.

When you are leading, you should not only be fair,
but should be perceived to be fair.

N. Vittal
Chairman
Vittal Innovation,
Bangalore

15

IS LEADERSHIP POSSIBLE IN RULE- BOUND BUREAUCRACY?

How you perform depends on your ability to get the best out of the
organisation. Some friends have described me as a person with
a school boy's enthusiasm. I adopted the attitude of a student
throughout my career, which probably led to my school boy label.

Who is a Wonderful Boss?

The word wonderful can cover a wide range of qualities. Eventually it is the judgement of the people with whom a person works which decides whether as a boss that person is indeed wonderful.

As I see it, wonderful means a person who always evokes our admiration and respect. The acid test is would you like to work with and slog for him or her? Is the boss a good mentor so far as the job is concerned? Above all is he or she fair and dependable in all his or her transactions, has integrity and a capacity to inspire you in your job?

I joined the Indian Administrative Service at the age of 22 in 1960 and retired after a long career of 42 years in public administration in 2002. How relevant can my experience of more than four decades in government be in a book meant for today's manager on *A Wonderful Boss?* What crunch advice can I give to the boss of today and tomorrow?

Nevertheless, I am writing this because I believe that even though the context, organisation, and the situation may change, when a group of people work together towards a common objective and somebody is the boss and others are reporting to him or her, a common set of dynamics evolve. Such dynamics have a degree of constancy and long-term applicability. I was a government servant and the main reason why government servants do not perform is thanks to the cast iron job guarantee provided under Article 311 of the Constitution. A government servant or babu is never in danger of losing his or her job unless he or she is incompetent or foolish. Even in a government organisation, competent bosses are required if the performance has to be good.

It is interesting that although the government and bureaucracy are perceived to be lost in red tape and performing with abominable inefficiency, there have been excellent bosses in the governmental system who have been able to get things done, motivate people and, more importantly, create generations of leaders who, inspired by them, in turn went on to become great bosses themselves. Some names strike my mind immediately. One of them is Mr. E. Sreedharan of Delhi Metro, who has emerged as a universally admired person. He has shown that in our corrupt system with all its inefficiencies and bureaucracy, one can still stick to principles, deadlines and complete projects without time and cost overrun. He has done this, not only with the Konkan Railways but also with the Delhi Metro. He has evolved certain set of basic principles which has brought this success. I am sure a whole generation of engineers have been inspired by him and are shaping into mini Sreedharans themselves.

Another legendary figure in the public sector is Dr. V. Krishnamurthy. He showed repeatedly in different public enterprises like BHEL, Maruti and SAIL, how huge organisations can be transformed by intelligent applications of organisational development techniques and cultural changes can be brought about.

Sam Pitroda is yet another example, who in a very short time coming to a totally different environment was able to create a new culture in C-DOT and a replica of the Silicon Valley start up in a century old department of Telecommunications.

In my 42 years in government, I have worked with different bosses. Unlike in the private sector, where one can quit and change bosses, in government this option is ruled out. So what happens is that every person learns to adjust and adapt to the situation in his or her career growth, and if lucky, evolve into an excellent boss himself or herself and of the types mentioned earlier.

I have enjoyed nearly every assignment given to me in my career. Some of my friends have described me as a person with a school boy's enthusiasm. I am not able to explain this enthusiasm. I had great pride in being an IAS officer. I called myself an IAS fundamentalist or the Ayatollah of the IAS. I believe that IAS is a very special and unique service, unlike any in the world where at a young age, a lot of responsibility and power are given to you. How you perform depends on your ability to get the best out of the organisation. I adopted the attitude of a student almost throughout my career and probably that led to my school boy label.

It is the attitude of learning all the time that confers happiness in work and deems no work as boring. Enthusiasm is a great psychological spark that gets easily transmitted. Even cynics working with such a person tend to develop, to begin with, a certain degree of indulgent amusement and in course of time, depending upon the age of the person, become a part of the team and get infected by enthusiasm if not positively motivated.

Enthusiasm, I find, is the most effective way of motivating people. If you are enthusiastic, you will take pleasure in doing your job and that changes the whole atmosphere and automatically a team develops. Those who align with you become a part of your team.

Some remain neutral and some hostile. A positive approach to work evolves and the result is that at the end of every assignment, there is a sense of satisfaction and that I think is how the wonderful aspect in work gets perpetuated.

Integrity

Doing what is right even when it is difficult.

The next quality which makes one a wonderful boss is integrity in all respects, intellectual, moral and financial. It is integrity that leads to credibility. After all, the basic requirement for being a boss is that there should be colleagues willing to work with him or her and be loyal to him or her.

The third aspect is empathy or human touch. You may call it emotional intelligence. It is the human touch that eventually makes an ordinary boss into a great boss or a wonderful boss. Once the human touch is there,

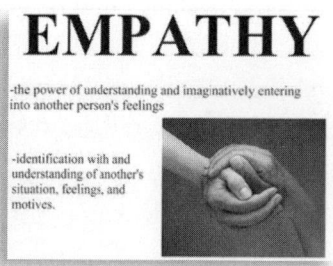

EMPATHY

-the power of understanding and imaginatively entering into another person's feelings

-identification with and understanding of another's situation, feelings, and motives.

it erupts in the right moments and adds on to the sense of the team spirit and commitment, loyalty and all that goes into making a person a wonderful boss.

These three qualities have nothing to do with financial incentives a boss can offer or the power of hire and fire he or she can wield. I think the three aspects of enthusiasm, integrity and empathy apply not only in government but right across the wide spectrum of management and governance of any organisation.

Any judgement about ones boss and grading them as good, bad, ugly or wonderful depends on ones perspective. I am now seventy five years old and my reaction to the bosses under whom I worked has undergone subtle changes so far as my ranking them and rating them is concerned. This I think is the uncanny impact of age and experience and must be common to all people. When I was young and in service, I used to admire bosses for their sheer brilliance in competence, expression, deportment style or image.

As I grew older, I tried to rate them and re-evaluate them. In fact, one of my colleagues told me when we were discussing about a common boss we had that he had qualities which we admired when we were in high school. As we get older we develop a different perspective and rate our bosses in terms of their intellectual and moral integrity. It is always worthwhile to remember that while one makes an effort to find out what goes to make a boss wonderful, ones assessment of a boss also depends upon ones emotional state and psychological maturity at the stage of interaction with the boss.

Stan Coelho, IAS (1956) is for me an excellent example of a wonderful enthusiastic boss who took every problem as an opportunity. He has been my model in the early days and his image got a tremendous boost when he had to handle the unexpected crisis of the India-Pakistan war, in 1965 when Ayub Khan's Pakistan attacked us in Kutch. He was the Collector of Kutch and for the excellent work he did, he was honoured with a Padma Shri.

But that was not all. He became Joint Secretary in the Ministry of Industry in 1977 and worked with George Fernandes in 1977 when in the post emergency excitement the Janata Government introduced new concepts like the District Industries Centre. He was then asked by the state government to come to Gujarat to give a boost to the huge Rs. 400 crore Gujarat Narmada Valley Fertilizer Company Project (GNFC). Although the company was formed, it was not making adequate progress.

He came straight from Delhi and settled in Bharuch which had no regular accommodation. Bharuch was a backward district and the project area was highly undeveloped. His daughter was going to one of the best schools in Delhi and thanks to his transfer; she had to attend the school in the fertilizer colony itself. His commitment to the task on hand was total. Unlike many other senior management members of GNFC who were living in Vadodra and commuting every day to Bharuch, which was an hour and half drive from the city, Coelho stayed in the project area itself so that 24 × 7 attention could be given. This display of commitment and enthusiasm for the project was the turning point in the life of that project which led to great success. Coelho as a student has been a great success in inter collegiate debates. He combined charm and logic and was very effective in persuading people to his point of view. In the five years when Coelho set up the GNFC project, he developed an excellent esprit de corps in the company. I was fortunate, I being his successor, could build on the sound foundation he had laid.

When it comes to integrity from all dimensions, the boss I admire is Smarjit Kumar Gangopadhyaya. He was collector of Vadodra and his capacity to tell the unvarnished 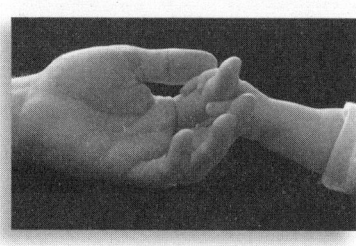 truth made him an outstanding collector. It is also the reflection of time that the political leaders in Gujarat then like Dr. Jivraj Mehta and others respected him for his honest and no nonsense approach.

When it comes to the human touch being the most admired element in a boss, there is none to beat Abid Hussain as a wonderful boss. In 1978, he led a team of 25 delegates from the ESCAP region to China and I was one of the two members from India. One could see the ease with which he mingled with people and his genuine concern for everybody he came across. Anybody who had met Dr. Abid Hussain can certify what a warm person he is. His success has been due to many factors but the most significant is his capacity to empathise. For example, he was brilliant in his perceptions and he could sum up with elegance and give an insight into long discussions involving different speakers which used to be a marvel for all of us.

When it comes to the humane approach which makes a boss, not only wonderful, but universally loved, there is none to beat Dr. Abid Hussain. His empathy for his colleagues was so obvious. In fact, I did not directly work under him in my career. It was only during the visit to China in 1978 that I was associated with him in a delegation and in subsequent years had occasions to work with him in different capacities. As the Chief Executive of the Rajiv Gandhi Foundation, he laid a healthy tradition in building it up as a centre

Is Leadership Possible in Rule-Bound Bureaucracy?

of excellence as far as policy analysis was concerned. The affection and ease with which he gets things done from his colleagues is something unbelievable.

I have also had other bosses who were role models when it comes to the technical aspects of work. In the older generation of ICS, L.P. Singh has been a model for bringing an intellectual approach and objective analysis to every issue one handles. His focus was an articulation of thought process and how policy options were evolved. Another person who had a systematic approach and ensured that there were no loopholes in implementing policies is H.C. Sarin, ICS. He was the advisor to the Government of Gujarat during 1974-75 and then in 1980. As advisor, he used to handle a very large number of departments and the systematic manner in which he kept his appointments and the points to be brought to the notice of the Governor in his scheduled meetings is something to be admired and copied (of course, I did).

Sivagnanam, IAS (1952) has been another boss; he is an amazing person with a phenomenal memory. He was a great master of detail. The enormous amount of work and the pains he took were beyond me. He knew almost every file he handled by heart. He was compared to a human computer and the manner in which he handled files was a source of inspiration for us. As junior colleagues, there is an uncanny process of osmosis by which we pick up the habits and approach of our bosses. In that sense, life is a continuous learning process and if you are in a service like the IAS, the learning never stops.

Explaining a beautiful vision in an elegant language was the strength of S.M. Ghosh, IAS (1951). Though he was nine years senior to me, he used to exchange very risqué or men only jokes, which brought us together. There is, I think, in human dynamics, a bond which grows among people who can share jokes.

Psychologists tell us that we normally remember things which we like and forget which we dislike. I think this is also true for the bosses we have. We pick up the qualities we admire and we avoid what we do not like. If one dislikes the boss, one avoids meeting him or her unnecessarily. I have also had such bosses where unless it is unavoidable, I would not go and meet them. The less said about them the better, particularly in a book about wonderful bosses.

So far, we have seen the factors which go to make a wonderful boss in organisations and bureaucracy in particular. Now we will go a little deeper and examine certain unique dimensions of the bureaucracy about a civil servant becoming effective and hopefully blossoming in to a wonderful boss.

As mentioned earlier, one of the important characteristics of a wonderful boss is integrity. Is it possible today for a bureaucrat in the system of public governance, where corruption seems to be the norm rather than an exception, to maintain intellectual, financial and moral integrity? Having passed through the mill for 42 years, I can clearly say Yes. It is possible for every bureaucrat who cherishes values of integrity to maintain his or her integrity and at the same time, become an effective bureaucrat and possibly a wonderful boss.

It is curious that some of the reasons I had mentioned in the earlier part as being responsible for the lack of accountability in governance could emerge as a strong tool helping an honest bureaucrat to retain his or her integrity and be effective. If job security under Article 311 of the constitution is the factor which enables many bureaucrats to idle away, not doing their job and continue to be part of the bureaucracy, the same job security can give tremendous courage to every honest bureaucrat to act according to his conscience. This is a luxury that is not available in the private sector or any non-government organisation. My own experience as Secretary in key departments which had dramatic impact on the economy and public life is a proof of this statement. You should not consider that I am boasting.

As a Hindu who believes in *sanathana dharma*, I realise there is lot of truth in what Lord Krishna says in the Bhagawat Gita. Addressing Arjuna he says, "*Nimithamathram Bhava Savyasachin*". "Arjuna, you are only an instrument in my hand." In my own case, I was Secretary, Department of Electronics at a critical time when the IT industry was about to take off.

There are people who believe that government has a negative Midas touch where whatever it touches, turns to ashes. In the 1990s when India was registering a remarkable success on the software front, our young women were winning laurels in international beauty contests like Miss World and Miss Universe, a popular joke those days was that our young women were able to take on the global competition in beauty because Government of India did not have a Ministry of Beauty. Our software and IT were growing because government did not interfere.

The reality is the opposite of this perception. In fact, there was a separate Electronics Commission set up in the 1980s by the Government of India on the lines of the Atomic Energy Commission which was abolished and converted into the department of Electronics (DOE). In June 1990, I was appointed as the Secretary to the DOE. I continued in this position till I retired from the IAS on 31 January 1996 with a break of 6 months from July to December 1993. The department was able to establish a strategic alliance with the industry and shape policies which were able to take full advantage of India's strengths and the emerging global scene.

The Software Technology Park which we pioneered became a model of how electronics in our environment can mirror the mystique of the Silicon Valley of the US—teams of technocrats starting up a company in their bedroom and nurturing it to global dimensions. Infosys, Wipro and all the iconic companies known collectively by the acronym SWITCH, Satyam, Wipro, Infosys, TCS, Cognizant, and HCL, registered remarkable growth because of the friendly and tailor-made policies designed and initiated by the DOE. In shaping these policies I also played a part as the Secretary of the department.

How was I able to play this part? This is again an example of how a bureaucrat can take advantage of what can be called benign neglect. When I became the Secretary, DOE, the department was under the Prime Minister. DOE has always been under the prime minister

(PM) since its inception. As the PM is too busy and has too many things on his or her plate, the Secretary of the department becomes the government of India.

Coming to think of it, who is the government? Right from the minister down to the peon are all part of the government and, in a sense, each one of them can claim to represent the government. For common people of the country, clerk or the peon in the office where they attend the government departments represent the face and are representatives of the government. The manner in which the DOE was able to nurture the electronics industry in India, from 1990 to 1996, when India registered a twenty six times growth in software exports from $100 million to $2.6 billion will always remain as a very glorious and significant chapter in the economic history of India.

I was fortunate and by the grace of god, to be the Secretary, Department of Telecommunication and Chairman Telecom Commission at a crucial time when the telecom sector and the century old department had to be thrown open to the private sector about the economic liberalisation policies introduced in 1991. I have always maintained that Indian political leaders exercise their political will only under two conditions. One, when there is a vote bank advantage, like the populist programs offering freebies. Here, there is a direct correlation between the freebies offered to the public and the dividends by the votes they get.

The second condition is when There Is No Alternative (TINA) factor operates. P.V. Narasimha Rao, as a PM was known to be the *Mauni Baba*. He was the one who said that not taking a decision itself was a decision. Such a person was able to introduce radical economic reforms because we were facing an acute financial crisis in 1991 and had to accept the dictates of the IMF under the so called Washington consensus.

While Dr. Manmohan Singh as Finance Minister and Narasimha Rao as PM realised the need for bringing out policy changes for setting up a new Telecom Department, Mr. Sukhram who was the Minister for Telecommunication and the whole set of officers of the department were opposed to any reform. The century old monopoly of the telecom department had given clout and influence and for those who are corrupt as well as excellent opportunities to make money over the years. If the telecom sector was opened and led to private competition, to that extent, their cosy existence was threatened. In fact, the service of Indian Telecom Service would come to an end.

The Minister was sympathetic to the ideas of the telecom department and opposed to reform through as Minister in the cabinet where the Prime Minister and the Finance Minister realised the need for reform, he had to go along. So his attitude was ambiguous. While he may not have openly opposed the policy of liberalisation, he silently could delay the process of reform to the extent possible by a simple act of not taking any decisions at all.

When I was posted as Secretary, Department of Telecommunication (DOT), and became Telecom Chairman on 1st October, 1993, I was fully committed to the need of the reform. As Chairman, I convened a series of meetings of the full Commission to hammer out a policy opening the sector for the entry of the private sector, corporatise the department to remove the anomaly arising from the state of diarchy in the department. It may be recalled that after Sam Pitroda became the Chairman of Telecom Commission, during the regime of Rajiv Gandhi, he was for corporatisation and making the whole department redesigned on the model of the Atomic Energy Commission and the Department of Atomic Energy.

Delhi and Bombay circles which represent 22% of the telephone density in the country were made into a corporation called Mahanagar Telephone Nigam Limited (MTNL), whereas rest of the country was run departmentally. This diarchy introduced lot of tension starting with the difference in the pay scales and working conditions of the same set of government servants who had till then a common service conditions. Corporatising the whole department would have eliminated this source of tension and provided many other benefits. While I was able to persuade the Telecom Commission to come to this conclusion by the end of December 1993, the minister and the senior members of the Telecom Commission from the department were opposed to the idea.

One of my early bosses, V. Eswaran, ICS, Chief Secretary, Gujarat used to say that he was a bad master who kept a dog and did the barking himself. I had to be like that bad master in DOT. Single handedly I prepared the papers for the policy changes to open the telecom sector, corporatisation of the DOE and raising resources for investment and improvement of telecom infrastructure. I submitted these papers by 5 January 1994 to the Minister. The Minister just sat on the file. In the first week of April 1994, I got a call from PM Secretariat when Amarnath Verma, Principal Secretary to the PM informed me that the PM was worried about the slow progress on telecom reform. The PM was to meet US President Clinton in May 1994 and telecom reform was one of the important issues to be discussed.

Eventually, the PM ordered a presentation on 11 April 1994 to be made by me to him and the Minister for Telecommunication when senior officials would also be present. I, therefore, made the presentation. So far as the policy of opening the sector was concerned, there was no difference of opinion on the issue of corporatisation, but the Minister raised an objection. This annoyed Mr. Narasimha Rao. He said that he was under the impression that enough homework had already been done and there was a consensus within the  department itself about the future course of action. He briskly ordered that the Minister Sukhram and I should reconcile our differences and meet him within a week.

We met him on 22 April 1994 at his residence at 4.00 pm. The Minister began by saying that corporatisation would lead to an enormous loss of approximately Rs. 9,000 crores. What he mentioned as loss was an exercise in misunderstanding. So long as the DOT was a government department, the profits of the department were not subject to income tax because the profit was an income to the government. But when DOT became a corporation, the corporation would have to pay income tax and this payment was interpreted as a loss of revenue. This was an extremely myopic view.

The Minister gave the PM a report of five pages on this view and I presented an eleven page report counteracting this argument. This further annoyed the PM, who said I should go along with the Minister. The result was that the policy was finally announced on 13 May 1994 opening the sector. The corporatisation issue hung fire for some time and later the entire department was corporatised as BSNL. MTNL continued its separate existence.

The telecom experience showed that it is possible for the Secretary to hold a view and present the case at the highest level and ensure the policy measures are carried out effectively. But there was a price to pay. I was transferred in less than four months on 5 September 1994 back to DOE. However, my association with Telecom continued because the Secretary, DOE, is the ex-officio member of the Telecom Commission.

This brings us to the issue of the bureaucrats and their political masters. Narasimha Rao knew that I was doing the right thing, but for political compulsions he had to transfer me. However, when I was about to retire on 31 January 1996, I was appointed as Chairman, Public Enterprises Selection Board (PESB). P. Chidambaram, who was then Commerce Minister, told me in a meeting in Bangalore that my posting as Chairman PESB was a delayed compensation by Narasimha Rao for me.

In fact, Mrs. Margret Alva who was then Minister of State for Personnel was handling the issue of postings of senior civil servants, gave another version. There was a story behind how I became the Chairman, PESB. Narasimha Rao kept the post of Chairman, PESB, vacant for more than two years. As a part of a cabinet reshuffle, he appointed Karunakaran as the Minister for Industry, this department is concerned with maximum number of Public Sector Enterprises. He, therefore, wanted a person who can be independent as the Chairman, PESB. Therefore, he called for the papers and appointed me as the Chairman, PESB. This shows that political leaders know the value of every civil servant and they use them for the purposes they deem fit. It was Narasimha Rao again who said that civil servants were like trained horses and the political leaders must be like the riders. If the rider is not competent, the horse has the uncanny sense of knowing the rider is not confident and would assert itself. But, if the political leader is mature and knows how to get the work from his trained civil servants then he can ensure that they deliver the goods.

This issue brings us to another issue which is discussed widely today. In the corrupt system of governance today, bureaucrats have started playing second fiddle to the politicians and, many times, they are  colluding with them. This also raises a question whether it is possible for a civil servant to be honest and continue in service. As my own career shows, that it is possible for a civil servant to be independent and still rise to high positions. I am not the only person. In fact, G.V. Ramakrishna, in his book *Two Score and Ten* has traced his own career and has clearly brought out how even though on the issue of HPJ Pipeline, he took an independent stand against formidable Quatrocchi promoting the case of the Italian firm Snam Projetti and the contract was awarded to the French company Spie Capag. He had a long interesting series of government assignments after retirement. He has described in detail how and when the French company offered a commission of $3 million. He forced that company to make that fund available to the Government of India by way of reduction in prices. G.V. Ramakrishna after retirement has had a series of assignments which were key appointments like advisor to the Governor of Tamil Nadu, India's Ambassador to the EU, Brussels, Chairman SEBI and so on. His autobiography is called *Two Score and Ten* because he has had a career of 50 years in public service.

Any number of honest civil servants, who maintained their independence and gave their unpopular advice to the government which they felt was right, have not suffered in their career. And even if the suffering comes, they can take it in their stride. In fact, when I became the Central Vigilance Commissioner and called on then

Is Leadership Possible in Rule-Bound Bureaucracy?

the Vice President in 1998, Mr. Krishna Kant, he told me, "Vittal, I have reserved one hour for you. I want to know how a person like you in our system came up to this position?" I told him that I followed what I call as the Vittal amendment to Franklin principle. Benjamin Franklin said, "Two things are unavoidable in life, death and taxes." But Vittal amendment says, "If you are a civil servant you must remember that four things are unavoidable in life, death, taxes, transfers and retirement." Once a person accepts this and goes wherever posted, he is bound to succeed.

That brings us to another dimension of how people interact with an officer. In the first five to ten years of an officer's career, based on his or her record of action taken, an image is created about

him or her. Thereafter it is this image that precedes him or her. In a way, your character becomes the career. In the Greek tragedies they say that the character is destiny. If you see the career of many officials, you find it is his or her character that decides his or her career. Those who get along with the malpractices of their political masters might have flourished in the short run but had to pay for success heavily in other ways. In My Fair Lady, Eliza Dolittle says, "I am a lady to Col. Pickering because he treats me as a lady but for Prof. Higgins, I will always be a flower girl." It is the way you behave with people and how they react to you. If it is a case of being courteous, courtesy is returned. If it is a case of straight forward and honest behaviour, people who interact with you adjust their behaviour accordingly. I have had Chief Ministers like Chimanbhai Patel tell me when they wanted a special treatment in personnel matters, "Vittal, I know you will not do anything out of the way, but because this particular request is for a student of mine (Chimanbhai Patel was earlier a professor before he became a politician) and therefore I am requesting you." This polite request from one of the powerful Chief Ministers of Gujarat is a proof that political leaders appreciate the quality of the civil servants. This is also a reflection of the fact that the political leaders are apt on judging people and emotional intelligence. And as far as political leader-civil servants relationship is concerned, the civil servants who want to be honest can still be honest and effective.

In fact, a civil servants life need not always be as dry as the files. One occupational hazard of the bureaucrat is that the word Life and File have the same alphabets but file is not life and life is not file. Many bureaucrats have been accused of being *Lakeer ka Fakeer* and lacking in the human touch. As we have seen in the earlier section, empathy is one of the basic requirements for a wonderful boss. It is obvious that bureaucrats who are only file minded can never be wonderful bosses.

Nevertheless, humour in files is the strength of some officers. The best example I can think of is B.S. Raghavan (West Bengal, 1952), who was my Deputy Secretary when I was the Under Secretary. In 1966–68, Ministry of Home Affairs, when L.P. Singh, ICS, was the Secretary, was fond of elaborate notes and his basic objective was that the notes should bring out the rationale for the evolution of different decision options. As I joined as the Under Secretary in 1966, Raghavan's first advice was: "Remember Vittal, in this division, brevity is the soul of nitwit." There was another equally brilliant Under Secretary, Satyam (1957, Karnataka), who used to write English poetry which was published by P. Lal in India and Allen and Unwin in Britain. In one file, Satyam had suggested about a decision, Let us hump it. Let us accept it and not pursue the matter further. When the file was put up by him as Under Secretary to the Deputy Secretary, Raghavan, he wrote, "If we hump it, we will look as ridiculous as a double humped camel." Puns were plenty. Sample: Deputy Secretary may please see in dark and through light.

The approach of every officer in handling files was different. Most of them just add their signature agreeing with the note put up by the juniors. The only contribution they make is the delay before putting up that signature. When I joined the service, I heard about what one of my seniors D.S Bhakle, ICS, who was for sometime

Chief Secretary in Bombay used to say about files. According to him files were like women. One cannot go to sleep with every woman one meets. Similarly, one cannot go into details of every file. Some are like a woman one meets over a date and some may be for a one-night-stand. Once in your lifetime, you meet a woman with whom you want to spend your life together. The same discretionary approach must be adopted as far as applying time and attention on the files, was his philosophy.

There are some civil servants who have an excellent sense of humour. We have been discussing the Minister and the civil servant relationship so far. On this topic one of my seniors who had a great sense of humour, H.R. Patankar (1956, Gujarat), had developed an elaborate theory of subtly varying degrees. It begins with the civil servant putting up a note in the file and the Minister passing orders in the file as every decision is recorded. Next is the stage where small chits replace elaborate notes. Then the Minister gives oral orders and the civil servants implement them after recording it in file. The fourth stage comes where detailed instructions are not necessary. Body language and cryptic words can carry many meanings. For example, when an application was given or a Minister made a phone call to the civil servant, he may merely say, "Please have a look at it." Remember Kamaraj's ubiquitous word *Parkalam* (Let us see). But the tone in which please have a look at it is uttered may communicate everything from immediate implementation of the decision to one which is merely a motion and positively rejecting the proposal. The last stage which Patankar used to call, the musical stage arrives. The Minister may merely utter a word like Hmm and the civil servant will understand what the Minister's view is. A still more evolved stage is when the civil servant anticipates what the Minister wants and acts accordingly. Unfortunately, what Patankar described in a humorous way became a sad reality when Indira Gandhi brazenly introduced emergency in 1975 and explicitly directed that she wanted committed civil servants and judges, who were committed in loyalty towards her. This is the tragedy which is at the root of poor governance today.

Humour has always been a significant factor in bureaucracy, otherwise perceived to be a very dull, boring, and a formal affair. This humour generally

slips in official meetings. There was a formidable ICS officer N. Subramaniam, known as Neruppu (which in Tamil means fire) Subramaniam. In a discussion about the movement of the iron ore in the Kiliburu Bailadila Vizag (KBV) Pipeline, somebody was explaining that as the crow flies, the distance was so much. Subramaniam interjected saying that crows did not carry iron ore.

I had a similar experience when as a Development Commissioner of the Kandla Free Trade zone, I was making enormous efforts to turn around the zone. My boss was Mr. R. Tirumalai, IAS (1948, Tamilnadu), Additional Secretary, Commerce who used to preside over the Kandla Free Trade Zone Board meetings. In one of the meetings when I presented my problems, a representative from DGTD said, "Sir, in the last meeting you said that with the new Development Commissioner, N. Vittal, the Kandla Free Trade Zone had turned the corner, then why are these problems raised." Tirumalai shot back: Kandla Free Trade Zone has many corners to turn.

Another issue about the bureaucracy is whether the civil servant should be anonymous. The *Statesman* used to describe the civil servants as the faceless non-entities of the South Block. There was a view in the past that civil servants should be faceless. They should be like the children of the Victorian age, seen but not heard. But in these days of 24 × 7 media ever hungry for breaking news, the anonymity of civil servant is almost an anachronism. In today's world, a civil servant to be effective has to be good in communication, not only in writing clear notes, but also with the media. This skill develops only by constant practice.

In my life, I have found that attending seminars has been a good training ground. My economic advisor, Dr. Pranab Sen, who today is the Member of the Planning Commission used to say that I was

the only Secretary to the government who was taking the seminars seriously. But by doing so, I found that I had to constantly think on issues and make some relevant points when I spoke. When you are asked to speak on the same subject repeatedly, for example, on corruption, you have to come up with new insights and angles. When I became CVC (Central Vigilance Commissioner), I used to deliver 100 lectures on corruption every year. If you have to talk on the same subject for more than 100 times every year, automatically you are forced to look in to different aspects. There is always the danger of one making contradictory statements. One also experiences the constant evolution and re-examination of their views. I think it is a healthy process.

To become an effective and a wonderful boss, such evolution of the mind is necessary. After all, we are all prisoners of biology and the iron rule of biology is Use it or Lose it. If we don't use our brains, we are bound to lose our thinking capacity. In the governmental system, the more senior a person becomes, the more accustomed he or she becomes to sending the papers he or she receives for examination. The only word he writes is Put up. By these putting up processes, the senior officers lose their capacity for original thinking. Remembering the iron law of biology, I consciously tried to avoid this by using a dictaphone and record my views in real time. I used to dictate the minutes of every meeting I held in the presence of the participants before the meeting was over.

Instead of Put up philosophy, I was using a Put down philosophy. I used to put down my views and my approach in real time. More importantly, when people met me or I received any complaint on the phone, I used to immediately record on the dictaphone, the gist of the discussion so that one is not left to the whims of memory to recall events. If you want to be effective in any organisation, get results or implement projects you may have to break the rules. You cannot make an omelette without breaking the eggs and cannot implement the projects without breaking the rules. But then, how does one overcome the problems and the eternal threat of the CAG?

It may be recalled that KPS Menon, ICS, has recorded his memoirs which are eminently readable. When, as Assistant Collector, he complained to his Englishman Collector that his increment was not released by the Accountant General because he had not appeared and passed in the Malayalam examination, even though Malayalam was his mother tongue. The Collector silenced him by saying, "Remember, as long as you are in government service, the Accountant General by his office is debarred from commonsense." In fact, the audit department is one of the key watchdogs of the government to ensure the canons of financial propriety are not breached.

In recent times, the manner in which the CAG is exposing the scams have brought home to the nation, the importance of constitutional authority called CAG and the need for observing due processes in taking decisions. If this fails, there is bound to be corruption and malpractices. One golden rule I followed throughout my life was to record on the dictaphone in real time, the details of decision I took, because mostly, when one decides under the pressure of circumstances, the nuances and the factors that make the decision are not clear. Even a week later, one cannot recall all the details. Because of this, whatever decision I took in my long career, when seen by the audit, were satisfied, because my notes and orders were self-explanatory.

As mentioned earlier, as the Secretary to the government, I used to record the minutes of the meeting before they were disbursed in the dictaphone and in the presence of the participants. This had a great a value in ensuring the decisions are correctly recorded and nuances of the different departments were reflected. The general practice in the Government of India is that a long time is taken to draft the minutes by the junior most officer entrusted with this responsibility and approval by the hierarchy of authorities. Much time is spent in the next meeting discussing the implications of the minutes as recorded.

This may raise a question whether I was giving the example of a bad boss, because my Under Secretary or the junior officer, who should have recorded the minutes of the meeting, did not have the opportunity to learn the art of recording minutes. My reply is that if he or she learns the basic art of how to dictate in the dictaphone then when he or she in turn becomes a boss would have no problem. Unfortunately, I found to my horror that I was practically the only Secretary in Government of India to use a dictaphone while I was in service. I do not know how it is these days in the Government of India, especially with the media breathing down the necks of the bureaucracy and 24 × 7 channels ever hungry for breaking news. But I suggest that if every Secretary to the government and every bureaucrat had to adopt my strategy of recording minutes in the dictaphone, there will be greater transparency and greater speed in decision making and greater effectiveness in governance.

When one attends a seminar, one has to speak in public, he or she has to necessarily develop the capacity of presentation of his or her view and has to have the element of ready width (wit) to carry conviction. Humour helps as a great weapon in these matters. Especially in my career as the Secretary, DOE, Chairman, Telecom Commission and later as CVC, I must have addressed a record number of seminars. As I went on meeting after meetings, I found that I have to organise my thoughts and the sequence in which ideas are presented so that the audience does not get bored. The risk of addressing too many meetings is that you may repeat the same jokes and stories. This has to be avoided at all cost. In fact, Prof. Sadagopan who heads the IIT, Bangalore, used to say that he had analysed my speeches and like Lotus 1-2-3, my speeches can be called Vittal 1-2-3, there will be 1 joke, 2 stories and 3 shlokas. I found this combination effective for communication.

Humour is the one thing which people remember. When I had to bring out the absurdity of the policies of the Government of India, as far as telecom is concerned, one striking case was that of the railways communication system. Under the 1885 Indian Telegraph Act, only the Government of India under Section 5 has the power for carrying out telecom services. The railway communication system was supposed to be used only for internal departmental requirements. And this system can be connected with the national P&T network only when there is a railway accident. I compared this practice with the story about how in ancient China, the pleasures of baked pork were discovered. It seems that a house caught fire and in the fire the pigs were destroyed. After the fire people found the pigs tasted well and thereafter, anyone who wanted to eat baked pork would have had to burn a house. This analogy brought the ridiculousness of the telecom policy followed by the Government of India as far as the railway network was concerned. Even today, I am afraid, the position has not improved. That shows the persistence with which the policy continues and the rigorous application of Newton's first law of inertia in government.

Railways have been using their network in later years and the possibility of using it for power transmission and telecommunication as well as the improved services on the computer network have been realised to some extent. But as a nation, because of our policy and the short-sightedness of individual departments, we are not able to make best productive use of sources of infrastructure we already have.

To bring the need for telecom on demand, I had to come up with couplets which are based on well known traditional verses so the message went home. For instance, when I became Chairman, Telecom Commission, the 8th Plan document of the department was drawn up with the help of the telecom department and the planning commission visualised that in the year 2000, the waiting period for getting a new telephone will not exceed two years. In 1993, the telephone density was 1. Only 1 telephone for 100 people and the waiting period was about 4 to 5 years. Reducing it to 2 years was the straight-line thinking of the technocrats. When I raised the possibility of telephone on demand which became the national telecom policy in 1994, I was greeted with ridicule.

Tulsi Das

To highlight the helplessness of the telecom customer, I came up with this version of Tulsidas's famous verse: *Raghukula reet sadaa chali ayee... Pran jaay par vachan na jaay. Doorsanchar ki reetisadaa chali aye. Saal jaaye par phone na aayee.* The situation did not improve ever after MTNL was formed and so the MTNL was called, *Mera Telephone Nahi Lagega.*

I took over as Chairman, Telecom Commission on 1st October, 1993, and was being referred to as the new Telecom Czar. While addressing a FICCI meeting I told them, "Don't compare me with a Czar, because we know what happened to a Czar and that too in October". The comparison with the unfortunate Czar Nicholas, who was killed in a revolution in October 1917, was too obvious and the audience could appreciate my critical position.

I adopted the same policy of being communicative with the media and the public when I became the CVC. Here this was with a conscious purpose, that is, if war is too important a matter to be left to the Generals, corruption is too important a matter to be left only to the CVC. I wanted to make the people sensitised towards the issue of corruption. The media all the time was saying that while fighting corruption is good but eventually, it is only a small fry that gets caught and the big fish escapes. I therefore, came up with this shloka based on an ancient shloka which shows that even in the age of yagnas and sacrifices; it was the weak animals that got sacrificed. *Ashwam naiva, gajam naiva, vyagram naivacha naivacha; ajaputram bhalimtatyat devan durbhala ghataka.* In sacrifice, only the chakravarthis are supposed to sacrifice the horse. Elephants cannot be sacrificed unless one had the stock of elephants like Veerapan, the dacoit. One cannot sacrifice the tiger, because it is too risky and the tiger may make a sacrifice of you. Ultimately, it is the poor goat, the helpless weak animal that got sacrificed. Even the English expression scapegoat refers only to this animal. *Aja* in Sanskrit means goat.

Modelled on this shloka, I came with a twentieth century version. So far as CVC was concerned, when it comes to corruption, it is not the big people who get caught, but the lower division clerk. Secretary *naiva*, Chairman *naiva*, Minister *naivacha*, LDC *bhalimdatyat*, CVC *dhurbala ghataka*. This I popularised as shloka, bringing home clearly the message of the legacies in our system of punishment when it comes to corruption.

All these jokes and addressing seminars are not an unmixed affair of fame and appreciation. I have faced critical positions also in this effort. One of the initiatives as CVC was to publish on the CVC website, the names of the IAS/IPS officers against whom there were corruption charges. Departmental enquiries were launched or major penalties were recommended. The message was to highlight that it is not only the junior people who have been acted upon. I took this initiative because, in case of criminal cases, the name of the accused is well publicised in the media and in the public domain, even though a person is innocent till he is proved guilty. That is how so many criminals are facing criminal cases in court. Unfortunately, there was a name of one IAS officer, who had passed away, in the first list I published in January 2000, against whom there was a major departmental enquiry going on. His wife sent me a letter threatening legal action. I had to rush to Ram Jethmalani, who was then the Law Minister, who said that under the Indian Penal Code, the case can be defended and reassured me legally. I was in the public domain in a TV program when I openly followed the healthy precedent of Mahatma Gandhi. It may be recalled when the Chauri Chaura incident took place in the quit India movement in 1920, Gandhiji stopped it openly confessing that he had committed a blunder.

I confessed on TV that I committed a Himalayan blunder in my anxiety to expose corruption. I wrote a letter also to the wife of the deceased officer. This taught me a lesson and I changed the policy to only publicise the names of senior officers against whom departmental enquiries

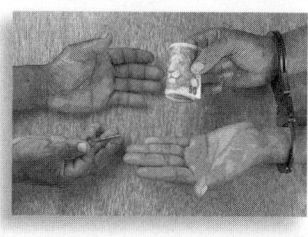

have been completed and major penalty recommended. This practice had a healthy impact and among the few things for which I am remembered today is the use of internet for the first time in the world for exposing corruption. Harvard University invited me to address a program in the School of Government on this issue in October 2000.

I worked with a number of Ministers and Chief Ministers both in the Government of Gujarat and the Government of India. I have had pleasant and smooth experiences. Probably, it is because as I earlier mentioned about how political leaders modify the behaviour knowing the reputation of an officer.

As I look back, perhaps the best Minister in the state I worked with was Mr. Manohar Singh Jadeja, the Prince of Rajkot, who was a member of the Congress party, but was opposed to Mr. Madhav Singh Solanki when he was the Chief Minister. Right from the beginning, we got along well together. In 1980, the earlier government of Janata Party was replaced by President's rule and after that the Congress Party came to power. I was appointed in February 1980, as Secretary, Civil Supplies, when the President's rule was on. Sometime in the middle of 1980 when the Congress government came to power, I had prepared a 28 point note on what should be the initiative to be taken by the department of Civil Supplies. I gave this note to Mr. Jadeja as soon as he took over as Minister. He took one week over it. Then after a week, he said, "I had gone through your note and I agree with you. Let us implement these ideas." In less than a year, we were able to initiate a lot of ideas like a comprehensive ration card covering multiple items ranging from cement, kerosene to food grain in a single ration card. We replaced the annual ration card with a five-year card, reducing the scope for the inspector raj and the frequency of the inspector visits to the fair price shop. We also set up a Gujarat State Civil Supplies Corporation on the model of Kerala, Tamil Nadu and Andhra Pradesh. This was an example of an ideal and proper understanding between a civil servant and the Minister in the approach so far as the policy was concerned.

Among the Chief Ministers I worked with, it is with Madhav Singh Solanki I had a long association. In 1963, three years into my career I was Under Secretary and Controller of Accommodation in Ahmedabad. Madhav Singh Solanki was one of the junior Ministers as Minister of State in Revenue then in Gujarat ministry of Jivrajbhai Mehta. He was one of the most sophisticated and unique politicians. I used to often run into him in book shops on Relief Road in Ahmedabad. Always pleasant and sophisticated, he always struck me as a new generation of politicians. Later, he twice became Chief Minister and was always forward looking. He made accurate assessment of the talents of the officers, which is one more proof of the general observation I have already made about how politicians have the uncanny capacity to assess the talent of the officers. He was also frank and open in discussions, so one could disagree with him.

When I was Secretary, Civil Supplies, there was a very sensitive situation that developed. In those days, there was a tremendous shortage of cement. That was the time of the Anthulay affair in which he set up a Trust in the name of Indira Gandhi for collecting funds using cement as an instrument. In Gujarat, the cement available in the black market came mostly from the irrigation department. The irrigation department was headed by another powerful politician who became the first tribal Chief Minister of Gujarat Amar Singh Chowdhury.

I had a very hard driving and strict Director, Civil Supplies C.J. Jose. He took the initiative of detaining an executive engineer of irrigation department under the Prevention of Black Marketing Act on the grounds that cement was being black marketed by him. The Irrigation Minister took up the case with the Chief Minister. Madhav Singh Solanki, as the Chief Minister, had to arbitrate between Amar Singh Chowdhury and Manohar Singh Jadeja who was in the opposite camp. I pointed out that the detention of the executive engineer under the prevention of black marketing act has been done because of the facts of the case and it was subject to a judicial review within three weeks. If the judge upheld the detention, then he will continue otherwise he would be released. Madhav Singh told me that we had created an embarrassing situation in our anxiety to check black marketing and an odd position where one senior government official in a department has been detained by another department. Anyway, the facts prevailed and the detention was upheld by the judicial review. Even in such situations, Madav Singh took the neutral stand and it was an index of the transparency and objectivity that prevailed in the administration of Gujarat in those days.

In the Government of India, the best Minister with whom I had a friendly relationship was Rangarajan Kumaramangalam. He told my wife that we got along not as a Minister and Secretary, but as a house on fire. The experience was opposite to the experience I was to have later as Secretary in the Department of Telecommunication. Eduardo Faleiro was another Minister who was very humane and when my mother was sick, he took the initiative to come and personally enquire about her health in my house. Hailing from Goa, he organised a function in Goa during one of our official trips where all the Goanese dishes were served.

Mrs. Margret Alva was also a friendly Minister. It so happened that she was a college mate of my wife and perhaps that is why she could share with us the details about how I got posted as Chairman, PESB. When I was Secretary, DOE, she was the Minister authorised to answer questions on behalf of the PM who was in charge of the DOE. In those days, there were lot of questions about using Sanskrit as the computer language and I had to brief Ms. Alva as normally done before the question day and every time she came in the leading list in her parliamentary performance. This was not surprising because in her college days she was an ace speaker and debater in inter collegiate competitions and won many trophies for her college Mt. Carmel.

Among the PMs, I have already mentioned about my interaction with Mr. Narasimha Rao. Later, when I became CVC and he was not in power, we were present in a function of Kumbabishekam of the Malai Mandir by the Shankarachariya of Kanchi Sri Jayendra Saraswati. With us Murali Manohar Joshi was also sitting who was then Minister for HRD. The discussion was about Indian culture and roots and not politics. One could sense the depth of Narasimha Rao's knowledge and his awareness of Indian tradition during his talk. I am sure the history will rank him as one of the best PMs the country ever had and as of the most under rated Prime Ministers. We are reaping the benefits of the economic reforms he introduced in 1991. I came to know from Mr. Meenakshi Sundaram, who was with Mr. Deva Gowda when he became the PM that it was Mr. Narasimha Rao who implemented the vision of Rajiv Gandhi who wanted 74-75th amendment to the Constitution to empower the local bodies and the Panchayats.

Chandrasekar, I found was one of the modest and pragmatic PM. I remember him telling me after a visit to Bombay where he had gone for a function. Some Jain muni had talked about corruption. And Chandrasekar was telling me why should the Jain munis talk about corruption we politicians are always anyway involved.

Atal Bihari Vajpayee was a more charming person among the politicians I have come across. He was the leader of the opposition when I was Secretary, Electronics and as Chairman of the Public Accounts Committee (PAC), he wanted to have a report about setting up of the project for manufacture of silicon which did not come through. The then government had decided that this report should not be given to the PAC. We claimed privilege. I remember the three or four times he called me and used his best charm to get the report and unfortunately, because of the government policy, I had to stick to the government stand of not making the report available to the PAC.

When he became the Prime Minister, I got introduced as CVC. The Vigilance Awareness Week, with Sardar Patel's birthday on 31 October, somehow he could not give a message. That was also the day when Indira Gandhi was shot dead in 1984. Sonia Gandhi, as Leader of Opposition, gave me the message for launching the first Vigilance Awareness Week on 31 October 2000. The PMO would not give, because PM would not give the message, the President K.R. Narayanan also would not give and he told me that for giving messages the President normally follows what the Prime Minister does. I spent 45 minutes with Atalji to persuade him to give a message and 31 October be declared as the date for Vigilance Awareness Week that was the date that continued till 2001.

Sardar Vallabh Bhai Patel

I explained to the Prime Minister that I wanted 31 October because it was Sardar Patel's birthday who was an example of absolute political integrity. Patel was the person who used to handle the cash of the Congress party during the freedom struggle and in spite of handling so much cash, not a finger can be raised against him, as far as his integrity is concerned. If there was any hesitation about the fact that Indira Gandhi's assassination was also on 31 October, Sonia Gandhi was the first to give the message should remove all doubts. After all, Gandhiji died on 30th January and that day is observed as Martyr's day. Nevertheless, Atalji would not budge. I could see the glint of steel under the smiling and ever pleasant Atalji's face.

After I got transferred, the Vigilance Awareness Week was not observed on 31 October anymore and instead was being observed in the last week of October or first week of November.

I came to know V.P. Singh when he was Minister of State for commerce in Indira Gandhi government way back in 1974-75. He was the Prime Minister when I got promoted as Secretary in the Government of India and took charge as Secretary, DOE. After he left power, I interacted with him in programs especially related to corruption. One could frankly discuss with V.P. Singh, ones ideas and he was always courteous and gentle.

Deve Gowda was the PM, when I was Chairman, PESB and I observed that he strictly followed the practice of respecting the decision and order of selection of the PESB. PESB not only recommends the panel of three names for every post, but also ranks the persons selected. During Deva Gowda period, it was always the number one person who was appointed. Later, I came to know Deve Gowda more personally when he agreed to release my book *Musings on Governance, Governing and Corruption* published by ICFAI. I was surprised that he had read my book and fully supported the stands I had taken and whatever one may say about Deve Gowda, one could see his attachment to certain basic principles. Actually, Meenakshi Sundaram, later on mentioned in a meeting that when he became the PM, he realised that he may not be there for a long time. He told Meenakshi Sundaram, "You pack your suitcase and come, we may not be there for more than one year". He had chosen the most reliable person Mr. Satish Chandran for his official decisions who was one of the distinguished members of the IAS. The decisions taken during the Deve Gowda period had been fair and correct as far as the Government of India was concerned.

I.K. Gujral, was another PM I met more in the precincts of the India International Centre. I had interacted with him in some seminars and found him to be very poised and balanced in his ways of thinking. The Gujral doctrine may be a subject of criticism, but when he held the office of PM, he always came across as a modest intellectual.

Rajiv Gandhi was the most technocratic PM this country has had. I was fortunate to interact with him when I was the Additional Secretary, Atomic Energy, when we had gone to present our scheme about how our department would handle a radiation emergency. One could see the quickness of his mind and the understanding he had about the technical matters, especially radiation. He said that it was directly related to his professional background. I had become Additional Secretary in the Department of Atomic Energy in 1988 just two years after Chernobyl. We were going through exercises in the nuclear plants to educate the public about how to behave in a nuclear emergency. As a person, Rajiv Gandhi was very charming, no wonder he captured the imagination not only of our people, but was seen as India's JFK.

The last time I met him was after he lost power, I had become Secretary, DOE and V.P. Singh as the PM came to preside a seminar on Electronics, in February 1991. I praised him as the person who for the first time talked about the twenty first century and introduced the concept of computers in governance. He liked my joke about lawyers and mothers- in- law which I mentioned while telling about the need for us to do everything possible to promote use of information technology. The joke is: There is a call for a lawyer from his undertaker. Your mother-in-law is dead. Do you want her to be buried, embalmed or cremated? The lawyer's reply: Do all the three, don't take any chance. When he got in to his van which he was driving , he mentioned to me about how he liked the joke and departed with a smile. That is the last I remember of him. The next I heard was the sad news of how he was assassinated brutally in Sriperumbudur on 21 May 1991. Rajiv Gandhi's Prime Ministership was a breath of fresh air in the musty corridors of Governance of India.

If you are a civil servant, you must remember that four things are unavoidable in life: death, taxes, transfers and retirement. Once you accept this and go wherever posted, you are bound to succeed.

What is Your Boss Quotient?

There are in all one hundred questions, divided into six sections. Each section reflects on a specific domain for which score interpretation is given at the end of the section.

For each of the statements/questions given below, mark yourself on a scale of 1 to 10. Write your score in front of each question.

How Competent Are You?

1. How competent are you in your work?
2. You are a quick decision maker.
3. You communicate with your team mates effectively and on several occasions.
4. You make efforts to keep yourself updated on the professional front.
5. You do detailed home work before every meeting and look fully in control of things in front of your team.
6. You always think of the future and keep planning mentally what may crop up as a challenge in the future.
7. You are able to simplify complex problems and thereby earn the respect of your team.
8. You do not hold back files, mails or issues, and take quick actions so that there are no bottlenecks for the team.
9. You are responsive to requests made by your team and do not procrastinate.

10. You are considered by your team members as a very clear headed boss.

11. You can judge situations and their seriousness very well.

12. You ensure that every employee/subordinate is clear about his role and has a proper job description.

13. You do a proper load balancing between team mates. This way you ensure that all employees have almost similar work pressure. There by it does not happen that in your team a few are highly over loaded and a few have little to do.

14. You move from macro management to micro management and vice versa very effectively.

15. When the circumstances require you roll up your sleeves and get into action on ground effectively.

16. You consult domain experts from your team and plug in their opinions into your decision making wherever required.

17. You believe in contingency planning and keep your back up or alternative plans ready for any eventuality.

18. You keep your office management very efficient and effective. For that you create processes, SOPs and good documentation.

19. You believe in building your image on competence rather than bragging.

20. You are compassionate and yet a hard task master.

21. You are diplomatic and handle people and situations with tact.

22. You do not set unachievable targets.

23. You do not sack, fire or write off a person because of one mistake.

24. You chose your words very carefully.

25. You are capable and hence able to give 'out of the box' or creative solutions to your team.

26. You are able to de complicate or simplify a complex problem.

27. When you are assigned a new role or you change your job, you give yourself adequate time to settle down and understand the strengths and weaknesses of the organisation and your team before initiating any changes.

28. You are polite, yet firm about your stand or instructions that you give to your subordinates.

29. You give instructions to your subordinates very clearly.
30. You have the courage to go against the advice of the experts in case you do not agree with the experts.
31. You are able to spot good talent easily.
32. You put the right person at the right place for the right job.
33. You have the ability to get things done.
34. You plan things in advance.
35. You are able to say a firm 'No' if you need to demonstrate and convey a dissent to something.

Score Interpretation: Your Total = (Max 350)

0–180 = C

Professionally you need to sharpen your axe. Examine your competence level on the parameters given in the book and constantly work on each of them to better your score.

181–280 = B

There is a scope for improving your professional competence and also in terms of dealing with you team in terms of professionally handling your subordinates.

Above 280 = A

You are a very competent boss who is respected by his team for his abilities. Ensure that you never lose this edge and make constant learning a habit for life.

Are You Able to Build a Good Culture?

1. You make a deliberate attempt to improve the culture of your company or your department.
2. You make a conscious effort to make your team mates happy at work place.
3. You do not play politics in your organisation.
4. You give subordinates (new joiners) sufficient time to settle down.

5. You ensure that people below you who are bosses to others treat their subordinates properly and with dignity.

6. You are particular about discipline of your team and make efforts to keep your work force disciplined.

7. You accord high priority to discipline and expect every employee to remain within the ground rules laid down by you or the organisation.

8. You do not believe in cheap popularity and try to keep everybody (your subordinates) happy all the time.

Score Interpretation

Your Total = (Max 80)

0–40 = C

You need to pull up things for yourself and your team as regards the culture of your organisation is concerned. You need to make a deliberate attempt to reign in a good work culture for your people.

41–64 = B

There is room for improvement in your understanding of the importance of culture in an organisation. Make efforts to improve upon all the points related to the culture of an organisation discussed in the book.

Above 64 = A

You have the ability and acumen to build a good culture in your organisation. Take this as a major strength and ensure that no team member ever messes up with your efforts to build a great organisation.

How Emotionally Intelligent Are You?

1. How polite are you with your subordinates?

2. You do not humiliate your subordinates.

3. You are humane towards your team.

4. You are considerate towards your team mates.

5. You make conscious efforts to bring emotional harmony within your subordinates to ensure that they care for each other.

6. You can judge people very well.

7. You are enthusiastic about work.

8. You display passion for your work.

9. By displaying enthusiasm and thereby bringing success to your organisation you are able to motivate your team.

10. You display patience to get rewards and achievements.

11. You act as a mood manager of your team. If your team is demoralised, you are able to get them back into good mood and are able to raise their moral.

12. You can bounce back after a failure. This has a positive impact on your team.

13. In case required, you are able to take unemotional or hard decisions.

14. You remain cool and very rarely lose your temper.

15. You do not panic. Even if you do, you manage not to display this.

16. You are a compassionate boss.

17. You do not hurt people emotionally.

18. You have a good corporate network. You make constant efforts to make a solid corporate network.

19. You never look helpless or ruffled up in any situation or a trying circumstances in front of your team.

20. You show grace when you are under pressure.

21. You look after the interest of your team mates and hence you are not a "Banana Boss."

Score interpretation

Your Total = (Max 210)

0–105 = C

Look at your emotional Competence seriously. You need to work on yourself and also on your interpersonal skills.

106–168 = B

You need to improve on your emotional Intelligence. Wherever you have scored a low, do work on this and make efforts to improve gradually. You have the ability to work on your weaknesses, provided you identify them.

Above 168 = A

You score a high on you EQ as a boss and have all the necessary qualities to deal with your people and also deal with yourself. Leverage you EI to your advantage in every aspect of your professional work.

Are You a Nasty or a Caring Boss?

1. You are not vindictive towards your subordinates.
2. You do not keep your team on tenter hooks by often pressing panic buttons.
3. You display that you care for your people.
4. You genuinely care for your team mates.
5. You are humble and down to earth.
6. You strongly believe in the credo, "Do to others what you would like them to do to you."
7. You care for your subordinate's emotions.
8. You never redicule anyone in public so as to hurt his self esteem.
9. You ensure that you never make a person feel small or feel criticised in front of his subordinates.
10. As a boss you do not make a mockery of any of your subordinates.
11. You are a benevolent boss. You help your team mates whenever they need your help especially on the personal front.
12. You are not an unnecessary stickler for leave and easily spare your subordinates to go on leave- provided the work does not suffer.

Score Interpretation

Your Total = (Max 120)

0–60 = C

You are not a very caring boss. Cause of concern as this kind of behaviour will create problems for you at your work. In addition it may be difficult for you to earn loyalty of your team mates.

61–96 = B

Need to improve on your people skill. Take a candid feedback from your peers and even your subordinates regarding your way of dealing with people.

Above 96 = A

You are a very caring and a matured boss. People will love to work for you and you command a genuine respect of your people.

How Supportive Are You as a Boss?

1. You hold the hand of your employees during a crisis or if anyone inadvertently makes a mistake.
2. You are tolerant to employees making some mistakes as long as they are not made repeatedly or deliberately.
3. You allow people to take reasonable risk but not at the cost of making a blunder.
4. You mentor and guide your subordinates on regular basis.

Score Interpretation

Your score = (Max 40)

0–20 = C

Be a little patient with your people and do not expect a zero error scenario. Accept that people make mistakes and allow your subordinates to take a bit of risk.

21–32 = B

You need to be more supportive. It is important to understand that your team will be able to deliver much more if you hold their hand whenever they require.

Above 32 = A

You support your team fully and your team loves you for that. Just because of your supportive nature your team is always prepared to do that extra mile just for you.

Do You Build a Feeling of Trust in Your Team?

1. You are transparent in your dealings.
2. Your team trusts you.
3. You as a boss do not encourage back biters.
4. You are impartial and treat everyone similarly under similar circumstances.
5. You do not have any favorites or blue eyed boys.
6. You point out short comings of employees during the year as they occur and do not wait for the appraisal time alone.
7. You do not like people buttering you or showering great praises, unnecessarily.
8. You are very honest and high on integrity.
9. You support whistle blowers.
10. As a boss you ensure you are always politically correct.
11. You always walk the talk and you do what you say.
12. You always keep your word.
13. You maintain your dignity, conduct yourself gracefully and do not act as a sychophant in front of your boss.
14. You protect your team from outside pressure.
15. You pay adequate attention to maintain your credibility in front of your subordinates.
16. You do not play the blame game by blaming someone for any mistake or a messed up job.
17. You do not waste time in postmortems and enquiries if something has gone wrong.
18. If required you display the big heart of a king in certain situations.
19. You are a royal boss who does not nag people for small trivial issues.
20. You do not view your subordinates in black or white mode. That means, you either love a person or hate him and not having a balanced view about individuals.

Score Interpretation

Your Total = (Max 200)

0–100 = C

Every boss needs to build trust with his team. Your organisation actually runs on trust if you want it to. Without trust you will never be able to get the best out of your team. You need to make genuine efforts to earn trust and respect of your people.

101–160 = B

Your team mates trust you, but you could make genuine efforts to work on some areas where you have scored low.

Above 160 = A

Your team trusts you and genuinely respects you. In fact your subordinates admire you because they feel that you will always treat them fairly.

Note:

(a) For which ever question your score is less than 5, you need to look at it very seriously. Make conscious efforts to improve in that area.

(b) Wherever you have scored between 6 and 8, you are doing average in that quality. Try and improve upon it.

(c) Wherever you score 8 and above, you are very strong there. Your effort should be to retain this as your strength and in fact leverage this quality in the best possible manner, to your advantage.

CONTRIBUTORS

Virender Kapoor...A Thinker, Educationist and an Inspirational Guru

Is an Indian who wears many hats. An educationist of repute, a former director of a prestigious management institute under the Symbiosis umbrella, is the founder director, president and chief mentor of MILE (Management Institute for Leadership and Excellence), Pune.

Having written books on information systems and telecommunication in the1990s he shifted his focus towards emotional intelligence, leadership and self-help. He has emerged as a leading think tank of human behaviour, motivation and success. His name appears with the likes of Thomas Friedman and Dale Carnegie. One of the most versatile authors, his books cut across subjects like *Passion Quotient—PQ*, *Emotional Intelligence*, *Leadership* and *Work Life Balance*. He brought "*Jugaad*"—an Indian concept of "getting things done" into the domain of formal management education with his book "*Rise and Rise of Jugaad.*"

His school books series "I can and I will" for classes 6 to 12 are the first of their kind to bring emotional intelligence in Indian schools. His books are now available in several regional languages like Hindi, Punjabi, Marathi, Gujarati, Telegu, Malayalam, Tamil as well as Vietnamese.

A telecommunication engineer, Kapoor did his Masters in Technology in Computer Science from the Indian Institute of Technology, Bombay, and later he completed his MA in International Relations and Strategic Studies from the University of Pune.

Virender has been writing for prestigious publications like *Data Quest*, *Times of India*, *Hindustan Times* and has been widely interviewed.

Email: virenderkapoor21@yahoo.com
Linkedin: http://in.linkedin.com/pub/dir/Virender/Kapoor
Website: www.virenderkapoor.com, www.mile.net.in
Twitter: @virenderkapoor
Blog: http://virenderkapoor.blogspot.in/

Ibrahim Ahmad

Is the Group Editor, Business Magazines Group, of CyberMedia (India) Ltd., South Asia's largest technology media company. In this capacity he heads three publications including *DATAQUEST*, *Voice&Data*, and *GlobalServices*, India's largest selling trade magazines for the IT, telecom, and BPO sectors. Under his supervision some of the country's most well known national industry surveys such as DQ Top 20 and V&D100 have been undertaken.

Ibrahim earlier had in his portfolio, *The DQ Week*, a weekly newspaper published from Chennai, Mumbai, Delhi and Kolkata for IT dealers and resellers across the country; and *DQ Channels*, a fortnightly tabloid for small and medium solution providers. He has been instrumental in guiding *DATAQUEST* and *Voice&Data* to take up an evangelist's role in bringing together various components of the industry - vendors, enterprise users, service providers, and policy makers - under the aegis of *DQ CIO Series*, and *Voice&Data Top View* panel discussions.

Platforms like *The DQWeek* led to the formation of IT channel partner associations in many cities.

Under his stewardship, the publications have been successful in championing some major industry issues like bandwidth (later taken over by NASSCOM), and Project W, for opening up and promoting Wi-Fi. Working as a professional journalist for the last 23 years, Ibrahim is also a successful project manager, and has been the driver behind the launch of a sister publication *PCQuest* in the neighbouring countries of Nepal, Sri Lanka, and Bangladesh.

He is an Economics graduate from the Aligarh Muslim University (AMU), Aligarh. Ibrahim later also pursued his MBA from AMU. He lives in Gurgaon with his wife and two daughters.

Email: ibrahima@cybermedia.co.in
Linkedin: http://in.linkedin.com/pub/ibrahim-ahmad/4/913/a98

Vinay Agarwal

Is a management consultant who works on the Profit and Growth Transformation (PGT) of companies, using the Theory of Constraints (TOC) methodologies. He is Chairman of the Theory of Constraints Institute and is also CEO Mentor, Corporate Advisor and a Company Director. Vinay has over thirty years of executive experience, including twenty years leading organisations as MD, CEO, COO, and Director with P&L responsibility. He served as an industry leader as Vice-President and President of the bearing industry association and was a member of the Association of Councils (ASCON) and National Council of the Confederation of Indian Industry. He has also been a member of the Global Management Committee of Saint-Gobain Abrasives.

Vinay holds a degree in engineering from IIT Kanpur, and in management from IIM Calcutta. He has worked with leading Indian and international companies namely, Blow Plast, TCS, SRF Group, BPL Mobile, RPG Group, Saint-Gobain, Dish TV and TVS Group. In his last corporate assignment he headed the business of Samtel Color Limited and Samtel Glass Limited.

Email: vinaynoida@hotmail.com
Linkedin: http://www.linkedin.com/profile/view?id=16631507 & trk=tab_pro
Website: http://www.pgtpartners.com

Raju Bhatnagar

Is a certified executive and business coach and an independent business strategy consultant who focuses on the IT and BPO verticals. Till mid 2011, Raju Bhatnagar was Vice President, Business Process Outsourcing (BPO) and Government Relations at NASSCOM, where he was responsible for providing leadership for various initiatives of NASSCOM and heading industry forums like BPO, labour, human relations (HR) and CFO forums.

The government focus included close interaction with ministries, quasi-government organisations and handling government relations for the IT and BPO industry both at the centre and state levels.

He has been associated with the BPO industry for 13 years having set up and run large third party BPO operations with companies including eFunds International, ICICI OneSource and Tata Business Support Services, where he pioneered India's first rural BPO delivery centre.

Prior to the BPO industry, he spent 19 years with ANZ Grindlays Bank, and eighteen months with HDFC bank.

Currently, he chairs ISO's International Work Group which is working to create a new ISO standard for the BPO industry and is also involved with the World Bank in advising developing countries on their ICT strategies to establish themselves as emerging destinations for the BPO segment.

He holds an MSc (Hons.) in Mathematics from BITS Pilani, and has completed post graduate studies in International Trade from IIFT, New Delhi. He is certified as a PCC (Professional Certified Coach) from the International Coaching Federation (ICF), USA, and has over 2,000 hours of coaching experience.

Email: bhatnagar101@yahoo.co.in
Linkedin: http://in.linkedin.com/pub/dir/Raju/Bhatnagar

Anshoo Gaur

Is the President and Head of Amdocs India and a member of the Global Amdocs Management, since 2007. Anshoo is also an Executive Officer of Amdocs Ltd. (NYSE: DOX). He was the winner of the Bloomberg-UTV IT CXO Award 2010 as business head of the year in APAC. Anshoo has over 22 years of cross cultural leadership experience, playing a wide variety of roles on strategic IT planning, operations management, process reengineering, product management and development, customer and P&L management.

Anshoo holds a Masters degree in Industrial and Systems Engineering from the University of Arizona, Tucson and a Bachelors Degree in mechanical engineering from National Institute of Technology, Surathkal, India.

Email: anshoogaur@gmail.com
Linkedin: http://www.linkedin.com/in/anshoogaur
Twitter: @anshoogaur
Blog: http://anshoogaur.blogspot.in/

Kallol Hazra

Having spent more than 28 years in the IT industry in various roles, Kallol has finally managed to downgrade himself from platinum to blue on Jet Privilege and is currently leading the Global Software Delivery Centre of CSG International as Managing Director, India based in Bangalore. His current assignment includes managing a highly technical team to solve CSG global customer's business challenges through delivery of solutions using CSG's products – better, faster and cheaper.

Previously he was with Hewlett Packard (HP) where he handled several assignments over 14 years.

His last assignment was Director–Application Services responsible for managing HP India's Application Services Business.

He holds a double Bachelor's degree in technology and physics from Calcutta University and a management diploma.

Email: kallol.hazra@gmail.com
Linkedin: in.linkedin.com/in/kallolhazra
Twitter: @kallolh

Dr. Samir Kapoor

A PhD in human resources from Symbiosis International University and a master's degree in personnel management from the Symbiosis Institute of Business Management, Samir is also a certified graphologist from the Institute of Graphology, Pune. He has held senior management positions in many organisations, and set up one of its kind-resourcing centre for Standard Chartered Bank, India.

He was also conferred with the 'Innovative HR Professional of the Year' award at the Deccan Herald Avenues Awards for HR excellence where he was the youngest person to win an individual award.

Email: samir.kapoor@mile.net.in
Facebook: https://www.facebook.com/samir.kapoor.9
Linkedin: in.linkedin.com/pub/dr-samir-kapoor/7/91a/453
Twitter: @samirkapoor

Huzaifa Khorakiwala

Is an eminent personality, an inspiring speaker, a brilliant thinker, a prolific writer, a committed social worker, and a loving individual.

At present he heads the non-profit organisation, Wockhardt Foundation, and is also the Executive Director of Wockhardt Limited and is a member of the promoter family of Wockhardt Group—a leading pharmaceutical and healthcare group.

Dr. Huzaifa Khorakiwala has an MBA from the prestigious Yale University in the USA. He has won numerous awards and is associated with many social causes.

"Service to man is service to God" is his motto in life.

Email: ceo@wockhardtfoundation.org
Website: www.drhuzaifakhorakiwala.org

Amit Malik

Is Director–Human Resource at Aviva life Insurance India Ltd. In his current role, he leads the human resource function and plays a significant role in contributing to and facilitating the achievement of the strategic business goals of the organisation by 'partnering' for success with key stakeholders (shareholders, internal and external customers and alliance partners). He is responsible for strengthening the HR Business Partnership, building a dynamic, vibrant and meritocratic culture and instilling a sense of pride and ownership and accountability in employees' actions.

Prior to joining Aviva he worked in HR leadership roles at the Bank of America, Royal bank of Scotland, American Express and GlaxoSmithKline Consumer Healthcare.

Amit graduated with Bachelors of engineering degree (major in mechanical) and is a management graduate in human resource from Symbiosis Institute of Business Management, Pune.

Email: malikamit99@gmail.com
Linkedin: http://www.linkedin.com/pub/amit-malik/2/2a8/ba
Twitter: @amitmalik99

Rajat Mathur

Is currently Executive Director of human resources at a leading multinational investment bank. He leads the talent function across the Asia region including talent acquisition, talent development and diversity.

He has a Bachelors degree in science from the prestigious St. Stephens College and a masters in human resource management from Symbiosis Institute of Business Management, Pune.

Email: rajat1901@gmail.com
Linkedin: http://www.linkedin.com/pub/rajat-mathur/0/65b/47a
Twitter: @runrajat

Tanaya Mishra

Is currently Senior Vice President – Group Human Resources, JSW, Mumbai.

She has vast experience in the field of HR and has spent approximately two decades in the industry. She has worked extensively in the fields of generalist HR, organisation development, talent management and succession planning. She is one of the rare lady HR Leaders who is conversant and at ease with both the service as well as the manufacturing sector.

She holds a PhD. in manpower planning and a Post Graduate Diploma in personnel management, and a Bachelors Degree in Law (LLB) and has been trained and certified by SHL, DDI, and Thomas. She is a Board member of NHRD Network, National and Regional Committee Member with the Confideration of Indian Industry(CII), subject matter expert with SHRM,General Secretary of the National HRD Network (NHRDN) – Mumbai Chapter and is a committee member of the Bombay Chamber of Commerce and Industry.

Email: tanayamishra@gmail.com

S.V. Nathan

Is the talent director for Deloitte in India, with over 28 years of professional experience in human resource (HR) management. Apart from his responsibilities in Deloitte, Nathan serves as a Fellow at Sumedhas, a not-for-profit education and research body on Organisation Development.

Nathan serves as the National Secretary of the National HR Development Network (NHRDN), and is the Chairman of the Global In-House Center, Hyderabad Chapter of NASSCOM, and the current Chair of the Indian Society for Training & Development (ISTD), Hyderabad Chapter. He is an active member of the distinguished WILL Mentoring Council of the "Forum for Women in Leadership" in India.

A man of letters, Nathan graduated in Mathematics and did his post-graduation from XLRI, Jamshedpur.

Blog: svnathan.com

Anu Vishwas Sarkar

Is the regional head of diversity (APAC) at Deutsche Bank and global head of diversity for service centre operations of the firm. She has been instrumental in establishing the diversity function for the bank in the region. As a member of the Global and APAC diversity council, she works with leadership teams and a wide range of employee networks to design and deploy the strategy around multiple facets of diversity. Her work revolves around creating a leadership agenda which is built around an inclusive workplace.

Email: anu.sarkar@db.com

Vandana Saxena Poria OBE (Order of the British Empire)

Was born and brought up in the UK where she qualified as a chartered accountant. She then spent 10 years living and working in a multitude of countries in Central and Eastern Europe before moving to India in 2005. Vandana's career started in the UK with HW Fisher, after which she joined Ernst & Young. She then went on to set up the international division of Europe's largest listed professional education company, BPP Professional Education, where she was the CEO for seven years. During that time, she set up several full-time centres across Central and Eastern Europe, with off-site training in Asia and Africa.

Vandana is currently the CEO of Get Through Guides (GTG), a content creation and training company that she set up in 2006. GTG develops and publishes materials for international professional qualifications in the BFSI sector, and provides training to top corporates in the Indian subcontinent. Within five years of

Vandana setting up GTG, it has gone on to become an accredited publisher for the ACCA qualification – one of only three publishers globally.

The quality of GTG's work has been further acknowledged in India. GTG was asked by the Insurance Institute of India to rewrite the Licentiate textbooks in 2010, and also has worked with the IRDA on producing the revised life insurance textbook. Around one million insurance agents are now using GTG produced materials to pass their insurance examinations. GTG is accredited for training by the Institute of Chartered Accountants of India, the Institute of Chartered Accountants Sri Lanka, the Institute of Chartered Accountants in England and Wales, the Chartered Institute of Management Accountants and others.

Vandana also works closely with the British government to foster international trade for the UK and has given numerous presentations to promote business and understanding between the UK and India. She has held several positions with the British Chambers of Commerce in several countries. Since 2006, Vandana chairs the "British Business Group" in Pune which was set up with support from the British High Commission. In the Queen's Birthday Honours list announced on 14 June 2008, Vandana was honoured with an OBE for services to trade and investment, one of the youngest female Asians to be given the honour.

Vandana is an acclaimed speaker and is often invited to speak at events about developing skills through broad interactive education. She is passionate about the fact that with the right methods, India can turn into—a nation of entrepreneurs into a nation of Infosys's and Tatas. She is the recipient of many national and international awards, besides her OBE honour.

Email: vsp@GetThroughGuides.com
Linkedin: www.linkedin.com/pub/vandana-saxena-poria-obe/6/677/85b
Twitter: @Vporia

Sunil Sinha

Is the Chief, Group Quality Management Services, Tata Sons, the holding company of the Tata group. He was appointed Chief Executive of Tata Quality Management Services (TQMS) in 2005 and five years later was elevated to the present position.

TQMS, which is a division of Tata Sons, is the nodal entity for the Tata group for the promotion and coordination of initiatives relating to business excellence, innovation, sustainability, safety, and corporate governance. In his role as Chief Executive of TQMS, the 53 year old Sunil has helped implement the Tata Business Excellence Model—a transformational and holistic improvement programme—in over 100 Tata companies.

He is also a member of the Tata Group Innovation Foundation (TGIF), which has been a lead player in the development and deployment of the Tata group's innovation agenda. Additionally, he heads a group that works with Tata companies on climate change. This group is involved in measuring the carbon footprint of Tata companies, and for minimising the impact of their businesses on the environment, and laying the ground for a low-carbon culture across the group.

Being at the hub of the business excellence journey undertaken by the group, Sunil has been an important part of the cultural integration efforts involving international enterprises acquired by the Tata companies. He currently serves on the boards and audit committees of Taco Hendrickson Suspensions. He also serves on the advisory boards of the Management Institute for Leadership and Excellence (MILE) and Symbiosis Institute of Distance Learning.

He has spoken in global forums on subjects such as innovation and business excellence, most recently at Harvard Business School. In 2009, Sunil was nominated by Business Week magazine as one of the world's "25 Masters of Innovation".

Mr. Sinha's professional career spans nearly three decades. During this time he has immersed himself in many different spheres of business, among them being Organisational Transformation,

Quality Management, Human Resources, International Operations, Project Management, Innovation and Climate Change. He has held a variety of leadership positions in the Tata group, including General Manager (Human Resources and Corporate Quality) at Tata International, and Human Resources Head (Sales and Marketing), Tata Steel. Prior to these responsibilities, he helmed the chartering function, and the marketing and sales of Tata Steel's long products in international markets.

Mr. Sinha was a founding member of the "Total Quality Implementation Group" at Tata Steel during the period when many change initiatives were undertaken in the company. He graduated in mechanical engineering from Bihar College of Engineering, Patna, in 1982 and completed an Advance Management Programme from INSEAD, Fontainebleau, France, in 2004 and Advanced Strategic Management Programme from IMD, Switzerland.

Email: sunilsinha3008@gmail.com
Linkedin: in.linkedin.com/pub/sunil-sinha/1/3b/7b3/

N. Vittal

Belongs to the 1960 batch of the IAS, Gujarat cadre. Mr N. Vittal was Secretary, IT (1990–1996) and later, Secretary Telecommunications (1993–1994) at a critical time. He introduced policies for software technology parks and was deeply involved in shaping the liberalisation of the telecom sector. Post-retirement, he was Chairman of the Public Enterprises Selection Board until 1998 and was Central Vigilance Commissioner until 2002. He has written on a wide range of issues about governance, management and IT and is the author of fourteen books.

Email: nagarajanvittal@hotmail.com